An Introduction to to Jewish Ethics

Louis E. Newman
Carleton College

PEARSON
Prentice
Hall

Upper Saddle River, New Jersey 07458

Library of Congress Cataloging-in-Publications Data
Newman, Louis E.
  An introduction to Jewish Ethics/Louis E. Newman—1st ed.
    p. cm.
Inlcudes bibliographical references.
  ISBN 0-13-238890-1
  1. Ethics, Jewish. 2. Jewish law—Moral and ethical aspects.
  3. Judaism—Doctrines. I. Title

BJ1285.N48 2004
296.3'6—dc22

2004000986

Editorial Director: Charlyce Jones-Owens
Acquisitions Editor: Ross Miller
Assistant Editor: Wendy Yurash
Editorial Assistant: Carla Warner
Marketing Manager: Karla Kindstrom
Marketing Assistant: Jennifer Lang
Managing Editor: Fran Russello
Manufacturing Buyer: Christina Helder
Cover Design: Jayne Conte
Composition/Full-Service: Pine Tree Composition, Inc.
Printer/Binder: Courier Companies, Inc.
Photography © by Bil Aron

Pearson Education LTD., London
Pearson Education Singapore, Pte. Ltd
Pearson Education, Canada, Ltd
Pearson Education–Japan
Pearson Education Australia PTY, Limited
Pearson Education North Asia Ltd
Pearson Educación de Mexico, S.A. de C.V.
Pearson Education Malaysia, Pte. Ltd
Pearson Education, Upper Saddle River, New Jersey

10 9 8 7 6 5 4 3 2 1

ISBN 0-13-238890-1

To my students

"I have learned much from my teachers, more from my colleagues, and from my students, most of all."
Babylonian Talmud, Ta'anit 7a

Contents

Conclusion: Learning the Language of Jewish Ethics

Preface

This book is designed to introduce students to Judaism and its ethics. In writing it, I have tried not to presume that readers have any prior background in Judaism or in the academic study of religion or ethics. Accordingly, I have tried throughout to summarize basic concepts in Judaism and key approaches to Jewish ethics in ways that do justice to their complexity but without overwhelming readers with more information than they can readily absorb. This approach, I hope, has the virtue of making this volume widely accessible, but comes at the price of reviewing what will be familiar ground to some readers.

In the interest of making this volume "user friendly," I begin each chapter with an overview and conclude with a review of key points. These should enable readers to identify quickly the central ideas presented and to track the argument of the book at it unfolds. I close each chapter with a list of questions for discussion and/or reflection. These point toward issues that merit further consideration and may help in digesting more fully material that is frequently presented in rather condensed form. The glossary at the end of the book may also be helpful in defining terms that very likely will be unfamiliar to most readers. Terms included in the glossary appear in bold when they are first introduced. For more advanced students, I have tried in the notes to draw attention to some of the complexities that I do not take up in the text. The suggestions for further reading may be especially valuable to those interested in pursuing more detailed study of matters that I have been able to cover here only in a general way.

Because textbooks of this sort are not written primarily for other scholars, they are not meant to break new ground, and this book for the most part is no exception. Its purpose is principally to present the tradition of Jewish ethics in a way that is clear and accessible. Still, this presentation of Jewish ethics has been influenced at many points by my own scholarship in the field, including essays that appear in my *Past Imperatives: Studies in the History and Theory of Jewish Ethics* (Albany, N.Y.: State University of New York Press, 1998). Chapter Five, which addresses the theoretical foundations of classical Jewish ethics, and Chapter Six, which categorizes contemporary approaches to Jewish ethics, rely on this previously published work. In this way I have tried to make even this introductory presentation sophisticated enough to sustain the interest of those for whom the material itself is very familiar.

This book has been many years in the making and could not have come about without moral, intellectual, and material help from many quarters. My interest in Jewish ethics began during my graduate studies at Brown University and owes much to my teachers, especially Wendell S. Dietrich, John P. Reeder, Jr., and Sumner B. Twiss, who introduced me to this field. Over the years I have learned much, too, from the many Jewish and Christian ethicists whose work I have read, as well as from theorists of religion. I want to acknowledge here especially Eugene Borowitz, Elliot Dorff, David Novak, Laurie Zoloth, James Gustafson, Stanley Hauerwas, and Clifford Geertz.

I am especially grateful to Prentice-Hall and its editor, Ross Miller, for their support of this project and their willingness to wait long beyond the original due date for me to complete it.

Over the years I have been blessed with wonderful colleagues, both in the Religion Department at Carleton College and beyond. Collectively, they have encouraged my work, both as teacher and scholar, and their influence is visible on every page of this book. I am especially grateful to the College for awarding me a faculty development grant in 1985–86 to support my research in connection with this project.

Many colleagues generously agreed to read this manuscript and offered numerous suggestions for improvement. I wish to thank David Ellenson, Richard Miller, and especially Elliot Dorff and John P. Reeder, Jr., for the many points that they urged me to clarify, expand upon, and qualify. I am also grateful to two Carleton students, Zach Pruitt and Alice Gorel, who read the entire manuscript and guided me in making this introduction more accessible to students. The Rev. Douglas Mork, a former student, served as a research assistant, and his able work was an enormous help to me. Any failings of substance or style that remain here are entirely my own.

Most of all, my life has been blessed by a loving family. I am grateful to my wife, Amy, and to our children, Etan, Jonah, and Penina, for their unwavering encouragement and support. Whatever I manage to accomplish in this world is due in no small part to the security and serenity I find in being surrounded by their love and laughter.

I have had the great privilege of teaching many students since I joined the faculty of Carleton College in 1983; indeed, I have had them very much in mind as I have written this book. Through their persistent questions, they have helped me again and again to see that something I thought I had just explained still was not quite clear. In the process, they have taught me how to be a teacher. To the extent that I have succeeded here in making Jewish ethics understandable, I am indebted to their intellectual curiosity, their love of learning, and especially their patience with me as I struggled to make this tradition that I know and love accessible to them. I dedicate this book to them, for it is in many ways the fruit of their work as much as mine.

Louis E. Newman
6 Av 5763
August 4, 2003

Introduction:
Preparing for the
Journey

Imagine that you are about to leave on a trip to a place you have never been before, perhaps to live in a foreign country on a study abroad program. You have packed your bags, trying to anticipate what you will need during your stay. Perhaps you have talked with others who have taken this trip before you to learn something about what to expect. If you are like most students, you probably face this adventure with some mixed feelings, a sense of excitement but also some uncertainty about what lies ahead. Will I find my way in this unfamiliar place? Will I be able to understand (or make myself understood in) the native language? Will I find this new culture attractive or distasteful? You have some sense of what to expect, but on reflection you also know that most likely some surprises await you, some pleasant and others less so.

If you reflect still more on your travels, you will undoubtedly realize that you are carrying more with you on this journey than the contents of your suitcases. You bring with you a host of assumptions about "the way the world works," things that you have been trained to expect since childhood, about how to respond in particular social situations (when you enter a classroom, when you meet someone for the first time), how people in certain positions (clerks, parents, police officers) should behave, how to dress, and what sorts of foods are palatable. In fact, one of the greatest pleasures (and challenges) of spending time in a foreign culture is that these many ingrained and often unconscious assumptions are forced into the open when you confront a culture with different assumptions from your own.

In all likelihood, your trip abroad will be more satisfying and more educational if you take some time before you leave to consider all of this and especially to expect the unexpected. The more aware you are of your own "cultural baggage," the more likely it is that you will be able to open to another culture's perspective and learn what it has to teach you. Nowhere is this truer than in the realm of interpersonal relationships, where most people have well-established expectations about what sorts of behaviors are "right" and "wrong," socially acceptable or unacceptable. It can be jarring, but also enlightening, to discover that what you have always taken for granted as simply "natural" is regarded as peculiar by others. And, of course, the more distant and exotic the country you plan to visit, the more you will need to prepare yourself for those differences and the more difficult it may be to suspend judgment about that culture's practices and values.

I begin by asking you to consider what is involved in this imaginary journey because, in a very real sense, you are about to embark on just such an excursion. On this trip you will explore Judaism and its ethics. Although this trip is intellectual rather than geographical, it is nonetheless an encounter with a culture and its values that are quite different from those you probably know from your own experience. Some of the features of this "place"—certain behaviors or values, perhaps—may be fairly familiar to you and thus readily understandable. Others are sure to appear rather strange and puzzling. These "natives" definitely speak a different language and use idioms that will be difficult to understand, even in English translation. Most of all, they take for granted certain beliefs about how the world works that influence their ideas about what is right and wrong; learning about these will be necessary if you want to find your way around this new intellectual terrain.

Like any physical journey, this intellectual adventure will be most educational if you take some time at the outset to reflect on your own beliefs and values. Take a moment to ask yourself some fundamental questions: What sorts of obligations do you have to those closest to you, such as family members, and why? How do you define justice? What personal moral traits are most important to cultivate? What makes an action morally right or wrong in the first place? Clarifying your own responses to these and similar questions will help you appreciate points of similarity and difference with your own culture as you navigate in this new environment.

It is important to prepare for this trip in another way as well, by learning something about the particular goals of the tour you have chosen, for not every tour of a foreign country covers the same ground. Some introduce you to the history of the country and focus on famous monuments, landmarks, and places of special historical interest. Another tour of the same country might highlight the special topographical features of this place, including its flora and fauna. Still another might attempt to take you down the back roads and introduce you to the folk practices of the people whom most tourists never meet. In short, it is possible to visit a new place with different agendas, different sets of questions and interests, and so learn very different things about the same place. No single trip, especially not one as short as this, can possibly expose you to every important and interesting feature of a country. So, as you begin this exploration of the world of Jewish ethics, you should know something about the orientation of the particular tour on which you are about to embark.

First and foremost, this introduction to Jewish ethics is about a particular religious tradition, Judaism, and the ethics that arises within the context of that tradition as it develops over time. This is to be distinguished sharply from the ethics of Jews, the ethics practiced by Jewish communities throughout their history. If you were to study the latter, you would have to rely on much sociological and demographic information, perhaps surveys designed to discover what Jews now, or in some previous era, actually did in their moral lives: how generous they were toward the poor, how respectful they were of their parents, or how honest they were in their business dealings with others. This study, by contrast, aims to discover what Judaism teaches about how Jews *should* live morally, quite apart from whether Jews actually live up to these standards. This is very much in keeping with the orientation of most books on ethics, which present morality as a system of values and rules that define a "good" life. Some moral systems also devote a good deal of attention to the problem of motivating people to actually adopt these values and live such a moral life and to the question of what sanctions to take against people who fail to do so. In this presentation of Jewish ethics, you will touch on these issues only briefly but will focus largely on what you might think of as the two most basic questions that all systems of morality must address: What is required of a person to live a moral life? How does a person come to know what his or her moral obligations are in the first place? As you will see, the answers to these questions, even in broad outline, are complicated and will require some detailed investigation.

So far, this exploration of Jewish ethics may sound much like other studies in ethics that you may have undertaken, perhaps in philosophy courses. Throughout history, many important thinkers have formulated systems of ethics that attempt to explain the requirements of the moral life and the foundations or source of common moral principles. Perhaps you have studied or encountered references to Aristotle's "golden mean," Immanuel Kant's "categorical imperative," or John Stuart Mill's "utilitarianism." Jewish ethics is different from these other ethical philosophies in one crucial respect: its religious foundations. Like Christian or Buddhist or Islamic ethics, Jewish ethics is an expression of a religious worldview and way of life. Therefore, these moral questions—about what is required to live morally and how people come to know their moral obligations—are answered with reference to Judaism's most basic beliefs about God and human nature, and to its sacred stories about God's role in human history. Jewish ethics, then, is thoroughly religious in nature because the specific moral ideals and standards that Jewish authorities have espoused over the centuries have been shaped decisively by their religious beliefs and practices. As a result, you cannot study Jewish ethics without to some extent studying Judaism as a whole. So this journey takes you first into the world of Judaism as a religious tradition and then explores the ethical values and obligations that arise within that religious system.

Because you will be considering Jewish ethics as part and parcel of Judaism, it stands to reason that this journey will be guided by scholarship in the field of religious studies. This means, first of all, that this investigation, like all scholarly work on religion, attempts to be descriptive and unbiased. It is not the goal here either to praise the merits of Jewish ethics, or, for that matter, to point out its shortcomings. As readers, you may wish to evaluate the strengths and weaknesses of this system of ethics at the conclusion of this study, just as you might evaluate the attractive and unattractive elements of another culture after having lived in it for some time. Even then, it is probably prudent to avoid "rushing to judgment" in your encounter with another culture as much as possible. After all, many of you have found that the

longer you spend in a foreign culture (either physically or intellectually), the more
you get "inside" its thought, the more sense it makes to you, and the more difficult
it is to dismiss. Quite apart from your assessment of Jewish ethics, however, the point
of this book is not to *judge* this system of ethics but to *understand* it. That, in itself, is
a formidable undertaking.

I draw on work in religious studies in a more specific sense, as well, when I utilize the insights of scholars such as Clifford Geertz or Stanley Hauerwas to illumi-
nate some aspect of Jewish ethics. Their work on other traditions, such as Islam or
Christianity, has value for this investigation because Judaism shares with other religious traditions certain basic features.[1] Of course, I cannot undertake here a full-
scale comparison of Jewish and other religious systems of ethics. The territory awaiting you is too vast and the space allotted here too limited to permit that. At various
points along the way, however, I will make observations about key similarities and differences between Jewish and especially Christian ethics. These comparisons may
help orient you, especially if you have some background in another religious tradition, in this unfamiliar terrain.

This commitment to studying Jewish ethics in the context of Judaism also
brings into focus one of the main challenges of producing an introduction of this sort.
Given that Judaism has a history dating back some thirty-five centuries and that
ethics has been a central feature of this religion from the beginning, how is it possible to do justice to this tradition in a single volume, much less one as short as this?
Between biblical times and the present, Judaism has evolved dramatically. The biblical record alone includes expressions of **Israelite** religion spanning nearly a thousand years, during which time Israelite social and political structures changed significantly. Biblical scholars have determined that the Israelites borrowed a number of
practices and ideas from their neighbors (which they often reinterpreted) while
defining themselves in opposition to many other aspects of pagan life. There is no
simple way to summarize the "core" of biblical religion, especially in light of the many
diverse forms in which Israelite religion expressed itself: the sacrificial cult of the
priests, the moral diatribes of the prophets, the laws of Moses, the psalms of David,
and the proverbs of Solomon. Far from displaying uniformity, the biblical text indicates that, at various times and places, Israelites imagined and worshiped God differently, held different sets of values, and expressed their religious devotion in many
different forms and venues.

In moving beyond the biblical period, the picture becomes still more complex.
At various times, Jews lived among Babylonians and Persians, Greeks and Romans,
Zoroastrians, Christians and Moslems, to name only a few. As a result of these many
cultural influences, Judaism evolved new ways of conceptualizing God, new ritual
practices as well as new ways of understanding old ones, and new institutional and
social structures. It is evident, then, that Judaism was something different for the
rabbis teaching in Babylonian academies in 400 C.E. than it was for those living in
the Islamic societies of Spain and North Africa one thousand years later. It was also
understood differently by philosophers in the Middle Ages who were influenced by
Plato and Aristotle than it was by those in the eighteenth century who tried to adapt

Judaism to the ideas of the Enlightenment and the social conditions of modernity. Moreover, Judaism has had its rationalists and its mystics (and many varieties of each), its idealists and its pragmatists, those with a more universal outlook and those with a more ethnocentric perspective. The challenge for scholars and students alike is how to draw these multiple "Judaisms" under a single umbrella, to introduce Judaism and its ethics in a way that does justice to the diversity of the data.

I have tried to respond to this challenge of describing both the diversity and unity within Judaism by offering an introduction to Jewish ethics that identifies coherence within the tradition but resists imposing it where it does not exist. Plainly, these are matters of scholarly judgment; others, relying on the same basic data, could surely present a different picture of Judaism and its ethics than I have presented here. It is important to acknowledge at the outset, then, that my interpretation of the territory you are about to enter has been shaped by several convictions.

First, at the most basic level, Judaism has retained some important ideas and values over the course of its long history. No matter how much they evolve, religious traditions tend by their very nature to be conservative, to preserve the inheritance of prior generations. By way of analogy, U.S. democracy is very different today than it was in 1789 when the Constitution was ratified, yet it is still recognizably the same form of government. Certain basic values, such as civil rights and the separation of powers, remain in place, even if these take different forms. Similarly, you are very different at age nineteen or twenty than you were at six, or at six months, yet you are recognizably the same person, not only genetically, but frequently in terms of core personality traits. Your identity may be evolving, but it is continuous. Identifying the "core" or "essence" of a religious tradition is a more complex matter, but within the tradition itself, adherents frequently point to certain beliefs and basic values that they perceive to be definitive of the tradition as a whole. This presentation of the continuities within Judaism across the centuries will attempt to identify these.

Second, within uniformity there is much room for divergent tendencies. Just as the U.S. system of government allows for different political orientations—for Democrats, Republicans and Independents of various sorts—and for Supreme Court justices to offer different interpretations of the Constitution, Judaism encompasses within it many different and even incompatible tendencies. Although this is true of every religious tradition with a long history, it may be especially so in the case of Judaism. As anyone who has studied classical Jewish literature knows, the ancient rabbis engaged in lively and extended debates on almost every subject they addressed; indeed, they often left important issues unresolved and even fashioned their literature in a way that highlighted their disagreements. To gloss over or minimize the disputes within this tradition, then, would be to seriously misrepresent it. I have been especially attentive to these alternative streams within the tradition, in part because much prior work in Jewish ethics has tended to homogenize them, thus leaving the mistaken impression that Judaism and its ethics is entirely unified and internally consistent.

In attending both to these broad areas of agreement within Judaism and to the many "variations on its themes," I have tried to produce an introduction to Jewish

ethics that is balanced and pluralistic. It is tempting to simplify the presentation of
Jewish ethics by holding up one orientation or expression within this tradition as normative. For some, this has been the universalism of the biblical prophets, the legal-
ism of the rabbis, or the pietism of the medieval mystics. Once some element has
been singled out as the norm or the "highest expression" of Jewish ethics, the other
dimensions of this tradition can justifiably be glossed over or set aside entirely. By
contrast, this presentation of Jewish ethics affirms the many divergent and even contradictory tendencies within the sweep of Jewish tradition, just as a historian of the
U.S. Supreme Court might explain the views of both conservative and liberal justices
but side with neither. In a sense, I have tried to be neither "Democrat" nor
"Republican" but simply to present the many aspects of this tradition, what they
share, where they diverge, and why. Not all perspectives get equal time, but all are
accorded equal respect. To do otherwise would be—returning to the metaphor—
to offer a very skewed and unrepresentative tour of this foreign land and to leave
you with the impression that it is a less complicated and interesting place than it
actually is.

Given all that I have just said, it will not surprise you to learn that this introduction will be broadly conceptual. Rather than attempting to summarize the details
of Jewish ethical teachings—plainly an impossible task—the goal here is to provide
you with a conceptual framework so that you can make sense of the Jewish ethical
tradition as a whole. Of course, the book includes many specific examples of Jewish
moral teachings on a range of subjects from justice and humility to abortion and war,
but always the focus is on the larger features of Jewish ethics as a whole. So I will
here hazard some fairly broad (though I hope not unsubstantiated) generalizations
about Jewish ethics, all the while keeping an eye on those persistent tensions and disagreements within the tradition. As you read, then, you will do well to keep the "big
picture" in mind as you encounter specific details. Like an astute traveler who notices
an unusual local custom, you will want to ask, What does this specific moral rule or
religious practice tell me about the nature of Jewish ethics as a whole?

OUTLINE OF THE BOOK

Having now prepared you for the type of journey that this will be, it is time to give
you a more detailed summary of this trip, your "intellectual itinerary," as it were. You
begin in Chapter One with a brief introduction to religion, ethics, and the intersec-
tion between them. Because you may be new to the study of these fields, some basic
orientation to the types of questions that religion and ethics address should prepare
you for the journey ahead. Here you will take special note of the ways in which ethical questions may be addressed differently in the context of religious life than they
are in a purely secular context.

Chapter Two presents an overview of Judaism, focusing on the ways in which it
grows out of the historical experience of the Jewish people but also shapes that experience. This chapter highlights key theological concepts, especially as they are pre-

served in the traditional daily liturgy. You will discover that the most fundamental categories of Jewish tradition derive from the Hebrew Bible but that they have been shaped decisively by the rabbis of ancient times, whose interpretations of the Bible produced "classical" (or "normative" or "rabbinic") Judaism. Even at this most basic level, you will learn that foundational beliefs about God, humankind, and the nature of the world can be interpreted in several ways.

Chapter Three delves into the world of Jewish texts, which present the ideas and values of traditional Judaism. Because this literature will be unfamiliar to most of you and because much of it is written in a rather peculiar style, it will be helpful to examine closely some representative selections of these classical Jewish books. The chapter notes the special features of this literature, the diverse genres it encompasses, and the historical circumstances in which various books were written. I hope that this will make it easier for you to understand the many quotations from and references to this classical Jewish literature throughout the book.

Having laid this groundwork, Chapter Four turns to a brief overview of traditional Jewish ethics. Following those scholars of ethics who have discerned three separate elements within ethical systems—values, virtues, and rules—you consider one example of each: justice (value), humility (virtue), and honoring parents (rule). These representative aspects of traditional Jewish ethics should help you understand something of the texture and scope of Jewish moral life. Here you will pay special attention to the ways in which each dimension of Jewish ethics is inextricably linked to specific religious beliefs and practices. The value of justice, the virtue of humility, and the obligation to honor parents are not unique to Judaism, of course, but the ways in which Judaism explains and develops these moral perspectives is quite distinctive.

Chapter Five investigates the theoretical dimensions of Jewish ethics, the questions of how people know their moral obligations and of what makes something a moral duty in the first place. This discussion is divided into two parts, for Judaism recognizes two domains of ethics. The tradition assumes the existence not only of universal moral obligations, which are incumbent on every human being but also of a much more extensive set of moral obligations that devolve on Jews alone as the result of their special relationship to God. After exploring the theoretical foundations of both ethical systems, the chapter concludes by considering the relationship between these two overlapping sets of ethical duties.

Chapter Six leaves the world of classical Judaism behind and takes up the many ways in which Judaism and its ethics have been transformed in the modern period. This chapter considers the historical and sociological changes that occurred within Jewish communities in the eighteenth and nineteenth centuries, the specific challenges that they posed to traditional Jewish belief and practice, and the ways in which different groups of Jews responded to them. This brief introduction to contemporary Jewish life will emphasize the various ways in which Jewish thinkers have attempted to fashion a Judaism (and a Jewish ethic) that is recognizably continuous with the tradition while acknowledging that the whole enterprise of constructing a Jewish ethic in the modern period necessarily involves rethinking the very basis of Jewish thought and practice.

Chapter Seven surveys a range of contemporary Jewish ethicists' work. Again, it is necessary to choose representative selections of ethical views on just a few issues and to let these suggest the spectrum of contemporary Jewish ethical discourse. The focus here is on three frequently discussed moral issues—sexual behavior, abortion, and war—and the chapter summarizes the views of a few prominent contemporary Jewish ethicists on each. The goal here is more than just to highlight the range of disagreement among these thinkers; it is to underscore the common challenges that each faces as he or she attempts to "do" Jewish ethics, to offer moral guidance that is grounded in traditional Jewish teaching but that is responsive to the realities in which contemporary Jews live.

The Conclusion invites you to look back on the distance you have traveled since embarking on this journey and to look ahead at the challenges of becoming even more of an "insider" to this tradition. Here I employ the metaphor of learning a new language and suggest that the challenges and rewards of becoming "fluent" in a foreign language closely parallel those of immersing oneself in the study of another moral system.

The world of Jewish ethics is vast and complex, and on this journey it will be possible to introduce you to its main features only in the most general way. Just as you could not reasonably expect to become an expert on another country after visiting for only a few weeks, you can expect to discover here only the most basic features of this new land: the most important ways in which Jewish ethics is distinctive and some of the ways in which the natives express themselves. If this introduction to the study of Jewish ethics is successful, you should feel at the end that you have a conceptual framework within which you could make sense of any information about Jewish ethics that you might ever come across even if the details are new to you. The measure of your understanding, then, should be not how much information you have absorbed, but whether you have at your disposal a set of questions and categories that would help you make sense of the information you know.

I hope that this exploration of Jewish ethics will also give you the tools to think in new and interesting ways about the ethics of other religious traditions, as well as about nonreligious systems of ethics. Above all, this journey should help you to think about the relationship between how a group of people sees the world, its convictions about what is real and true, the moral life that it advocates, and the way it suggests that its members should make their way in the world. At base, all systems of ethics—Jewish and non-Jewish, religious and secular—are grounded in distinctive ways of perceiving reality.

I also hope that the journey on which you are about to embark will be rewarding—eye opening, intellectually stimulating, and enjoyable. I hope, too, that for at least some of you, it will also be morally instructive, for it is my conviction that no moral system has a monopoly on moral wisdom. When you open yourselves up to the insights of another moral tradition, you may well discover that it has something to teach you about how to think and behave morally. Many of you who have traveled to other countries know that, on returning, you integrated something of your experience abroad into your life at home. I invite you to think of this intellectual journey in the same way, as a chance not only to learn new and interesting ideas but also to join with those Jewish thinkers (and with their counterparts in every tradition) who have grappled with the existential questions of moral life: What is the good I should seek? What are the virtues I should cultivate? What are the duties I owe to others? If you are prepared to set out on this journey keeping an open mind about these questions, I believe you will discover that the people you encounter in this book are not only interesting to visit but also make excellent fellow travelers.[2]

Chapter One

Religion, Ethics, and Religious Ethics

Summary

People in all times and places have confronted certain basic questions about the meaning of human existence and the proper way to live. Religion and ethics represent two distinct but related spheres of reflection on these basic questions. This chapter explores the characteristics of human life that make these questions urgent and the ways in which religion and ethics address them. It pays particular attention to the ways in which questions of ethics arise in the context of religious traditions. Finally, descriptive and normative approaches to these questions are differentiated, laying the groundwork for an academic study of religious ethics.

◆ ───

> *[The] demonstration of a meaningful relation between the values a people holds and the general order of existence within which it finds itself is an essential element in all religions, however these values or that order be conceived.*[1]

All of us as human beings live in a world we did not create and, in certain basic respects, we cannot change. The natural cycles of day and night and of seasons that rotate in a regular pattern, as well as the astounding variety of plants and animals, the movements of heavenly bodies, and the array of elements that make up the physical world—are all part of a universe that exists independent of human beings. Humans are born into a vast and complex world for which we can take no credit. Since the beginning of recorded history, we have pondered the nature of this universe and our place within it. In the last few centuries, of course, our understanding

11

of the world has advanced dramatically. As we learn more about the complexity of the world at all levels—from the behavior of subatomic particles to that of distant galaxies—we have more reason than ever to pause and marvel at how the world came to be and what role, if any, we play in this extraordinary universe.

Yet the world around us is not the only source of wonder and speculation. Human life itself is structured in ways that give rise to still more questions. Human life is limited in numerous respects. Most obviously, our physical existence ends in death, and we live (at least as adults) with the knowledge that time will not be ours forever. Moreover, during the course of our lives, we inevitably face the facts of our own vulnerability—to disease and other forms of suffering, to "the slings and arrows of outrageous fortune,"[2] to our own inability to do all that we can, or believe we should, do. Of course, we all have the ability to think abstractly and creatively, yet our powers of cognition are not adequate to answer all the questions we are capable of formulating. Human life is full of wonder and surprise, as well. We are capable of forming deep emotional bonds with one another, of performing acts of great generosity and self-sacrifice, of bravery, but also of foolishness.

These features of human life, along with the features of the natural world that surround us, define the human condition, which is constant across the millenia of recorded time and in all human cultures. Technological advances have enabled us to alter the circumstances of human life somewhat, but not fundamentally. We have learned how to eliminate certain diseases, but we cannot relieve all suffering, nor can we conquer death. We have learned how to calculate the size of distant galaxies, but we do not know for certain how the universe began or what its fate will be billions of years hence. In addition, of course, we cannot escape the quirks of fate that can change the course of our lives radically, for better or worse, from one day to the next. In all these ways, we remain the same limited and vulnerable creatures that we have been throughout human history.

These very aspects of the human condition give rise to a series of questions about the purpose or meaning of life as we experience it. Some of these questions relate to what philosophers call *ontology,* the nature of reality: Given that so much of the world appears to be changing and in flux, what is ultimately real? Is there a reality that transcends the ebb and flow of ordinary life and, if so, what is it? In the final analysis, is the universe one (though it appears in many guises), or is it many? Is the world constructed in a way that promotes or inhibits human strivings, or is it indifferent to them? Other questions concern *soteriology,* the nature and possibility of salvation: Is there a way to escape from the conditions that create human misery and, if so, how? On the other hand, how can we explain human goodness and the many blessings we have? Is there a life beyond death and, if so, what must we do to attain it? Still other questions concern *eschatology,* the end of time: Is there a purpose or direction to human history? Will human history—marked as it is by strife, pain, and failure—someday give way to another kind of existence? How can we know when the culmination of history will come and what, if anything, can we do to hasten it?

Of course, many different answers have been proposed to these questions over the centuries and it is not the purpose here to attempt to review all, or even most, of the alternatives. Rather, the point is to note that these questions are as old and persistent as the human condition itself. In addition, although the questions themselves are not inherently *religious*, many answers to them have been. It is time to turn to the nature of religions and to the distinctive perspectives they bring to these fundamental human questions.

RELIGION, RELIGIONS, AND RELIGIOUS STUDIES

To some extent, everyone is acquainted with religions. Whether through direct personal experience or simply through observation of others, everyone recognizes certain rituals and forms of worship, certain beliefs and institutions, as religious. When scholars try to define precisely the characteristics that mark these as religious, however, two related issues arise. First, because the world's religions exhibit enormous diversity, it is not at all apparent what common feature (or features) unite these disparate phenomena into a single set. The times and places that are considered sacred, the nature of religious authority, the structure of the religious community—all of these differ widely as we survey the world's faiths. What do all religions have in common?

Second, there are rituals and practices that are not commonly thought of as "religious" but that exhibit some of the same traits we commonly associate with religion. For instance, everyone knows that a political rally is not quite the same thing as a religious revival meeting, yet both have distinctive rituals and symbols that move people to identify with a cause greater than themselves. Both of these events often create powerful emotional responses and shape the participants' attitudes and values in profound ways. What distinguishes specifically religious modes of belief and behavior from others that have many of the same effects?

Although there is no single definition of religion on which adherents and scholars of all persuasions can agree, it is apparent that some of the most popular, or commonly proposed, definitions are inadequate. Many people have assumed that religion is defined in terms of belief in a supernatural deity and/or the worship of a power greater than themselves. This appears to be too narrow for, although it accords with the dominant traditions of the West, it cannot account for many religions of the East, such as Taoism and Buddhism, which do not affirm the existence of a supreme being. Others have suggested that religions are defined by "reliance on a pivotal value" around which all of life is oriented. The famous twentieth century Protestant theologian Paul Tillich claimed that religion was whatever people held to be their "ultimate concern."[3] This appears to be too broad, however, for it provides no way to distinguish religions, such as Judaism or Christianity, from ideologies, such as Marxism or even Nazism. Even if some followers of these ideologies adopted them in lieu of a religion or adhered to them with religiouslike fervor, people typically think of religion as involving something more than commitment to a particular ideal.

In this text I will follow those who have defined religion in terms of the experience that underlies it rather than in terms of its psychological or social effects or its institutional forms. The eminent historian of religion, Mircea Eliade, who championed this approach throughout his career, spoke of religion as based on "an experience of the sacred" that was qualitatively different from other sorts of experiences. This experience could not be reduced to or translated into any other category of human experience.[4] In this sense, Eliade's approach to religion is often referred to as *phenomenological,* for he was interested in explaining the phenomenon of religion, the experience of religion, in its own terms. For Eliade, religion arises in "a primary religious experience that precedes all reflection on the world."[5] The sacred manifests itself as something apart from, and more real than, ordinary experience. A religious person encounters this sacred reality as evidence of another realm of existence, more enduring, more powerful, and more awesome than anything occurring in day-to-day, mundane life. Indeed, one of the most powerful effects of this religious experience is the immediate desire to maintain a sharp distinction between this realm of sacred reality and the profane or ordinary reality in which people live most of the time.[6]

Eliade believed that at the core of every religion lies some such experience of the sacred. It is that experience that the religious individual then takes to be the primary point of orientation for his or her life. It provides a way of delineating time and space, for the times and places in which sacred reality is experienced become themselves sanctified, set apart as utterly different from mundane time and ordinary places. Experience of the sacred also provides an orientation toward the natural world and a foundation for one's values. Fundamentally, the religious person strives to orient all of life in relation to this sacred reality. Religious traditions, then, develop as a way of preserving and fostering a connection to this sacred reality. They offer adherents a means by which they can reconnect with or even re-experience this sacred reality, even if the primary experience occurred centuries earlier. Through religious ritual, with the help of specific words and actions, the sacred experience can be made perennially present, and believers can renew their religious orientation to the world.

The precise characteristics of this sacred reality and the particular type of orientation (physical, moral, or spiritual) that it provides are as varied as the human cultures in which religious experience has occurred. Still, it may be helpful to consider some of the salient features of Jewish religion as exemplary of religious experience in general. Judaism asserts the existence of a supernatural being, God, who created and sustains the natural order and who has blessed human life as the culmination of creation. The multiple forces of nature that sometimes threaten humans are actually part of a unified whole, created with purpose and designed to sustain human life. Traditional Judaism has asserted that human history is purposeful as well, and is anything but a clash of blind forces, "full of sound and fury, signifying nothing," as Shakespeare wrote.[7] Instead, history is a drama in which God calls humankind to divine service and in which humans sometimes succeed and sometimes fail to realize God's will. Judaism has asserted that the physical existence that ends in death is not the whole of life. Rather, human beings possess a divine element, a soul that can outlive the body and return to its source. In all these respects, Judaism affirms the existence of a supersensible reality, one that transcends ordinary life and thereby provides it with meaning and orientation.

At this point, it is possible to answer the question posed at the outset of this section. Religious answers to the basic questions that the human condition forces on us can be distinguished from nonreligious answers by the sort of experience that religions take to be central. Whatever else religions do, they assert that "ordinary experience" is secondary in importance to "sacred experience," and that it is the latter that provides a true and proper perspective for thinking about all questions of existence, purpose, and value.[8] To adopt a religious perspective toward life, then, is to believe that there is a supermundane reality and that by placing ourselves in proper alignment or relationship with that reality we gain insight (if not ultimate truth) about the basic questions of human existence. It is this aspect of religion that William James had in mind when he formulated his famous definition of religion as "the feelings, acts, and experiences of individual men in their solitude, so far as they apprehend themselves to stand in relation to whatever they may consider the divine."[9] The point is that religious people do not merely conceptualize or experience "the divine"; they stand in relation to it. As this study will illustrate, this relation is a multifaceted one.

One other important aspect of religion distinguishes it from many other approaches to human life: its intrinsically social character. To be sure, many religions begin with the profound experience of a single individual, such as Mohammed (Islam) or Mary Baker Eddy (Christian Science). However, a religion, to be worthy of attention, must be sustainable, which means it must be communicated to and shared by a group (however small) of adherents. Because this experience of sacred reality provides a distinctive orientation to all of life, the social life of any group of religious devotees will likewise be shaped in some way by religious experience and belief.[10] That is, the form that a religious group takes and the way it organizes and perpetuates itself will be another facet of its religious practice, often a very significant one. Some religious communities are very hierarchical; others are egalitarian. In some religious groups, authority is acquired through direct lineage to great leaders of the past; in others, it is acquired through personal visions or ecstatic experiences; and in still others, it is acquired through years of rigorous study. So religious views of human life are distinctive in part because they are shared by a group and serve to define the characteristics of that group. Just as the twentieth century philosopher Ludwig Wittgenstein noted that there is no such thing as a "private language," so too there are no private religions.[11]

Because religions are social, they often create institutional structures that facilitate the communication and perpetuation of religious beliefs and practices. Everyone is familiar with the institution of the clergy, a specific group of individuals whose training or preparation qualifies them to represent the religion, transmit its teachings, perform its rites, or otherwise serve the needs of the religious community and give it direction. Similarly, many religions institutionalize the places where religious activities occur. Synagogues, churches, and mosques are but a few examples of places devoted to the purposes of the religious community, including worship, study, contemplation, and social interaction. Religions, of course, vary in the types of institutions they foster and in the degree of complexity those institutions exhibit. Few, if any, religions can perpetuate themselves, however, without institutional structures of some sort. So a study of a religion must attend not only to its beliefs and practices but also to the social structures that it employs.

Because religions are social phenomena, and because the experience of the sacred at the core of a religion can be symbolized and ritually celebrated and shared among a group of people, religions can be preserved and transmitted from one generation to the next. We speak of a *religious tradition* as a system of symbols, beliefs, practices and institutions that have been perpetuated across time. Some traditions, such as Judaism, can be traced back across many centuries. Many of its ideas (such as monotheism) and rituals (circumcision), as well as its institutions (synagogues and rabbinic leaders) were first developed in ancient times. Any attempt to understand such a religious tradition faces certain challenges. Because these will be a central focus of this book, it is important to discuss them at the outset of this study.

Religious traditions are complex, very stable in certain respects and yet ever changing. On the one hand, certain symbols and rituals (the cross and the Eucharist in Christianity, for example) persist over time and exhibit strong resistance to change. It is difficult to imagine a group that identified itself as Christian but that rejected the cross as a symbol. Yet it is clear that over many centuries, Christians have used this symbol in many ways: as a model for the design of cathedrals, on Crusaders' flags when they went into battle, it as a piece of jewelry around their necks, and on the front cover of their bibles. Even more significantly, they have understood the meaning of the cross differently. It can symbolize God's love and forgiveness, the redemptive power of suffering, Christian dominion over a place or a people, and/or the fate awaiting those who would reject Christ's message. Any study of a religious tradition, then, must be sensitive to the multiple meanings that religious symbols have taken on over time.

But symbols are not the only aspects of religious traditions that change over time. Basic religious doctrines may change as people develop new understandings of the sacred reality, often in response to new knowledge in other spheres of human life. For example, in the light of Copernican perspectives on the solar system (or Darwinian perspectives on the evolution of animal life on earth), some religious groups have reinterpreted biblical texts about creation. In addition, the scope and locus of religious authority may change as social conditions change. So with the advent of feminism and the recognition that women should share in the opportunities traditionally reserved for men, many religious traditions have ordained women to the clergy. Often new religious rituals develop and old ones are discarded in response to the changing needs and beliefs of a religious community. For example, Jews once celebrated the exodus from slavery in Egypt (Passover) by slaughtering a lamb and placing its blood on the lintel of their homes.[12] Later this practice was replaced by putting a symbolic lamb shank on a special plate (along with other symbols of the exodus) and retelling the story of God's deliverance. More recently still, the story itself has been retold as a lesson about the struggle of the Jews for liberation from political oppression and related to similar struggles among contemporary groups. It is not necessary here to explore the various factors that account for these changes in the celebration of Passover over the centuries. The central point is clear: Certain aspects of a religious tradition, like the presence of a particular symbol or the celebration of a particular holy time, may remain constant. At the same time, the way in which that symbol is interpreted or the meaning associated with the celebration of that holiday may shift dramatically over time.

The fact that religious traditions are constantly changing makes it difficult to study a tradition such as Judaism that has spanned centuries and been influenced by many different intellectual trends and cultural contexts. The tradition, taken as a whole, exhibits enormous diversity. One can reasonably ask whether there is any single, coherent thing called "Judaism" that could be the subject of this textbook. At the very least, it is not obvious how to summarize such a tradition or capture its "essence" and draw any firm conclusions about it. In some respects, the problem is analogous to studying the development of an individual over the span of his or her life. Certainly, the abilities and needs of a person evolve dramatically from infancy through adolescence to adulthood. Even a person's most distinctive traits—physical features or personality quirks—that are evident throughout his or her life change notably over time. Yet who would deny that there is a consciousness of continuity, of being somehow "the same person," throughout all of these changes? Similarly, religious traditions undergo enormous transformations throughout their history yet retain a sense of their distinctive identity.

How shall we locate and describe the distinctiveness of a religious tradition? I suggest that, while it is impossible to draw together every detail of a tradition and to encompass all the variations within a single coherent model, it is surely possible to identify the most enduring characteristics and to trace their development. In introducing a religious tradition, it may not be possible to account for every development, but it is possible to sketch the range of variation with respect to a given idea or ritual or institution. In Chapter Two I will discuss this approach in relation to Judaism specifically, but for now it is sufficient to note that studying a religious tradition requires attention both to persistence and to change. In addition, it forces people to seek patterns of coherence among those changes. The distinctive identity of a tradition, like that of an individual person, lies in the complex interplay of elements that fluctuate over time and those that endure.

Approaching religious traditions in this way does not begin with any presuppositions about the truth (or falsity) of the phenomena studied. A scholarly approach to the study of religion takes no position pro or con on the merits of particular religious views or practices. Its goal is not to defend or promote the cause of a religious tradition but simply to understand it. This approach does not entail making any claims to "objectivity." As careful observers of the historical development of a religious tradition, people can readily concede that what they observe as well as how they understand it is limited by their situation. Other observers, situated differently, using other tools of analysis, might well see other patterns and draw different conclusions. The distinguishing feature of this academic approach to religion, however, is its unwavering neutrality with respect to the truth claims of the tradition it studies.

This approach to the study of a religious tradition is markedly different from that often taken by adherents of the tradition itself. Those who stand within the tradition are committed in some measure to the truths that their religion proclaims. At least to some degree, they choose to live their lives in relation to those experiences of the sacred that are central to the community. This, of course, does not preclude critical reflection on their own experience or on the reflections of those who have explored the meaning of this tradition before them. They are *participants in,* not only *observers of,* this religious tradition. For that reason, they typically defend the validity of their tradition even if they maintain a critical distance from some aspects of it.

The academic study of religion, although perhaps new to some readers, has been a part of the scholarly world since at least the middle of the nineteenth century. Since that time, numerous approaches to the analysis of religious phenomena have been developed by philosophers, psychologists, sociologists, anthropologists, and historians, among others. There is no need here to survey the history of scholarly studies of religion, which are continually being developed and refined, but it is important to indicate the approach represented in this study of Judaism and its ethics so that the control questions are clear from the outset.

This analysis of Judaism's ethics takes its orientation from the work of the noted anthropologist, Clifford Geertz.[13] Among the many insightful aspects of Geertz's work is his insistence that religions must be understood as "cultural systems," which create meaning through the synthesis of "worldview" and "ethos." In Geertz's words,

> sacred symbols [and, by implication, all religions] function to synthesize a people's ethos—the tone, character, and quality of their life, its moral and aesthetic style and mood—and their world view—the picture they have of the way things in sheer actuality are, their most comprehensive ideas of order.[14]

This means that, in the context of religious systems, beliefs about ultimate reality are intimately connected with values about how one ought to live. Each religious symbol, practice, or ritual, fuses some aspect(s) of the believer's worldview with some aspect(s) of the believer's way of life.

Geertz makes the same point when he notes how religious symbols function simultaneously as a "model of reality" and a "model for reality."[15] By this he means that some models are symbolic representations of a reality that already exists in the world. A highway map is a symbol in this sense, representing through various lines and other markings the roads of a particular geographical region. Other models are symbolic representations of a reality that has yet to be created. A blueprint is a good example of this sort of symbol, for it functions to tell a builder how to create a particular structure. While some symbols represent the *world as it is,* other symbols represent a *world that needs to be created.* In Geertz's view, religious symbols serve both functions simultaneously. A religious symbol, like the cross, both represents a reality that already exists (the event of the Crucifixion) and a reality that believers are being called to create (for example, a world filled with God's love or one in which suffering is accepted willingly).

This insight into the interrelationship between worldview and ethos, the world as it is perceived to be and the world as we wish it to be, has important implications for the way people study religious ethics. To understand the ethical views of a particular religious group, for example, the Jews, people must first take account of the group's ontology, its ideas about reality—its worldview. Then the moral guidance it offers, the virtues it promotes, the course of action it advocates—its ethos—must be examined. Finally, the study must look for the ways in which these two elements of a religious system are mutually reinforcing. Later this chapter will examine some more concrete ways in which this interaction can be traced by looking at the function of specific rituals. For now it is sufficient to note that Geertz's approach to religions as systems of meaning provides an orientation to the study of religious beliefs and values. Before this relationship between worldview and ethos can be examined, however, it is necessary to consider the nature of ethics as a distinctive sphere of human concern.

MORALITY AND ETHICS

Ethics, like religion, arises in response to basic features of human existence. Just as people are driven to ask questions about the nature of the world around them and their place within it, they also inevitably confront practical questions about how to live in a world with others. If religions respond to questions about the very nature of the cosmos and of humankind, ethics responds to questions about human interaction, how to orient our lives in relation to others.[16]

Questions of morality probably long predate civilization as we know it. Long before the dawn of recorded history, our primate ancestors began living in groups. We may never know exactly how or why human sociality began, but we may surmise that the reasons were at least partly pragmatic. In groups, people could more easily provide resources for essential human activities: hunting or gathering food, raising offspring, defending themselves from hostile forces (either natural or human) that threatened, and caring for the weak and elderly. Of course, social life satisfied other needs as well: for companionship, for sharing stories, and for learning and transmitting knowledge beyond the limited sphere of one's own experience.

Living with others is at the heart of ethics. If people were absolutely alone in the world, there would be no moral questions to consider. By contrast, living in society forces people to confront the multiple ways in which their interactions with others affect both them (as individuals and the groups to which they belong) and themselves. For example, consider the many ways in which groups make claims on individuals creating rules to follow; making demands for their time, energy, and/or resources; and restricting their personal freedom to do or say whatever they please. This immediately gives rise to one basic type of moral question: How does an individual act in situations when the individual's needs conflict with the needs of another or of the community as a whole? Consider, too, the ways in which even the most basic choices that individuals—make about what to eat, the words to speak to and about others, the way to use the natural resources at their disposal—affect others, perhaps including others they will never meet and whose names they will never know. Living as social animals, such issues are inevitable. How people address them is, in part, the subject of ethics.

Ethics involves more than resolving conflicts between the individual and the group, however. Humans are endowed with the intellectual capacity to consider alternative courses of action and to foresee (though not perfectly) the consequences that our actions will have on others. Moreover, as humans, we are free to choose to act in ways that either benefit or harm others (and ourselves). We also have the ability to experience suffering and joy and, through our actions, to create these experiences in others. We also can imagine a social world quite different from the one in which we actually live and so work toward making the actual world conform more closely to our ideal model.

These basic human capacities—abstract thought, free will, emotional experience, and the ability to affect others by our actions—are the preconditions of the moral life. Those who lack one or more of these features, such as the mental capacity to understand the consequences of their own actions, are not held morally accountable for their actions as competent adults are. These capacities express themselves in many ways. Humans have the ability to decide what we will say to others (and how) and what we will conceal from them, the extent to which we will help or ignore them, and the degree to which we will facilitate cooperation or hinder it. We also have an ability, apparently unique among animals, to reflect on our own behavior and judge it in relation to abstract standards. We can formulate moral standards ("it is morally wrong to lie"), and exceptions to them ("unless telling the truth would be more hurtful to the people involved") and inculcate these moral standards in others (our children, for example). We often assign moral praise or blame to others and/or to ourselves for upholding those standards or failing to do so. We can seek forgiveness from those we have harmed, and we can bear grudges against those who have harmed us. We also are capable of feeling guilt for our own misdeeds (or even immoral intentions). In short, given the complexity of human interactions and the nature of moral agency, hardly any encounter between persons lacks moral consequences.[17]

At this point, it is necessary to attempt to bring some conceptual clarity to this discussion of ethics. What exactly is ethics? Like religion, ethics is notoriously difficult to define with precision. People commonly think of ethics as having to do with what is "right" or "good." Yet they recognize that when they say, It is good to change the oil in a car every 3,000 miles, they mean something quite different than when they say, It is good to help those who are frail. In the first instance, "good" means merely "useful" or "beneficial" in relation to some goal (having a car that runs well), while in the second, "good" points to a moral action. But what exactly is it that defines an action as "moral" or "immoral?"

Although philosophers have offered various answers to this question, they have generally agreed on this much: Moral questions involve defining those actions (or attitudes or character traits) that establish and maintain proper relationships among people. So, for example, in the ordinary course of things, deciding what shirt to wear is not a moral question but deciding how to talk to our children is, for only in the latter case does the action have consequences for sustaining a relationship with another person. Philosophers have sometimes used the term "other regarding" to refer to this dimension of ethics, which always involves concern for others and a person's relationship to them. It is important to note that the "others" who command ethical attention need not themselves be moral agents. They may be infants who are incapable of making moral judgments themselves or people not yet born (as when we talk about having a moral obligation to preserve our natural resources for future generations). Nor need morality even be focused on definite actions, as when we are told that it is morally wrong to harbor hatred toward others in our hearts. Whether the focus is on actions or attitudes, rules or values or virtues, however, morality always concerns relationships with others.

The problem with this minimal definition of morality is that it does not yet delineate morals from other "other-regarding" systems of behavioral norms, for example, law or etiquette. Although the relationship between morality and law continues to be debated by ethicists and legal philosophers, several things seem to be clear. First, a system of law is (in principle, if not always in fact) finite, capable of articulation in a set of rules specifying proper and improper actions. Morality, by contrast, is not necessarily reducible to such a catalog, for it may enjoin people to be "benevolent" or "caring" without specifying precisely what this might mean in every situation. Second, law (again generally, though not always) entails a notion of enforcement. That is, laws are typically accompanied by the threat of force against those who would disobey them. By contrast, morality is not "enforceable," at least not by physical force. Morals do, of course, often carry social sanctions of other sorts, as when those who act callously are shunned by their acquaintances. These sanctions fall far short of the types of punishment typically associated with violating the law, however.

The relationship of morality to other sets of behavioral norms, such as etiquette, points to a second basic feature of morality: It typically carries a kind of "weight" or "authority" that overrides other action guides. How we serve food to guests at the dinner table and how we address invitations to a social event may have consequences for our relationships with others, but we do not regard these as moral issues. *Morality* concerns what is good or right in a more "ultimate" sense; its authority is not merely what is conventional or accepted social practice, for morality sometimes calls such social practices into question. Rather, moral judgments are grounded in principles that people regard as universal, more enduring, or more rational than other social norms. This is the reason that moral concerns "trump" other social norms when the two conflict; indeed, some have argued that morality takes precedence over law, as well.[18] Although philosophers have disagreed about exactly what gives morality this sort of weight, most have agreed that this feature is intrinsic to morality.

THEORETICAL AND APPLIED ETHICS

Up to this point, I have been using the words *morality* and *ethics* interchangeably, which is the way they are often used in ordinary conversation. Some, however, have given these terms more technical meanings that help delineate the practical from the theoretical aspects of the subject. This distinction needs to be explored, for I will refer to it regularly throughout the remainder of this book.

Some reserve the word *morality* to denote the practical questions of what is right and wrong, good and bad. How ought people to treat their aging parents or their disobedient children? What obligations do people have to the disadvantaged: people who are poor, handicapped, or who have mental or emotional disabilities? Under what circumstances, if any, can people terminate the life of an unborn child or of someone in a persistent vegetative state? How should people regard those who have harmed them or those they love? What responsibility do people have to do what is right for others when this entails negative consequences for themselves? These are all *moral* questions, for they concern attitudes and behaviors that pertain directly to our relationships with others.

It is important to recognize that all such practical (or as some call them, "first-order") moral questions concern *values*. Any claim that another person should be treated in a particular way must rest on a view of what makes a person valuable and how the value of a human being should be reflected in his as her treatment. When people face a moral quandary, uncertain which of two options represents the more moral choice, they are really confronted by conflicting values, each of which has a claim on them. The ultimate subject of morality, then, is what people value in human beings and in human relationships, how they express those values, and how they prioritize them when they hold values that cannot both be expressed in the same situation.

Over and above these practical questions, scholars have raised numerous theoretical issues about the nature of morality itself. These "second-order" questions, some of which I have touched on already, concern the way people understand moral judgments. How do they differentiate the realm of morality from that of law or other normative dimensions of life? How do they justify their moral stands? Is there a rational or objective basis for choosing between opposing moral views? What are the goals of the moral life? What are the necessary criteria for being a moral agent, that is, for being capable of making moral judgments? These questions and others like them are *ethical* insofar as they concern the theoretical foundation of moral practice and judgment. Morality, then, concerns practical questions of what is right and wrong; ethics concerns abstract questions about the nature of right and wrong. Employing this distinction, I might say that all of us make *moral* judgments in our daily lives, but relatively few of us contemplate *ethical* issues on a regular basis.

It is important to stress the character of this academic approach to the study of morality and ethics, as I did earlier in this chapter with respect to religion. My task here is to analyze the moral views and to some extent the ethical theories articulated within one religious tradition, Judaism. In doing so, I must be careful to bracket my own moral judgments. At times, I may feel that what Judaism teaches about some moral problem (for example, abortion or euthanasia) is problematic, but my purpose here is to understand the basis for these views, to explore the ways in which they are connected to other dimensions of Judaism, rather than to assess whether they are right or wrong. Although I am examining a system of moral norms, I must remain *descriptive*, not *normative* in my focus. Of course, it may happen that as I come to understand the moral views of others, they will have an influence on my own. For many, one of the attractions of studying religious ethics is that it helps them hone their own moral sensitivities.

RELIGIOUS ETHICS

By this point, it will be obvious that religion and ethics represent at least partly overlapping spheres. In both our religious and our ethical lives, we ask questions about our place in the world, how we are related to others, and what makes us distinctively human. Both raise questions of *value*, and both concern the meaning and purpose of human life. In one sense, religion is broader than ethics, for it encompasses questions not only about human interaction but also about "the sacred" and our relationship to the whole of the world around us. Religion includes teachings not only about our moral obligations but also about our proper ritual and ceremonial behavior. Of course, ethical reflection need not be tied to a particular religious tradition or to religion at all. Indeed, much contemporary ethics is secular in nature and rejects any intrusion of religious views. But while ethics can be independent of religion, it is rare for religion to ignore ethics. Most often, religious traditions have rather well-defined ethical components. Certainly, that is the case for Judaism.

What is distinctive about "doing ethics" in a religious context? How is religious ethics different from secular ethics? What types of distinctive challenges await you as you begin to examine the ethics of a particular religious tradition?

First, you will discover that religious groups often appeal to an authority for their ethical judgments that those outside the religious community would not recognize. For Jews, as you shall see, one such authority is the will of God, particularly as codified in Scripture and in a vast corpus of rabbinic writings that interpret Scripture and expand on Jewish religious (including moral) responsibility. Within this context, it makes perfect sense to cite a passage from Scripture or from the **Talmud** as a "prooftext" that a particular action is required or proscribed. When no traditional text quite applies to the situation at hand, it may be necessary to argue using a combination of logic and analogy to derive from the traditional sources a principle that fits the moral situation. In any case, Jews have an inherited body of religious teachings that their religious tradition has vested with authority and to which they appeal for moral guidance. This contrasts with secular ethicists who generally hold that moral truths must be grounded in human faculties alone, independent of any religious authority.

Second, and more substantively, religious ethics are shaped by religious beliefs, for example, about God, the moral capacity of human beings, the perfectibility of the created world, the purpose of human life, and the afterlife, to name just a few. These types of beliefs can influence morality in a number of ways: (1) by giving rise to new moral obligations, (2) by providing a religious grounding for moral duties that others could justify on nonreligious grounds, and (3) by providing religious sanctions, either positive or negative, for moral behavior. In addition, religious communities often shape morality (4) by providing a context in which moral development is fostered and moral dilemmas resolved and (5) by creating and supporting religious leaders who exercise some manner of authority over the moral life of the community. Although this list is by no means exhaustive, it helps you to see that religious ethics may differ from secular ethics in both content and tone. It is worthwhile to examine briefly each of these aspects of religious ethics using examples drawn from the Jewish tradition.

First, most of us at one time or another have been in a situation in which a friend or acquaintance hurt us in a way we felt was unwarranted. Perhaps the other person was genuinely remorseful and asked for our forgiveness. At that point, we were faced with a moral question: Should we grant forgiveness and, if so, why? Forgiving entails a willingness to maintain this relationship in some form *despite* the offense that has occurred. It may not mean that the offense is entirely forgotten or that the relationship will be exactly as it was beforehand. The request for forgiveness is a plea to look past the offense in question and not to terminate the relationship on its account. Under what circumstances, if any, do we have a moral obligation to forgive?

Although the answer to this question may depend on the nature of the offense and of the relationship involved, in general it has been claimed that on secular grounds, we can never be morally required to preserve a relationship in the aftermath of a breach by the other party. Our relationships with others are, in this sense, like contracts; if the other party breaches his or her duties, we are released from our responsibility to continue in the contractual relationship.

Judaism does, however, recognize a duty to forgive others. Analyzing the sources that discuss this, we discover that certain religious beliefs underlie this duty. In particular, it is believed that God is merciful and forgives both those who deserve such compassion as well as those who do not. Jews are expected to emulate God in this respect. As one traditional source puts it, when Scripture admonishes us to "walk in God's ways" (Deuteronomy 28:9), this means:

> As the ways of Heaven are to be gracious, graciously bestowing gifts not only upon those who know Him but also upon those who do not know Him, so you are to bestow gifts upon one another. And, as the ways of Heaven are to be long-suffering, long-suffering with the wicked and then accepting them in repentance,

so you are to be long-suffering [with the wicked] for their good and not impatient
to impose punishment upon them. For, as the ways of Heaven are abundant in
lovingkindness, ever leaning to lovingkindness, so are you ever to lean toward
doing kindness to others rather than lean toward doing them harm.[19]

The tradition suggests that as beneficiaries of divine compassion, Jews should do no
less for others than God has done for them. This is but one instance of Judaism's
postulating a moral duty that arises in a context of particular beliefs about God's
attributes.[20]

Second, Judaism provides a new justification for moral rules that could be (and
have been) established on secular principles alone. The prohibition against taking the
life of others without cause and the requirement to help save the life of another (at
least if this does not entail significant risk to a person's own life) are two examples of
widely accepted moral rules. In the context of Jewish teaching, however, these are
presented as corollaries of the belief that human beings are created in the image of
God, as Genesis 1:27 states. The ancient rabbis reflected as well on the enormity of
these moral duties in relation to the story of God's creating Adam and in propagat-
ing the entire human race beginning with a single man.

Man was created alone in order to teach you that if anyone destroys a single soul,
Scripture regards that person as if he had destroyed the entire world; and if anyone saves a single soul, Scripture regards that person as if he had saved the entire
world.[21]

Again, this Jewish religious teaching does not change the substance of the moral pro-
scription concerning murder or the moral requirement to save another's life. Indeed,
some authorities include these sorts of laws in a category of things that humans could
know through reason alone, without the benefit of the **Torah**,[22] yet the biblical creation story provides a rich source of reflection on the meaning and basis of these
moral rules.

Third, among the persistent questions that philosophers have debated is why
people should be moral. Granting that people can determine what their moral duties
are, what reason is there to fulfill them? Some, like the eighteenth century philosopher Immanuel Kant, argued in effect that acting in accord with reason necessitates
acting in accord with moral principles. Others have noted that it may be impossible
to offer a purely prudential justification for acting morally because doing so sometimes requires people to make sacrifices that are not in their immediate, egoistic self-
interest (as when a moral individual returns a wallet full of money to its owner).[23]

Within Judaism, by contrast, it is often claimed that those who act morally will
indeed be better off, for they will receive divine rewards for their behavior. In the
Bible, God promises to grant the Israelites various blessings and to protect them
from various maladies if they honor their parents (Exodus 20:12; Deuteronomy 5:16)
and do what is "good and right in the sight of the Lord your God" (Deuteronomy
12:28). Later rabbinic sources suggest that those who visit the sick and help support
the poor and who clothe the naked and help to make peace will benefit in the world

to come.[24] Jewish authorities frequently claim that one's moral action in this life can decisively affect one's eternal destiny. Of course, the threat of punishment for violating moral rules goes hand in hand with the promise of blessings for those who observe them. Jewish tradition is replete with such threats, including the famous set of curses and blessings presented, in graphic detail, in Deuteronomy, Chapters 28 and 29. These passages and others like them are obviously calculated to motivate people to fulfill their moral duties. It should be noted that the tradition also offers other motivations: In light of God's benevolence, people should demonstrate their gratitude by observing God's laws and that living morally will bring them into a closer, deeper relationship with God. All of these represent religious sanctions for moral behavior.

Fourth, religious rituals and symbols, shared in the context of a religious community, can heighten awareness of the moral dimensions of life, reinforce moral responsibilities, and provide moral guidance. Within Judaism, perhaps the most powerful example of this is the ritual surrounding Yom Kippur, the Day of Atonement. In ancient times, this was the day when the high priest engaged in an elaborate rite of purification and expiation on behalf of the Israelites. It was understood that if the rite were performed properly, God would forgive the Israelites for the sins of the past year. In the words of Scripture, "You shall be clean before the Lord" (Leviticus 16:30).[25] Since the destruction of the ancient **Temple** in 70 C.E. and the advent of worship services in synagogues, Yom Kippur has become a day of intense supplication and self-reflection, accompanied by fasting and other acts of self-denial. Through the course of the day, certain liturgical texts such as the following are recited repeatedly, cataloging the moral failings of the community and the moral weakness of human beings whose life and fate are in God's hands:

> For the sin which we have committed against You under compulsion or of our own will,
> And for the sin which we have committed before You by hardening our hearts,
> For the sin which we have committed before You unknowingly,
> And for the sin which we have committed before You with utterance of the lips,
> For the sin which we have committed before You by unchastity,
> And for the sin which we have committed before You openly or secretly.[26]

The overall effect of reciting this litany throughout the day is to heighten Jews' awareness of their moral tasks, holding up a model of genuine repentance for the past and holding out the possibility of renewed moral purpose in the year ahead.

Finally, within traditional Jewish communities, the rabbi functioned as a religious/moral authority. He (all traditional rabbis were men) was expected to be both learned and pious, knowledgeable about the teachings of the tradition, and a model in his personal life of virtuous behavior. Faced with moral dilemmas, it was common for Jews to bring their questions to the rabbi in their community or, in some instances, communicate their concern to an eminent authority in another place. The rabbi would then offer moral guidance, either orally or in the form of a written **responsum**, which was presumed to be authoritative for that individual. In this way,

Judaism provides a living authority figure who speaks for the tradition to the individual situation of the adherent. This represents one more way in which this religious tradition shapes the moral life of individual adherents.

In all, religious ethics is distinctive for many reasons. Potentially every aspect of moral life—moral reasoning, moral development, the content of moral responsibility—is shaped by religious faith and practice. As James Gustafson, a prominent Christian ethicist, has said, the central moral question for Christians is "what is God calling us to be and to do."[27] Being a member of a religious community, people face moral questions, not ultimately as an isolated individual, but in dialogue with coreligionists across space and time. Moreover, as Stanley Hauerwas, another important Christian ethicist, has suggested, the moral life of people who belong to religious communities is shaped by distinctive religious myths or stories. These give believers both a particular vision of reality and a corresponding orientation toward God and other people. In Hauerwas's words, "we can only act in the world we see, a seeing partially determined by the kind of beings we have become through the stories we have learned and embodied in our life plan."[28] In significant ways, religious people see the world differently from those who are secular and so are motivated to act in the world and toward others in ways consonant with that vision.

It follows that the primary task for students of Jewish ethics is to discern the distinctive ways in which Judaism has conceived the world in general and human life in particular. This will then enable them to notice the myriad connections that religious beliefs, rituals, and institutions have on the moral life of the Jewish community. This will make it possible to analyze the connection of Jewish religion to Jewish ethics only in an introductory way, but even this limited task will require students to have a somewhat detailed knowledge of classical (or rabbinic) Judaism as it took shape in antiquity and has persisted through the intervening centuries. Some of the examples discussed in this chapter, have already introduced you to some features of Jewish religious life and thought. It is time now to continue laying the foundation for this study of Jewish ethics by exploring some of the salient features of traditional Jewish belief and practice.

KEY POINTS

- Religions address persistent questions about the human condition: the origins of life, the purpose of human existence, and the nature of what is real, among others.

- Religions focus on an experience of something "sacred," beyond the realm of the ordinary; they attempt to orient human life in relation to that sacred reality, to preserve and recreate a connection to that sacred experience.

- Religious traditions are both conservative and dynamic. They preserve certain narratives (myths), symbols, and rituals as key means of understanding and approaching ultimate reality, yet the meaning of these narratives, the use of these symbols, and the practice of these rituals may change dramatically over time.

- The academic study of religions remains neutral with respect to the truth claims of the religion under study; its goal is neither to advocate nor to discredit any religious belief or practice, only to understand it.
- Ethics concerns what is "good" in human life and what is "right" in relationships with others in the most basic and ultimate sense.
- Because human life is inherently social, ethical issues—about what character traits to cultivate, what values to adhere to, and what obligations we have to others—are inescapable.
- Ethics encompasses both practical and theoretical questions. Practical questions include how to avoid harming others, whether certain sorts of people are entitled to preferential treatment, and how to resolve conflicts between values. Theoretical questions include how people come to know their ethical obligations, how to distinguish ethics from other normative aspects of human life (like etiquette or law), and why they should be moral altogether.
- Within the context of religious traditions, ethical questions (both theoretical and practical) are raised and addressed in distinctive ways. Religions can (1) give rise to distinctive moral duties, (2) provide distinctive reasons for moral duties that could also be justified on nonreligious grounds, (3) specify rewards and punishments for acting morally or failing to do so, (4) create a context for the moral development of individuals, and (5) provide religious authorities who offer moral guidance to members of their communities.

QUESTIONS TO CONSIDER

1. Think about a time when you debated a moral issue (e.g., abortion, war, capital punishment) with others. What principles did you (or they) appeal to? Were any of them religious? If not, think of religious beliefs that could influence someone's position on these issues.

2. We all know people who are not fully religious in Eliade's sense, who do not completely orient themselves in relation to a sacred reality, but who are also not entirely secular. How does religion influence someone's life when it is just one of many points of orientation? What role does, or could, it play in that person's moral life?

3. Consider a famous religiously based moral leader (e.g., Mahatma Gandhi, Martin Luther King, Jr., Mother Teresa). How would you describe the relationship between his or her religious faith and moral life—the values the individual upheld and the roles he or she played in society?

4. We know that religion does not always have a positive moral effect on people. Sometimes religions motivate people to commit acts most of us would describe as terribly immoral. What aspects of religion make it susceptible to functioning as a force for moral as well as immoral behavior?

5. What specific obstacles do you have to overcome in order to engage in this academic study of Jewish ethics? Are there specific religious beliefs or moral viewpoints that you will need to set aside in order to make sense of Judaism's worldview and moral system?

Chapter Two

Judaism and Jewish Ethics

Summary

Judaism as an evolving religious tradition is introduced. Its origins in ancient Israelite belief and practice are explored, and the basic characteristics of rabbinic or classical Judaism are explained. This chapter explains some salient features of Jewish ethics in relation to these fundamental dimensions of Jewish life and thought.

To the philosophers: the idea of the good was the most exalted idea, the ultimate idea. To Judaism the idea of the good is penultimate. It cannot exist without the holy. The good is the base, the holy is the summit. Man cannot be good unless he strives to be holy.[1]

WHAT IS JUDAISM?

Judaism is a religious tradition whose origins lie in the distinctive worldview and way of life developed by the ancient Israelites. Rooted in the Hebrew Bible, it is the religion of a particular people who have always understood themselves to stand in a unique relationship with God. The Israelites (later Jews) viewed themselves as "a kingdom of priests and a holy nation" (Exodus 19:6), which is to say, as a national group with a fundamentally religious identity and purpose. For this reason, to understand the specific beliefs and practices central to this religious tradition, this chapter begins with a consideration of the people themselves, their origins, and the special religious destiny to which they felt and continue to feel called. This presentation will provide a framework within which you can make sense of their religious experience or, as discussed in the last chapter, the way they understand "sacred reality" and their relationship to it. As you will see, a few basic categories have remained central to Jewish religious experience across the ages. The task here is to explore those categories that structure Jewish religious life and begin to examine the ways in which they shape Jewish ethics.

Story and Law: The Narrative and the Normative

The story of the Jewish people, where they came from, and how they have understood themselves, begins with the Hebrew Bible, which records that the Israelite people begins with the journey of one Abram (later renamed Abraham) from the city of Ur in Mesopotamia to the land of Canaanin about 1800 **B.C.E.** God commands Abraham to take this journey and promises him that his destiny is to be the father of a great nation, with descendants as numerous as the stars in heaven, and that the land of Canaan will belong to them in perpetuity (Genesis 13:14–17). The book of Genesis is devoted primarily to relating stories about Abraham's sojournings, his family, their relationship with God, and their encounters with their Canaanite neighbors. Abraham's grandson Jacob (later renamed Israel) fathers twelve sons who become the ancestors of the Israelite tribes. The descendants of this familial clan become enslaved in Egypt for several hundred years and then, in fulfillment of the divine promise to Israel's ancestors, God dramatically liberates the people and leads them back to their homeland, which they conquer with divine assistance. As you will see, this exodus from Egypt and liberation from slavery become a paradigm for Jews of God's acting within history to ensure the redemption of the Jewish people from oppression.

The defining moment in Israel's history occurs along the way, in the wilderness between the slavery in Egypt they have left behind and the "promised land" they are preparing to enter. God speaks directly to the Israelites and to their leader Moses at Mt. Sinai, revealing a body of divine instruction (**Torah**) to guide them from that time forth. Through this act of divine revelation, God and Israel enter into a covenant, a relationship of mutual obligations. Israel's life as a nation is to be governed by God's law and their destiny is to be God's own people.

Whether historians can confirm the veracity of this account, in whole or in part, does not concern us here. The Biblical story clearly captures the Israelites' own understanding of their origins. The story itself is encapsulated in a ritual proclamation that Israelites recited each year when they brought the first fruits of their land to the Temple in Jerusalem as an offering. It continues to occupy a central place in the **haggadah,** the traditional text recited on the holiday of Passover, which commemorates the Exodus (Deuteronomy 26:5–9):

> My father was a fugitive Aramean. He went down to Egypt with meager numbers and sojourned there; but there he became a great and very populous nation. The Egyptians dealt harshly with us and oppressed us; they imposed heavy labor upon us. We cried to the Lord, the God of our ancestors, and the Lord heard our plea and saw our plight, our misery, and our oppression. The Lord freed us from Egypt by a mighty hand, by an outstretched arm and awesome power, and by signs and

portents. God brought us to this place and gave us this land, a land flowing with milk and honey.

In response to God's beneficence, Israelites believed it was their duty to observe God's Torah and that, if they did so, they would continue to enjoy God's favor (Deuteronomy 4:39–40):

> Know therefore this day and keep in mind that the Lord alone is God in heaven above and on earth below; there is no other. Observe God's laws and command- ments, which I enjoin upon you this day, that it may go well with you and your children after you, and that you may long remain in the land that the Lord your God is giving you for all time.

The Jews' understanding of themselves, then, is rooted in this epic story of promise and fulfillment, of being singled out by God for a special purpose, of being liberated from slavery, and especially of being the recipients of God's law, which they are to cherish as a sign of God's love.

This story lies at the heart of the Jews' traditional understanding of themselves; by paying close attention to its themes, we can discern the core elements in classical Jewish religious life. The elements are principally these:

- God's love of Israel and Israel's corresponding duty to love and honor God.
- Torah as a body of divine revelation communicated exclusively to Israel.
- The study of Torah and the observance of God's law as the primary means of demonstrating devotion to God.
- The covenant between God and Israel, often symbolized as a kind of marriage.
- The assurance that Israel's historical destiny will rise or fall depending on its devotion to God or lack thereof.

You can see how these themes are woven together into a coherent whole by examining the central prayer of traditional Jewish life. The **Sh'ma,** which stands at the heart of the morning and evening worship services, is not strictly speaking a prayer but a collection of three scriptural passages. The first paragraph (Deuteronomy 6:4–9) reads as follows:

> Hear, O Israel, the Lord is our God, the Lord alone. You shall love the Lord your God with all your heart and with all your soul and with all your might. Take to heart these instructions with which I charge you this day. Impress them upon your children. Recite them when you stay at home and when you are away, when you lie down and when you get up. Bind them as a sign on your hand and let them serve as a symbol on your forehead, inscribe them on the doorposts of your house and on your gates.

The subsequent paragraphs of the *Sh'ma* (Deuteronomy 11:13–21 and Numbers 15:37–41) assert that Israel will prosper or suffer insofar as it heeds or ignores God's law and that Israelites are to wear a special fringed garment to remind them of their obligation to observe God's law. Given the importance of these themes—God's love and protection of Israel, observing the divine commandments as the means by which

Israel shows its love of God, and the history of Israel as a reflection of its relationship with God—it is hardly surprising that the *Sh'ma* was placed by the rabbis at the very center of the morning and evening worship services or that these were prescribed as the last words a traditional Jew was to say before dying.

Beginning in the first century C.E., the rabbis greatly developed each aspect of this religious system, particularly through their voluminous explications of Scripture and their interpretation and expansion of the law. Rules that receive only scant attention in the biblical text, treated perhaps in only a verse or two, were developed into whole treatises; rules were reinterpreted in light of contemporary social realities, and whole bodies of law were generated with no direct basis in Scripture at all. The justification for all this legal development was clear to them: *since it is above all through proper observance of God's law that Israel demonstrates its devotion to God, the law must govern every aspect of life, infusing even the most mundane activities with holiness.*

Expounding the details of the law was the ultimate form of service to God in two separate respects. First, insofar as the Torah is divine, exploring its every detail enabled one, as it were, to probe God's mind. Studying Torah thus offered insights into the very nature of the universe. Second, by developing the law as they did, the rabbis believed they were making explicit God's will for Jews in every aspect of their lives. The study of Torah, then, was an end unto itself, as well as a means for determining the full extent of the Jews' duties to God. Ultimately, through expounding and observing the law, traditional Jews confirmed their status as God's special people whose holy way of life was the source of their communal identity and the key to their ultimate redemption. Torah, then, was both God's gift to Israel and Israel's primary form of devotion to God. In terms of Geertz's theory discussed in Chapter One, Torah for Jews is both a model of reality (the Jews' being chosen by God for a special destiny) and a model for reality (in that its laws direct Jews to follow a holy way of life). The central themes of their national story—promise and fulfillment, exile and redemption—were concretized in a way of life focused on study of Torah and observance of the law.

It is no wonder, then, that rabbinic literature is replete with passages praising Torah and honoring those who study and teach it. Torah is God's gift to Israel, the tangible expression of God's infinite love for this people. It functions as the equivalent of a "marriage contract" that binds God and Israel to one another forever. It is variously described as the most precious thing in the world,[2] the source of all truth,[3] something that itself antedates creation, the source that God consulted in creating the world.[4] Torah cannot be praised highly enough; its teachings are Israel's greatest treasure. It follows that Torah study is honored as the central ritual of traditional Jewish life. Through engaging the words of Torah, traditional Jews commune with God, feel God's presence in their midst, renew their commitment to God, and re-experience God's commitment to them. No word of the text is superfluous, no aspect of Torah too trivial to be studied again and again. In the words of one traditional Jewish prayer, "for they [the words of Torah and God's commandments] are our life and length of days; we will meditate on them day and night."

Israel's history was likewise a major preoccupation of the ancient rabbis, for they needed to square Scripture's statements that Israel is God's chosen and much beloved people with the fact that Israel's history was marked by much suffering and repeated defeats at the hands of its enemies.[5] Several possibilities were explored. Sometimes they asserted that God tests those whom God loves, to determine the extent of their devotion. God, like a king who has been away on a lengthy trip, can be counted on to return to his beloved wife (Israel) and to reward her for her fidelity during his absence.[6] On this view, Israel's suffering is paradoxically turned into evidence that this people is the recipient of special divine attention. Alternatively, Israel's fate was sometimes understood as just punishment for its infidelity.[7] From this perspective, Israel's fate is in its own hands and its fortunes will be restored when it demonstrates renewed devotion to God's Torah. In yet another reading of Israel's history, the rabbis sometimes suggested that Israelites will be rewarded in the world to come for their suffering in this world.[8] They taught that God's love for Israel endures, even if the events of this world do not always appear to confirm this. All of these attempts to understand the meaning of Israel's history testify to the rabbis' enduring belief that God's relationship with this people was writ large in their historical experience and that God's special love for Israel remains unshakeable.

PARTICULARISM AND UNIVERSALISM

Thus far, I have focused on God's special relationship to Israel, on the central place of Torah in that relationship and on the view of Israel's history that follows from these beliefs. Indeed, these are the themes that most preoccupied biblical and later rabbinic authors, yet this narrative of the special bond between God and Israel is set within a larger narrative that is universal in scope and significance. The same God who established this covenantal relationship with Israel also created the world, cares for all humankind, and has a plan for history that extends to all nations, not to Israel alone.

These more universal themes are also well attested in Scripture. The very opening lines of Genesis tell that God created heaven and earth; in the words of the psalmist, "the earth is the Lord's and all that it holds, the world and its inhabitants" (Psalm 24:1). God is also the "father" of all humankind and so is concerned for the fate of the entire world: "Have we not all one father? Did not one God create us? Why do we break faith with one another, profaning the covenant of our fathers?" (Malachi 2:10). God's dominion is complete in every respect. The natural order is God's creation, testifying to God's power and wisdom: "The heavens declare the glory of God, the sky proclaims God's handiwork" (Psalm 19:2). All human beings, as "children" of the same God, are accountable for their deeds to the same divine being. Finally, God is understood as the author of all human history, rewarding and punishing all the nations of the world, along with Israel, for their deeds: "Let the sea and all within it thunder, the world and its inhabitants; let the rivers clap their hands, the mountains sing joyously together at the presence of the Lord, for God is coming to rule the earth; God will rule the world justly, and its peoples with equity" (Psalm 98:7–9).

God's universal dominion and God's special concern for Israel were intertwined in many aspects of Israelite religion, but nowhere is this connection more evident than in the concept of the **messiah**. Initially, the messiah (literally, "anointed one") was to be an Israelite king from the line of David, who would reunite the divided kingdoms of Samaria and Judea, as they had once been united and powerful under David's rule. These kingdoms, which had been defeated and their people exiled by the Assyrians in 722 B.C.E. and the Babylonians in 587 B.C.E., respectively, would be restored to their land. There they would dwell in harmony, enjoying God's protection as they had centuries earlier in the "golden age" of David's rule (Ezekiel 37:21–22, 24–25):

> Thus said the Lord God: I am going to take the Israelite people from among the nations they have gone to, and gather them from every quarter, and bring them to their own land. I will make them a single nation in the land, on the hills of Israel, and one king shall be king of them all. Never again shall they be two nations, and never again shall they be divided into two kingdoms. . . . My servant David shall be king over them, there shall be one shepherd for all of them. They shall follow My rules and faithfully obey My laws. Thus they shall remain in the land which I gave to My servant Jacob and in which your fathers dwelt, they and their children and their children's children shall dwell there forever, with My servant David as their prince for all time.

This vision of national restoration and sovereignty came over time to be linked with a conception of universal peace. Israel's restoration would signal a new era in human history, the dawning of the "kingdom of God" when all nations of the world would recognize God's sovereignty, seeing themselves as subjects of a single divine king. In this vision of the messianic end of time, all people would flow to Zion where Israel's Temple would be the locus of God's presence on earth. Mihca (4:1–5) continues:

> In the days to come, the mount of the Lord's house shall stand firm above the mountains, and it shall tower above the hills. The peoples shall gaze on it with joy, and the many nations shall go and shall say, "Come, let us go up to the Mount of the Lord, to the house of the God of Jacob, that God may instruct us in His ways, and that we may walk in His paths." For instruction shall come forth from Zion, the word of the Lord from Jerusalem. Thus He will judge among the many peoples, and arbitrate for the multitude of nations, however distant. And they shall beat their swords into plowshares and their spears into pruning hooks. Nation shall not take up sword against nation, they shall never again know war. But every man shall sit under his grapevine or fig tree with no one to disturb him. For it was the Lord of Hosts who spoke.

Here the particularism of Israel's historical destiny and the universal thrust of monotheism have been fused into a common vision encompassing all nations and all of human history.

In short, the central narrative of traditional Jewish life, which focuses on Torah and Israel, on exodus and covenant and law, is embedded within a larger narrative that extends from the creation of the world to its ultimate redemption. God's special relationship to Israel unfolds in the context of God's relationship to the world as a whole. Indeed, some have suggested that God, Torah, and Israel—the central elements of Jewish theology—can be understood fully only against the backdrop of a larger set of concepts—*creation, revelation, and redemption*—which encompass all of human life. It was the twentieth-century Jewish thinker Franz Rosenzweig who first systematically explored creation, revelation, and redemption as the triad of relationships at the foundation of Jewish life and thought.[9] Although I have already touched on these theological concepts, they merit more sustained attention because, like recurring themes in a musical composition, they weave their way throughout every dimension of traditional Jewish life.

CREATION, REVELATION, AND REDEMPTION: CORNERSTONES OF JEWISH LIFE AND THOUGHT

As noted earlier, God is portrayed in Judaism as the creator of the world and humankind, as the revealor of Torah to Israel, and as the one who redeemed the Israelites from slavery in Egypt and guided them to freedom in the promised land. Scripture describes each of these events as occurring at a particular time in the past. Within the religious perspective of classical Judaism, however, creation, revelation, and redemption were perennial dimensions of life that could be experienced again and again. The ways in which this is so can be seen most readily by turning to the **siddur,** the traditional prayerbook, and to the yearly cycle of holidays that establish the rhythm of traditional Jewish life.

The traditional liturgy that Jews recite each morning illustrates the many ways in which the themes of creation, revelation, and redemption are interwoven. After an opening set of morning blessings and psalms, the service proper begins with the following passage:

> Blessed is the one who spoke and the world came into being, Blessed is God.
>
> Blessed is the one who does the work of creation, blessed the one who says and does, blessed the one who decrees and establishes, blessed the one who has compassion for the world, blessed the one who has compassion for the creatures, blessed the one who rewards those who revere Him, blessed the one who lives forever and endures eternally, blessed the one who redeems and saves, blessed is His name.[10]

Each verb in this sequence after the first line is in the present tense, emphasizing that God, whose existence is eternal, creates and establishes the world continually. The morning service begins with the acknowledgement of God as the author of all creation, who not only formed the world and everything in it, but who continues to manifest concern for all living things.

This opening section of the service concludes with the reading of Exodus 15:1–18, "the Song of the Sea" that the Israelites sang just after their dramatic redemption from slavery in Egypt. Here again, however, the point is not to recall some historical event. Immediately following the biblical text, the liturgy continues:

> For sovereignty belongs to the Lord, who rules the nations. Deliverers shall arise on Mount Zion [site of the ancient Temple] to judge the mountain of Esau [Jacob's brother and, in rabbinic lore, the perennial antagonist of Israel], and the Lord shall be sovereign. The Lord will become King of all the earth. On that day the Lord shall be one and His name one.

The redemption of Israel in the past immediately evokes the anticipation of a future redemption, when Israel will be freed from the oppression of its enemies and all nations will recognize a single God. Then humanity will be truly united and God's dominion over the earth fully manifest. The freedom that caused ancient Israelites to sing praises to God was but a precursor to the freedom that Jews, in unison with the rest of humankind, hope one day to experience.

The next main section of the traditional liturgy, which is central to both the morning and evening services, again reiterates the ways in which creation, revelation, and redemption are ongoing experiences in the life of the Jewish community. In the morning, the prayer service continues,

> Praised are You, Lord our God, King of the universe, creating light and fashioning darkness, ordaining the order of all creation.
>   You illumine the world and its creatures with mercy; in Your goodness, day after day You renew Creation. How manifold Your works, O Lord; with wisdom You fashioned them all.

In the evening, this paragraph is replaced with,

> Praised are You, Lord our God, King of the universe whose word brings the evening dusk. You open the gates of dawn with wisdom, change the day's divisions with understanding, set the succession of seasons and arrange the stars in the sky according to Your will. You create day and night, rolling light away from darkness and darkness away from light. . . .

Thus, at the beginning of the day and at its conclusion, Jews sense God's immediate presence in the orderly sequence of natural events. God's creation is evident each and every day, which is both a source of wonder and a cause for praise.

The passage that follows in the liturgy shifts from creation to revelation. In the morning service, it reads,

> Deep is Your love for us, Lord our God, boundless Your tender compassion. You taught our ancestors life-giving laws. They trusted in You, our Father and King. For their sake graciously teach us. Father, merciful Father, show us mercy; grant us discernment and understanding. Then will we study Your Torah, heed its words, teach its precepts and follow its instruction, lovingly fulfilling all its teachings. Open our eyes to Your Torah, help our hearts cleave to Your mitzvot [commandments]. . . . Praised are you, Lord who chooses his people Israel in love.[11]

The Torah may have been revealed on Mt. Sinai, but it needs to be understood and received anew each day. The gift of Torah, in this sense, is continual, for each time a

Jew opens his or her heart to understand its message, it takes on new life. In this sense, it is no accident that the blessing recited immediately before the public reading of the Torah scroll is "Blessed are you, Lord our God, who *gives* the Torah." Whenever Torah is read and heard by the community, revelation occurs again.

This portion of the morning service concludes with further references to the redemption from slavery in Egypt, followed by an invocation: "Rock of Israel, rise to Israel's defense. Fulfill Your promise to deliver Judah and Israel." In the evening, the invocation changes, but the basic thrust remains the same:

> Help us, our Father, to lie down in peace; and awaken us to life again, our King. Spread over us Your shelter of peace, guide us with Your good counsel. Save us because of Your mercy. Shield us from enemies and pestilence, from starvation, sword and sorrow. . . . Guard our coming and our going, grant us life and peace, now and always. Praised are You, Lord, eternal guardian of Your people Israel.

Again, God's protection is something Jews hope to experience each day. The God who was present when Israel's ancestors needed to be redeemed from slavery is the "eternal guardian of Israel." Whenever and wherever Israel is in distress, God can be called on to renew the work of redemption and can be expected to act again on Israel's behalf.

These experiences of creation, revelation, and redemption not only structure the daily worship of traditional Jews but also animate the yearly cycle of holidays as well. The biblical calendar has three central festivals: Passover (*Pesach*), Pentecost (*Shavu'ot*), and Tabernacles (*Sukkot*). Each has its origins in the agricultural cycle of planting and harvesting that structured the agrarian life of ancient Israel: Passover marks the beginning of the grain harvest, Pentecost the beginning of the fruit harvest, and Tabernacles the conclusion of the harvest season. Each of these holy days also acquired additional significance in relation to Israelite history: Passover celebrates the redemption from slavery in Egypt, Pentecost marks the giving of the Torah at Mt. Sinai, and Tabernacles recalls the period of the exodus when the Israelites dwelled in temporary structures or booths. Each year the Jewish people effectively relives its earliest history as Jews celebrate these holidays, no longer by bringing offerings of grain or fruit to the Temple but by rehearsing their sacred history.

Among these annual festivals, Passover is richest in symbolic and ritual celebration. In remembrance of the exodus from Egypt, the story of divine deliverance is retold, and a feast is held that symbolically reenacts the events of that time. Unleavened bread is eaten to recall the hasty departure from Egypt; bitter herbs and salt water are part of the ritual, to re-experience the bitterness of slavery. Most dramatically, the story of the exodus is retold, beginning with the testimonial, "We were slaves to Pharoah in Egypt, . . . and had the Lord our God not brought us out of Egypt, then we, our children and our children's children would still be slaves to Pharoah in Egypt." The traditional liturgy exhorts every Jew to internalize the epic story of this ancient journey from slavery to liberation. "In each and every generation, one must see oneself as having personally experienced the exodus from Egypt." Not surprisingly, this reenactment of the drama of liberation concludes with an expression of messianic expectation, "Next year in Jerusalem."

The revelation of Torah is celebrated on Pentecost, when Jews traditionally spend the entire night in study of scriptural or other sacred texts. The teaching and learning of Torah in this intensive way emphasizes again that divine revelation occurs whenever and wherever Jews engage God's word. In the synagogue, the assigned scriptural reading for Pentecost is Exodus 19–20, which recounts the dramatic way in which God descended on Mt. Sinai and spoke to all the assembled people there. Standing as the Ten Commandments are read aloud, the congregation symbolically reenacts the receiving of Torah and reconstitutes itself as a holy community.

The feast of Tabernacles, which concludes the harvest season, is celebrated by building and living in a special booth (*sukkah*) for eight days. Eating and sleeping in the *sukkah,* covered with boughs and yet open to the sky, brings one in touch with the natural world and the bounty of the earth. In its historical significance, Tabernacles provides a way to re-experience the wanderings of the ancient Israelites on their way to the promised land. Though fragile and temporary, the *sukkah* symbolizes God's protection, both in the past and in the future. It is invoked in the daily liturgy when Jews implore God, "Spread over us the *sukkah* of your peace," and during the holiday itself, Jews pray, "May the merciful one raise up the fallen *sukkah* of David," in anticipation of the time when the coming of the messiah will signal the ultimate redemption.

Throughout the year, then, Jews liturgically rehearse their history as a people and symbolically reenact the events that forged their special relationship with God. In doing so, they reflect again and again on the themes of creation, revelation, and redemption, for these are the ways in which God was, and remains, present in their lives. In Judaism, the sacred is manifest through God, Torah, and Israel, and the life of holiness is shaped by experiences of creation, revelation, and redemption.

I turn now to the question that will remain central throughout the remainder of this book: How does this religious system, anchored in God, Torah, and Israel, animated by experiences of creation, revelation, and redemption, structure the moral life of this people?

WHAT IS JEWISH ETHICS?

Jewish ethics is the sum total of the moral values, virtues, and rules that arise in the context of Jewish religious life, together with the critical reflection on these that has developed in the context of Jewish religious thought. That religious life is complex and richly textured, consisting of interrelated beliefs, ritual and liturgical practices, and patterns of living, all of which contribute to the context within which Jews think about and strive to live out their moral ideals. Chapter One observed that within religious systems, ethics takes on a distinctive form and tone. The way in which moral obligation and the moral life is understood flows directly from the distinctive features of a people's religious experience. So the ways in which this tradition understands both practical questions (such as how to behave in concrete situations and which moral virtues to cultivate and how) and theoretical ones (how to understand the ground of moral obligation and how new moral rules are generated) are shaped by the distinctive beliefs and values, motifs, and theological categories of this religion.

Within Judaism, the moral life in its entirety is lived in the context of the covenantal relationship between the Jews and God. This means, at the very least, that all moral obligations are responsibilities, not only to other persons, but also to the God who created all people and who is the source of all value. Moral obligations to others ultimately are grounded in a common relationship to God, which entails a common origin and a common destiny. As the preceding discussion of revelation indicated, however, the specific content of Jewish moral obligation is ultimately determined by the words of Torah and the interpretation of those words. For Jews, all religious (including moral) obligations are part and parcel of their special covenantal relationship with God. In the words of one rabbinic dictum, "On three things is the world founded: on Torah, on worship and on acts of lovingkindness."[12] The triad is not arbitrary. Torah, as noted, represents the way in which God communicates to Israel. Worship, in turn, is the way in which Israel communicates with God. Acts of lovingkindness—moral behavior—finally, are the way in which people bring God's presence into their relationships to one another, thus completing the circle of interconnection between God and humankind. Each act of lovingkindness helps to infuse our earthly existence with godliness and so makes God's presence in the world more real and active. So when examining Jewish moral life, you should not be surprised to discover that questions of moral value—what is good and right in human relationships— are explored in the context of the grand divine-human drama that moves from creation through revelation to redemption. Each of these central theological categories needs now to be explored in greater detail.

CREATION: SOURCE OF MORAL CAPACITY AND FOUNDATION OF MORAL VALUE

How does God's creation of the world, and of humankind in particular, shape the way Jews understand the moral life? What bearing does creation have on the classical Jewish view of human nature and the moral purposes of human life? What moral virtues and obligations derive from the belief that humans are all creatures who owe their very existence to a divine creator? The answers to these and similar questions throughout the remainder of this chapter necessarily draw from a multiplicity of (sometimes conflicting) sources, for the goal is to sketch in very broad strokes the spectrum of views on these matters found within Jewish tradition.

From the perspective of classical Judaism, certain aspects of morality are embedded in the structure of the universe, as much a part of the cosmos as the regularities of nature. The earliest stories of Genesis presuppose that there is a moral order that human beings are expected to recognize and observe. Long before the giving of the Torah on Mt. Sinai, in other words, human beings are supposed to have known not to murder and deal treacherously with one another. Hence, God first punishes Cain for murdering his brother Abel (Genesis 4:11–12) and later punishes the entire generation of the flood for its misdeeds (Genesis 6:11–13), although these people had never been instructed that these behaviors were immoral. In short, the biblical text implies that there is a natural moral order, known (somehow) to humankind from the very beginning, without benefit of specific divine instruction. In later rabbinic parlance, such moral laws or principles are designated as those humans would know through the exercise of human reason and by virtue of human experience "even had the Torah not been given."[13]

God thus is the creator, not only of the physical universe but also of the moral universe. The natural order and the moral order are but two aspects of God's all-encompassing power. From this perspective you can understand why the author of Psalm 19 juxtaposes God's work in the natural world ("The heavens declare the glory of God, the sky proclaims God's handiwork;" verse 1) with God's establishment of the moral order ("The teaching of the Lord is perfect, renewing life; the decrees of the Lord are enduring, making the simple wise; the precepts of the Lord are just, rejoicing the heart; the instruction of the Lord is lucid, making the eyes light up . . ." verses 8–9). It follows that by acting righteously we bring ourselves into alignment with the divinely ordained moral order.

Yet the fact that there is a divinely created, natural moral order does not mean that human beings by nature act morally but that they are created with the capacity to make moral decisions—for good or ill. God created us as creatures who possess the capacity for both good and evil and whose primary existential struggle is to curb our impulse to do evil and nurture our propensity to do good. This characterization of humankind is reflected throughout the Hebrew Bible, and it remains a cornerstone of rabbinic views of human nature. Indeed, as later Jewish thinkers rightly have noted, there would be no reason for God to ordain the many laws found in the Torah if human beings did not possess the free will to make choices either to obey or to disobey them.[14]

Much rabbinic reflection is devoted to the problem of cultivating the necessary strength of character to actualize our potential for acting righteously. Often the rabbis suggest that if people only reflect deeply on the basic features of the human condition, we will be able to resist our temptation to do evil:

> Ponder three things and you will not fall into sin. Know from whence you come, whither you are headed, and before Whom you will be required to give an accounting. Whence you came? A putrid drop [of semen]. Whither you are headed? A place of dust, worms, and maggots. Before Whom will you be required to give an accounting? Before the King of kings, the Holy One, who is blessed.[15]

If we truly consider the fact that our existence is transitory, that we come from nothing and return ultimately to nothing, we will come to recognize that our physical existence is without permanent value. Ultimately, then, it is our moral behavior that is the measure of our worth in God's eyes. If we remind ourselves regularly of our proper place in the scheme of the universe, this text suggests, we will give appropriate attention to cultivating our capacity to live a righteous life before God.

The recognition that humans are divine creations has further implications for the moral life. When we consider how utterly dependent we are on God for all the blessings that sustain human life, we confront the fact that, in relation to God, human life is ultimately without substance or merit. Our moral deeds are paltry in relation to divine goodness. As we stand before the creator of heaven and earth, there is little we can say on our behalf to justify our existence; certainly there is little in the way of moral virtue to commend us. The traditional liturgy says it most directly:

> Master of all worlds! Not upon our merit do we rely in our supplication, but upon Your limitless love. What are we? What is our life? What is our piety? What is our righteousness? What is our attainment, our power, our might? What can we say, Lord our God and God of our ancestors? Compared to You, all the mighty are nothing, the famous nonexistent, the wise lack wisdom, the clever lack reason. For most of their actions are meaningless, the days of their lives emptiness. Human preeminence over beasts is an illusion when all is seen as futility.

This means that humans must depend for moral justification on divine grace, on God's willingness to look past our repeated moral failings, on divine forgiveness. Within Judaism, to be humans standing in God's presence entails being acutely aware of our moral weakness and the frailty of human goodness. This finds expression in another frequently repeated piece of liturgy: "Our Father, our King, be gracious to us and answer us, though we have no deeds to plead our cause; save us with mercy and lovingkindness."

God's creation of humankind has immediate implications for the substance of Jewish moral duties as well. In the Genesis account, only human beings are singled out as reflections of God's own image. This suggests that human life is invested with sanctity in and of itself, and so possesses intrinsic value. The value of human life is not quantifiable and not relative to the value of anything extrinsic to it. For this reason, traditional Jewish authorities generally have refused to terminate medical care for those whose "quality of life" is lacking in some respect.

Moreover, the fact that human life comes from God means that our lives are not ours to do with as we please. We are forever indebted to God for the very fact of our existence and live with the knowledge that one day God will take back what we have been given. Indeed, Jews still recite the phrase "The Lord has given and the Lord has taken away; blessed be the name of the Lord" (Job 1:21) prior to the funeral of a loved one. It is not surprising, then, that classical Jewish ethics allows little room for notions of personal autonomy that figure so prominently in much secular (especially Kantian) ethics. By the same token, the widespread contemporary notion that our bodies belong to us and that we have an inherent right to do with them what we will is completely absent in traditional Jewish ethics.

If you stand back from the views presented thus far, you cannot help but notice a certain tension. Within this religious tradition to be created "in God's image" means both (1) that humans have a godlike capacity for moral judgment and the ability through our moral choices to uphold the divinely ordained moral order and (2) that we live at an infinite distance from God's moral perfection, that all our moral deeds and strivings could never justify our existence without the benefit of God's unending forgiveness and compassion toward us. On the one hand, our moral worth derives from our being created in "God's image," and we are the only creatures so created, yet over against an omnipotent and perfect God, our moral worth is ultimately negligible. Human beings are both exalted insofar as our lives are invested with divine moral purpose and infinitesimally meager insofar as we can never measure up to God's moral demands on us, despite our most fervent efforts. The religious obligation in Judaism to atone for our sins embodies this tension, for it simultaneously presupposes both the divine moral seriousness of human action and the view that we are utterly dependent on God for moral justification.

This tension is captured nicely in a famous debate attributed to the first century sages Hillel and Shammai.

> For two and a half years the school of Shammai and the school of Hillel debated. The former said that it were better for humankind not to have been created than to have been created. The latter said that it were better for humankind to have been created than not to have been created. They voted and concluded: It were better for people not to have been created than to have been created, but now that they have been created, let them search their deeds.[16]

Given the enormous human capacity for both good and evil—as we today know only too well—these ancient Jewish teachers rightly questioned whether the world would be better off without humankind. Their answer does not resolve the tension within the tradition so much as embrace it: It would indeed have been better had humans *not* been created, but *after the fact*, we should turn our attention to living the best moral life of which we are capable. In effect, this compromise between Hillel and Shammai reinforces the point of the passage cited earlier about "Pondering Three Thing,": ultimately human worth can be measured in deeds alone. In this sense, Jewish ethics is a search for the proper way to live that, if followed, will justify after the fact what we could not have justified beforehand, our right to a place in God's created order.

The same issue is addressed in a teaching of the **hasidic** master, Simha Bunam of Pzhysha, who lived some 1700 years after Hillel and Shammai debated the question of human worth.

> Rabbi Bunam said to his disciples: Everyone must have two pockets, so that he can reach into the one or the other, according to his needs. In his right pocket are to be the words: "For my sake was the world created," and in his left: "I am earth and ashes."[17]

Both ways of viewing humankind are valid, and there are times, Bunam suggests, when we especially need to cultivate either a sense of our profound importance or a sense of humility. The main point for our purpose is that both of these apparently contradictory ways of viewing humankind reflect the fact that we owe our existence to an act of divine creation. Both the exaltedness and the lowliness of human existence are reflections of where we stand in relation to the God who created us. Neither side of the equation alone tells the whole story.

Thus, classical Judaism understands the challenge of living morally to be framed by this paradoxical reality, that we are both "little less than angels" (Psalm 8:6) and little more than "earth and ashes." From these facts stem both our duty to become partners with God, upholding the moral order of creation, and our duty to be humble and contrite, ever ready to admit our moral failings and to forgive others for theirs. To live morally, then, it is necessary to remember both aspects of our creatureliness and to live each day in the awareness that our existence is ever so transient and that, through our deeds, we have the opportunity to justify our existence in the eyes of our Creator.

REVELATION: THE SOURCE OF MORAL AUTHORITY AND THE CHARACTER OF MORAL DISCOURSE

How does God's revelation of Torah to Israel shape Judaism's view of moral authority? How does Scripture, the written record of this revelation, function in the moral life of traditional Jews? And, given the centrality of revelation in Judaism, what role does reason play in moral decision making? Here, as in the foregoing discussion of creation, the focus is largely on the ways in which revelation as a theological category gives a distinctive shape and direction to Jewish ethics. As you shall see, the entire character of Jewish ethics as a system of thought and practice depends crucially on the fact that it is built on the foundation of God's revelation to Israel.

I have already noted that classical Judaism regards Torah as God's definitive revelation to the Jewish people and law as the primary form in which God directs human behavior. This revelation occurs in the context of a special covenant or contract between God and Israel, which itself arises in the context of a unique, loving relationship in which God singles out Israel for special attention and protection. God's revelation to Israel could be described as (1) exclusive, (2) verbal/legal, and (3) communal. Because these features of revelation are interrelated, it is not possible to draw a simple one-to-one correspondence between them and specific aspects of Jewish ethics; still, it will be useful to organize this discussion of Jewish moral authority and moral discourse in relation to these three basic characteristics of revelation.

First, and perhaps most obviously, the exclusivity of revelation lends a certain ethnocentric character to Jewish ethics and, indeed, to Judaism as a whole. God's revelation, after all, was given to Israel alone. Whatever obligations others may have, the Torah's overriding concern is to spell out Israel's responsibilities. By extension, the rabbis interpreted these scriptural rules, legislating for their own community, which felt bound by their authority. (Historically, the rabbis were never in a position to exercise authority over non-Jews, even if they had been inclined to do so.) The vast body of Jewish law, then, concerns Israel's covenantal obligations; the moral obligations of non-Jews are taken up only secondarily.[18]

Moreover, the sharp delineation between Jews and non-Jews has affected the content of Jewish ethics. Many sources address the moral obligations of Jews toward those outside the community, but rabbinic authorities routinely assumed that Jews' responsibilities to other Jews were different (and greater) than to non-Jews. As

members of God's covenanted people, Jews understood themselves to have more
extensive religious and moral obligations than others; God expected more from them
and, accordingly, they expected more of each other. This tendency was further reinforced by the history of Jewish-gentile relations in the ancient and medieval world,
which was often marked by attitudes of indifference, prejudice, suspicion and, not
infrequently, open hostility. Given this history, coupled with the fact that in all cultures closer emotional and familial ties give rise to higher levels of interaction and
responsibility, it is hardly surprising that Judaism assumes that Jews have greater
moral responsibilities to other Jews than to non-Jews.[19]

Fundamentally, then, Jews saw themselves as having access to and being bound
by the highest possible moral authority—the will of God. God's directives for the
Jews filled the Torah and, if they were but followed scrupulously, the people's very
lives would become embodiments of God's will, and a model for all to follow. Indeed,
the text of the Torah (Deuteronomy 4:5-8) seems to anticipate this when it imagines how other nations will look on the Jews and their observance of God's law:

> Behold, I have imparted to you laws and rules, as the Lord my God has com-
> manded me, for you to abide by in the land which you are about to invade and
> occupy. Observe them faithfully, for that will be proof of your wisdom and dis-
> cernment to other peoples, who on hearing of all these laws will say, "Surely, that
> great nation is a wise and discerning people." For what great nation is there that
> has a god so close at hand as is the Lord our God whenever we call upon Him?
> Or what great nation has laws and rules as perfect as all this Teaching that I set
> before you this day?

The people, then, are to exemplify God's will on earth, demonstrating for all to see
how the moral life at its highest is to be lived.

Second, revelation in classical Judaism refers primarily to the verbal communication of God to Israel as recorded in Torah. God, of course, interacts with Israel in
other ways as well. As noted earlier, Israel's own history was understood classically as
containing implicit messages from God that prophets interpreted for the people, but
the word of God remained primary and, once the word was reduced to writing, the
text of God's communication became the highest authority. There is an important
contrast here to classical Christianity, in which God's revelation takes human form.
Living a moral life for the believing Christian becomes a matter of emulating Christ,
doing as he did during his life on earth. For Jews, by contrast, the challenge is to
embody the words of Torah, to so integrate the meaning of the text into one's life
that, in a classic expression, "Israel and Scripture are one."

It should be noted in this context that not all parts of the Torah are equally
important for Jewish ethics. The law is preeminent, and it is the legal sections of
scripture that are normative for Jewish ethical practice. To be sure, the extensive narratives in the Torah are the subject of rabbinic exegesis, and many moral lessons are
derived from them. Other genres within biblical literature also contribute to Jewish
ethics: proverbs, psalms, and the wisdom of Ecclesiastes, for example. Yet, the rabbis were especially drawn to the explication of legal norms, perhaps because all areas
of Jewish religious life—rituals, holiday celebrations, diet, dress, and so on—were

treated almost exclusively in legal texts and provided the basis for an extensive system of injunctions and prohibitions. Ethics, too, the rabbis assumed, fell within the purview of **halakhah,** Jewish law, even if many moral truths could be found in non-legal sources. As you shall see in the discussion of contemporary Jewish ethics, many rabbis today continue to debate moral issues primarily by citing legal sources (both biblical and rabbinic), for these texts address most specifically what God expects morally of Israel.

Finally, the irreducibly communal nature of revelation further underscores an important contrast between Jewish ethics, on the one hand, and secular, philosophical ethics, on the other. In the context of Judaism, ethical questions are almost invariably addressed on the social, rather than the individual, level. The primary ethical question for Jewish thinkers has related to their rights and responsibilities as a community rather than rights and responsibilities as an individual. This is hardly surprising given that the revelation at the heart of this religious system is communal. The Jewish people as a whole stood at Sinai and took upon themselves the "yoke of the commandments," and the acceptance of this responsibility is ongoing in the life of the Jewish community. Hence, ethical demands are conceptualized in terms of corporate responsibility: "All Israel is responsible for one another,"[20] and so all are implicated in the deeds of fellow Jews (for better or worse). The liturgy for Yom Kippur, the Day of Atonement, reflects this when it consistently places the confessional prayers in the plural—"For the sin that *we* have sinned against you"—and asks God's forgiveness for the community as a whole.

Given this communal orientation, classical Judaism attaches little importance to the notion that God has some unique moral demand for particular individuals in particular circumstances. The path of righteous living has been revealed in Torah to the entire community; it needs merely to be understood and followed. Hence, the task is to determine what the tradition has taught about the obligations of Jews as a whole in each situation that arises. When an unprecedented situation arises, one defers to those rabbinic authorities who alone are qualified to extrapolate from the traditional teachings and to interpret God's will as it applies to the case at hand. Traditional Jews, then, would be unlikely to pray for special guidance about "what God wants from *me* in this situation," for divine guidance is assumed to be public and communal, not private and individual.

Perhaps the most important way in which revelation shapes Jewish ethics, however, becomes evident with the consideration of the role of reason in this moral system. In a word, given the centrality of revelation, reason as an independent source of moral knowledge plays a relatively minor role in Judaism. To be sure, some rabbis believed that reason alone was sufficient to establish the truth of certain moral laws, such as the prohibitions against murder and incest, as well as the need for certain social institutions, such as law courts. It is ultimately God's law, however, that defines the moral life for Jews. Moreover, the entire covenantal relationship between God and Israel reinforces this fact. God rewards and punishes Israel, not for the way in which they exercise their reason to discern their moral obligations, but simply for the extent to which they follow God's law. Whatever human reason may discern of the moral life on its own, it is the Torah as a vehicle of divine instruction that Jews are to use as their moral compass.

In the context of such a system, philosophical reflection on the moral virtues and obligations (and on the nature of moral duty, the character of the "good," etc.) is tolerated but not encouraged. At least in the western tradition that begins with Greek thought, philosophical speculation assumes that (1) truth is fundamentally universal and (2) humans can discover that truth through the exercise of human reason. This is in tension with the traditional Jewish view that truth is entrusted to a particular people through an act (or ongoing acts) of divine revelation. In this sense, it is not surprising that classical Christianity, with its doctrine that salvation is fundamentally universal, available equally to both Jews and gentiles (Romans 1:16, 3:29, 10:12–13), could more readily embrace the universalist and nonsectarian modes of reasoning characteristic of Greek philosophy than could Judaism, given the latter's insistence that God's revelation is communicated to a particular people.

Moreover, the idea that human intuition alone could be a source of moral knowledge, which figures prominently in modern moral philosophy, makes little sense in a Jewish context. From the perspective of classical Jewish tradition, God's will governs the moral life of traditional Jews, just as it governs all other aspects of religious practice. Whatever innate moral capacities God has given humans, they are not sufficient to determine the proper moral course without benefit of God's specific injunctions, nor are they sufficient to motivate consistently moral behavior without God's promise of rewards for the righteous and threat of punishment for the wicked.

Yet reason does play a role in this system, though rarely an independent one. As noted earlier, the rabbis of talmudic times and beyond devoted immense energies to the elaboration and exploration of biblical law. In doing so, they developed their own system of logical rules and principles for textual interpretation that often (though not always) guide their interpretation of the biblical text. Indeed, their own logical argumentation often led them to change radically the straightforward meaning of a biblical law, as when they determine that the infamous injunction to take "an eye for an eye" (Exodus 21:23–25) refers to the payment of monetary compensation, not physical vengeance.[21] At other times, they simply expanded the moral meaning of a biblical passage beyond its literal sense, as when they interpreted "you shall not place a stumbling-block before the blind" (Leviticus 19:14) to include taking advantage of another's disadvantage, for example, by offering bad advice to someone who will rely on it or by encouraging those who are prone to sin.[22] In short, the rabbis regarded the exercise of reason as a legitimate, indeed necessary, enterprise, for only in this way could the full, true meaning of God's law be spelled out.

Any investigation of the authority behind Jewish ethics, then, must confront a tension between two opposing views. On the one hand, the Torah, which is the definitive expression of God's revelation to Israel, is the ultimate moral authority for this religious community. On the other hand, the rabbis, through rational argumentation and endless textual explication, determine the substance of Jewish moral obligation. If, as noted earlier, Jews' moral responsibilities are obligations to God, it should follow that God's word is decisive. On the other hand, Jewish tradition assumes that the consensus of rabbinic opinion, not the words of sacred scripture themselves, govern Jewish religious and moral life.

This tension between revelation and reason is addressed and ultimately resolved in the following famous story from the Talmud:

> On that day, Rabbi Eliezer brought forward every imaginable argument, but the sages did not accept any of them. Finally he said to them, "If the *halakhah* agrees with me, let this carob tree prove it!" The carob tree was uprooted [and moved] 100 yards away from its place. . . . They said to him, "No proof can be brought from a carob tree."
>
> Again, he said to them, "If the *halakhah* agrees with me, let the channel of water prove it!" The channel of water flowed backward. They said to him, "No proof can be brought from water."
>
> Again he said, "If the *halakhah* agrees with me, let the walls of the house of study prove it!" The walls tilted as if to fall. But Rabbi Joshua rebuked the walls, saying, "When disciples of the wise are engaged in halakhic dispute, what right have you [to interfere]?" In deference to Joshua, the walls did not fall, and in deference to Eliezer they did not resume their upright position; they remained tilted.
>
> Again Rabbi Eliezer said to the sages, "If the *halakhah* agrees with me, let it be proved from heaven!" A divine voice cried out, "What do you have against Rabbi Eliezer? The *halakhah* always agrees with him." But Rabbi Joshua stood up, "It [the Torah] is not in heaven" (Deuteronomy 30:12). What does it mean, "It is not in heaven"? Rabbi Jeremiah said, "We pay no attention to a divine voice, since long ago the Torah was given at Mt. Sinai. And it is already written in the Torah, "After the majority must one incline." (Exodus 23:2).[23]
>
> Rabbi Nathan met [the prophet] Elijah and asked him, "What did the Holy One do in that moment?" Elijah [said], "He laughed, saying, 'My children have defeated Me, My children have defeated Me.' "[24]

On the most obvious level, this intriguing story exemplifies the tension between two different ways in which God engages with Israel, through miracles and through the text of scripture. Although miracles are dismissed as ultimately irrelevant when it comes to determining Israel's obligations, scripture remains fundamental. But what does scripture require? The striking conclusion of this story is that the text of scripture means precisely what a majority of the rabbis says it does. The Torah, that repository of divine revelation, is "not in heaven," but on earth, subject to rabbinic deliberation. Its meaning, then, is ultimately determined by human judgment and consensus, and this is precisely the way God wants it! Indeed, God is delighted with the fact that the rabbis have become the voice of God, supplanting not only dramatic divine pronouncements from heaven, but even (potentially) the plain meaning of the scriptural text itself.

If the meaning of the Scriptural text depends inescapably on rabbinic reasoning, however, the authority of the rabbis to make binding pronouncements on the community depends on scripture's sanction. That is the reason that the sages defend their position by noting that scripture itself authorizes them to decide its meaning ("After the majority must one incline."). The rabbis' authority is divinely ordained and they, in turn, determine what this divine text requires of the community. In such a system there can be no conflict between what God wants (scriptural authority) and what the rabbis decide (human authority), for the former has been defined in terms of the latter.

In classical Judaism, then, the authority of scriptural revelation and that of rabbinic reason are wedded to each other. It remains true, as noted earlier, that Jewish moral obligations are determined primarily by the content of God's revelation in Torah, but it must be added that revelation is mediated by a process of human, rabbinic reasoning. It follows that Jewish ethics develops through ongoing rabbinic interpretation of biblical law and, of course, interpretations of earlier rabbinic interpretations. In the context of such a process, reason is necessary but not sufficient on its own to determine moral obligation. Nor can reason function properly in solitude, for only when a community of scholars reasons together can God's will be discerned. The interpretation of revelation, like revelation itself, is a communal event.

REDEMPTION: THE POWER AND PURPOSE OF MORAL ACTION

In Judaism, redemption connotes an historical event that dramatically transforms life in this world. The paradigm of redemption is the exodus from Egyptian slavery by means of which God transformed a band of slaves, suffering oppression under a cruel pharoah, into a nation free to worship God in their God-given land. This theme constitutes a recurring refrain in traditional Jewish liturgy. The later redemption of the Israelites from Babylonian exile similarly entailed the movement from political subjugation to freedom, from an alien place to their homeland, from a condition in which God seemed absent to one in which God's power to act decisively on Israel's behalf was manifest to all. To the biblical prophets especially, the promise of God's redemption was a central article of faith and a source of comfort to a downtrodden people (see Isaiah 40–55, Jeremiah 30–31, Ezekiel 34–37).

How does God's action of redeeming the Israelites from slavery in Egypt (and, later, from exile in Babylonia) affect Jews' understanding of their moral responsibilities toward others? Given the decisive role that God plays in world history, to what extent can Jews' moral actions affect the course of human history? How does the biblical concept of the "end of days" shape Jewish moral vision and motivate Jewish moral striving?

God's redemption completes the theological triad that begins with God's creation of the world and God's revelation of Torah to Israel. Redemption, like creation and revelation, refers not only to these great events of the distant past but also to an ongoing mode of God's action in the world. It was assumed that God's redemptive action could (and would) burst onto the stage of history at any time. Yet redemption differs from both creation and revelation in one important way. While the decisive acts of creation of the world and of the revelation of Torah already happened in the past, the decisive act of redemption has yet to occur. The redemption from slavery in

Egypt or from exile to Babylonia is only a precursor or preamble to the ultimate act of redemption, the dawning of that idyllic state that humankind will experience "when the messiah comes" in the distant future.[25] As you shall see, even though the ultimate redemption may have been far off, the vision of a world redeemed by God influenced decisively the ways in which Jews understood both the significance and the purpose of moral actions.

As Jews throughout the ages retold the story of their redemption as a people, they derived distinctive moral lessons from that experience. First and foremost, God's redemption testifies powerfully to the truth that God desires human freedom and will not tolerate political tyranny. Human power is to be used to further *God's* purposes, for all humankind is subservient to God's authority. Thus, political oppression is contrary to God's purposes, for it perverts the natural, moral order that God created. At least one strand within the biblical tradition takes this line of thinking a step further. Israel owes its allegiance to only one sovereign—God—and any human ruler (oppressive or otherwise) represents a potential rival for that allegiance. Indeed, the prophet Samuel is extremely reluctant to acquiesce to the people's desire that he appoint a king, for this represents a rejection of God as their ruler (see I Samuel 8:7–8).

It is but a short step from this view of God as the author of human freedom to the moral principle that Israel must not oppress others or take advantage of the vulnerable within society. Within the Torah, the prohibition against wronging the stranger, the widow, and/or the orphan is repeated more often than any other, frequently with the appended admonition, "for you were strangers in the land of Egypt" (Exodus 22:20, 23:9, Leviticus 19:34, Deuteronomy 10:19). The Israelites' experience of slavery is invoked in these texts to remind them of the bitterness of slavery and so to heighten their sensitivity to others who are socially disadvantaged. Plainly, the point here is not only about the bitterness of slavery but also about the sweetness of liberation and the ideas of self-worth and responsibility that it entails. That experience of slavery ended with God's dramatic intervention in Israel's history, freeing them, and carrying them "on eagles' wings" (Exodus 19:4) to the place where they received God's revelation, and leading them into their own land. It follows that those who value God's gift of freedom dare not deny a similar freedom to others. The redemption that God has wrought in the lives of the Israelites they in turn must extend to others. In this context, it is not difficult to understand why the Bible, while permitting the institution of slavery, placed severe restrictions on the ownership of slaves, a trend that continued and intensified with subsequent rabbinic legislation.[26]

This concern for the disadvantaged and the stranger represents one way in which the experience of redemption shaped Jewish moral life. On the level of ethical theory, redemption has even more profound implications, for it places the entire system of Jewish moral norms in a new context. To understand how this is so, we must review briefly the characteristics of redemption as Jews have traditionally understood it.

Redemption represents the intrusion of God into the historical process, causing events to unfold in accord with God's will. The great messianic redemption in the future, like the redemptions from Egyptian slavery or Babylonian exile in the past, will be a world historical event. For the biblical writers as well as the later rabbis, redemption is the culmination of God's plan for human history, a plan that encompasses both Israel and its adversaries and that ultimately signals the fulfillment of human destiny. To be redeemed, then, is to be liberated from the historical forces that thwart God's will on earth, to be liberated by God for the purpose of serving God. The ultimate result of redemption is that condition that comes to be called "the kingdom of God (or heaven)" in which all nations of the world in common recognize the one God as their sovereign so that God's will and power become manifest in all human relations. As the prophet Zechariah put it, "And the Lord shall be king over all the earth; in that day there shall be one Lord with one name" (14:9).

This concept of redemption contrasts sharply with the more internalized, spiritualized view of redemption that arose within some Jewish circles in late antiquity and that is reflected in many New Testament writings. In that view, the purpose of redemption is the freedom from human sinfulness and its consequences, that is, death (both physical and spiritual). In the classical Christian conception, this can be accomplished only by the liberation of the spirit from the shackles of the body, for it is the latter that facilitates human sinfulness (i.e., straying from God). It follows that redemption is necessarily a personal affair, for the struggle between the forces of good and evil, of spirit and body, occurs in the depths of each human soul. So God's saving power is manifest in the personal rather than the political sphere. It must be noted that this internalized, spiritualized view of redemption does continue as a theme within Jewish ethics, particularly in the writings of pietists and mystics, yet the dominant view builds on the tradition of the biblical prophets and so understands redemption first and foremost as an event in the life of nations and only secondarily in individuals; it occurs on the plane of history more than in the depths of the soul.

Implicit in this national, political concept of redemption is the belief that human history is infused with divine significance. History is not merely the result of blind forces acting chaotically on people over which humankind has no control. Rather, history is always the product of God's will acting purposefully and, in some measure, predictably. Because God has revealed the overarching plan for human history, Jews have the ability to understand their history as it unfolds and to make decisions that either further or thwart God's purposes. Historical events, then, are never merely "historical," for they mirror stages in the unfolding relationship between God and humankind. So history unfolds through a dialectical process of human action and divine reaction continuing across the centuries until this divine-human drama reaches its final act, the messianic culmination of history.

The precise role that Israel plays in this drama of redemption remains a point of some disagreement within the tradition. On the one hand, much of the **Pentateuch** and many prophetic writings assume that Israel's history (and the world's) depends on how fully Israelites observe God's law. When Israel lives a life of holiness, as God has prescribed, God will bless and protect them and ultimately will send the messianic redeemer. On the other hand, later prophetic and apocalyptic writers believed that redemption depended not on human action, but solely on divine grace. The messiah would come not when Israel had "earned" it through its righteous action but as a divine gift, an expression of God's love, which overlooks and forgives Israel's past transgressions. The prophet Ezekiel expressed this latter view forcefully (Ezekiel 36:22–23):

> Thus said the Lord God: Not for your sake will I act, O House of Israel, but for My holy name, which you have caused to be profaned among the nations to which you have come. I will sanctify My great name which has been profaned among the nations—among whom you have caused it to be profaned. And the nations shall know that I am the Lord—declares the Lord God—when I manifest My holiness before their eyes through you.

Each of these positions on redemption must be considered in turn.

The view that redemption depends on Israel's deeds presupposes that human beings, through their actions, have a decisive role to play in history, which God has given them, though not specifically scripted for them. What transpires on this earthly plane depends in no small measure on the seriousness with which Jews take their divinely ordained task, to move the historical drama forward toward its ultimate conclusion. Moral action is among the primary ways in which Israel participates in shaping its history and, as the later prophets believed, all of human history. Indeed, the significance of Israel's moral deeds (and often, its moral transgressions) is one of the preeminent themes of all biblical literature. The message throughout is clear: if Israel will only take seriously its responsibilities to God, especially its moral responsibilities, it will be blessed immeasurably; failure to do so will result in divine recriminations and ultimately in historical calamities (Deuteronomy 11: 13–21). The divine import of human history entails the belief that Israel's moral action in the present has far-reaching implications for the future of the world.

This theme is developed extensively by the rabbis and is now popularly associated with the concept of **tikkun olam,** the "repairing of the world." On this view, Israel is understood to be God's partner in bringing about the redemption of the world. In the deepest sense, observing God's commandments (especially the moral injunctions) is doing God's work in the world, the work that furthers God's purposes. Indeed, God depends on Israel for this because the world cannot be redeemed except by Israel's performing deeds of lovingkindness. In some **kabbalistic** traditions, the notion of tikkun olam is expanded to encompass the view that the cosmos as a whole is in a state of brokenness and can be restored to wholeness only through Israel's action.[27]

This way of understanding redemption and the power of Israel's actions to bring it about places an enormous responsibility on human beings for the destiny of the world. In this context, a person can readily understand why Jews have frequently been overrepresented in radical and/or utopian social and political movements. If the goal is to transform the world into "the kingdom of God," a radical reorientation of political relationships is necessary. If God is depending on human beings to effect this transformation, then Jews dare not fail to fulfill their responsibilities as God's partners in the redemption of the world.

Even apart from such radical views, there was no escaping the implication that each righteous deed brings the world closer to messianic redemption, just as each sinful act impedes the progress toward that divinely ordained goal. In this sense, God has placed enormous trust in human beings, for the very destiny of the world depends on our behavior, for good or ill. The rabbis were fond of proclaiming that the coming of the messiah depended only on Israel's repentance, or only on Israel observing two successive Sabbaths perfectly, or only on the fulfillment of some other provision of the law.[28] The twentieth-century Jewish philosopher Martin Buber expressed this view succinctly, "God's grace consists precisely in this, that He wants to let Himself be won by man, that He places Himself, so to speak, into man's hands. God wants to come to His world, but He wants to come to it through man."[29] So the moral task entrusted to human beings, and preeminently to Israel, is necessarily an infinite one.

The second, contravening view continues to surface in the history of Jewish thought. Israel, through its actions, cannot force God's hand in history. The "end" is something about which humans dare not speculate, for doing so entails the arrogant belief that we can know the mind of God. A more modest assessment of human knowledge and of the power of human action seems more appropriate. In support of this view, it could be noted that, on the individual level, divine reward and punishment did not always correspond to human righteousness and sinfulness; maybe the same was true on the national level. If so, Israel could not be certain just how its behavior contributed to the coming of the ultimate redemption. Furthermore, it could be argued that humans, prone to sin as they are, were not a dependable vehicle for effecting the redemption of the world. Surely, God would not place the destiny of the world in our human, ever so fallible hands. The culmination of this line of thinking emerges in the view that God will send the messiah precisely when humankind has fallen so low that it cannot save itself. Only when the world is so depraved, when licentiousness runs rampant, will God intervene to bring the promised end.[30] This position correlates with the idea noted earlier in the discussion of creation that human beings have little moral worth, little to recommend them as agents of redemption. After all, doesn't scripture itself teach that "the Lord saw how great was human wickedness on earth, and how every plan devised by the human mind was nothing but evil all the time" (Genesis 6:5) and that "man is born to [do] mischief, just as sparks fly upward" (Job 5:7)?

If this latter view remains a minority position within rabbinic tradition, it is probably because the rabbis were reluctant to sever the connection between human morality and divine blessing and reward. To do so would be to undermine the belief that what we do in the moral sphere is of ultimate concern to God altogether and so to deprive moral action of its higher purpose and goal. Better to assert an (undemonstrable) belief in the cosmic significance of moral action than to open the door to the view that such action had no ultimate meaning.

There is, then, an unresolved tension in the classical view of redemption, as noted earlier in the discussions of creation and revelation. Here, too, the tradition overall tries to steer a course between two extreme positions or to assert the provisional truth of both possibilities. The challenge is how to balance God's power to effect redemption with ours. To stress God's role is to risk minimizing the importance of human action and the divine significance of the moral deeds people perform. To stress Israel's role is to risk arrogance, to suppose that humans, not God, are the true authors of human history. In the classic rabbinic view, redemption implies a partnership between God and Israel, each of whom plays a role in bringing history to its culmination, "the end of days." Yet the precise ways in which each partner contributes to this process is never fully clear, for humans can never be certain just what role we play in God's master plan for the world. Perhaps the most important point is that, on both views, the ultimate conclusion of the divine-human drama is not in doubt. The world will be redeemed, humankind will be united in its service of the one God, whether *through* human effort or *in spite of* it. This steadfast belief in redemption provides an enduring source of hope that humankind is perfectible and indeed one day will be perfected in its service of God. That vision of a world redeemed reinforces the basic truth about creation, that the world as a divine creation is "good," a place of ultimate concern to God, an arena in which human beings have been given a divine task. However they measure up in their devotion to that task, the world remains a place in which redemption is not only possible, but certain.

This chapter has sketched in very broad strokes some basic features of Jewish religious experience and pointed to some of the ways in which these shape Jewish ethics. Subsequent chapters will provide more of the details that will enable the reader to understand both the content and the character of Jewish ethics more fully. Before proceeding, however, it is important to consider briefly the sources that constitute the basis of Jewish ethical reflection. Some of these have already been introduced in the form of quotations from the Bible, rabbinic literature, and traditional liturgy, but a great many other works figure prominently in the history of Jewish ethics. At this juncture it is important to look more extensively at these sources, for this will enable readers to appreciate the texture of ethical deliberation in this tradition.

KEY POINTS

- Judaism's distinctive worldview and way of life is grounded in the communal narrative of the Jews: that they were a people enslaved and then liberated by God and chosen to have a special relationship with God and to live a holy life in the land of Israel, which God gave them.
- The Torah (Scripture) preserves this narrative and the laws that God revealed to the Jews; studying the Torah and following its dictates is the essence of traditional Jewish religious practice.
- The covenant between God and the Jews, established through the giving and receiving of the Torah, is the context within which Jews traditionally have understood themselves, their obligations to others, and their history.

- This particular covenantal relationship between God and Israel is set within a larger narrative about God's relationship to all human beings, which begins with God's creation of the world and will end with God's redemption of all people from discord and strife when the messiah comes.
- These themes of creation, revelation, and redemption weave their way through traditional Jewish liturgy and are reflected in the cycle of Jewish holidays.
- Different ways of understanding creation, revelation, and redemption have developed within Jewish tradition; these have shaped both Judaism's specific moral teachings and the way in which Judaism has understood the whole meaning and purpose of moral life.

QUESTIONS TO CONSIDER

1. Many scholars of religion and ethics have argued that the values we hold grow out of the stories we tell about ourselves. Can you think of stories that Americans tell about themselves and identify the moral lessons or values seem to be embedded in them? How do these compare with the stories and values that Judaism presents?

2. As noted, Judaism has a strong emphasis on community: God's covenant is made with the people, redemption will be a national (really a global) event, many prayers are recited in the plural, and so on. How does giving priority to the life of the community over that of the individual affect Jewish ethics?

3. How does Judaism's belief in the special status and moral obligations of the Jewish people fit together with its more universal teachings about all people being created in God's image? Do you see ways of resolving this implicit tension within the tradition?

4. Each of the three major theological themes in Judaism—creation, revelation, and redemption—has been interpreted in diverse ways. What are the implications for Jewish ethics of the core beliefs themselves—that God created the world, that God revealed the Torah to Israel, and that God redeemed the Jews from slavery and will redeem all humankind at the end of time? What, on the other hand, are the moral implications of the various ways of interpreting these basic concepts?

5. In studying religion it is always helpful to look at what is familiar with new eyes and to notice what is startling about it; conversely, it is helpful to look closely at what appears alien and peculiar to see if, on deeper examination, there is something familiar about it. From this first exploration of basic Jewish beliefs and values, what seems familiar and understandable to you? What seems alien and peculiar, perhaps even unintelligible? What can you do to move beyond these initial reactions to a deeper appreciation of these ideas and values?

Chapter Three

The Sources
of Jewish Ethics

Summary

This chapter introduces the major literary sources of Jewish ethics and examines representative excerpts from each. Special attention is given to the ways in which these sources contribute to the particular character of Jewish ethical discourse.

◆ ───

> *. . . the Jewish textual tradition is one of the great literary achievements of human culture, representing a system that is unique, important, and deeply compelling to anyone interested in literature itself. . . . In reading them we come face to face with those issues that form the universal core of all great literature, as we see those concerns refracted through the lens of the particular consciousness of the Jewish literary imagination.*[1]

To understand the character of Jewish ethics and to appreciate the ways in which it has developed over time, it is necessary to examine the various sources through which Jewish ethical views have been expressed. This is particularly important given two distinctive features of the Jewish ethical tradition. First, much of traditional Jewish literature takes the form of commentary on earlier literature. As a result, later layers of this literature are virtually unintelligible unless the reader is familiar with earlier ones. Moreover, much of this literature is written in a genre quite foreign to modern readers, who are more likely to be familiar with western philosophical modes of expression. Only by examining this literature closely, mastering its peculiar idioms and its distinctive logic, can you understand traditional Jewish ethical thought.

Indeed, as Chapter Seven especially discusses, contemporary Jewish ethicists continue to cite these classical sources frequently in their work. It would be impossible to include here excerpts from every major source for Jewish ethics, but it will be sufficient for my purposes to present some representative selections of the most frequently cited texts. Several major literary sources are sampled below in roughly chronological order: Hebrew Bible, **Mishnah, Talmud,** rabbinic **midrash,** medieval ethical treatises, law codes, and **responsa.**

As a focal point for this brief introduction to the sources of Jewish ethics, I have chosen the topic of repentance (*teshuvah*), surely a central concept in Jewish religious thought. **Teshuvah,** from the Hebrew meaning "return," has been a major subject of ethical reflection from biblical times to the present. As a result, there is a rich corpus of material on which to draw, with many examples from each of the genres of literature mentioned. In addition, the concept of repentance exemplifies many aspects of Jewish ethics discussed in the previous chapter. Even a brief overview of classical discussions of repentance, therefore, will enable us to see clearly how this particular ethical concept is permeated with religious significance, how it is tied to the individual's relationship to God, and how this practice of repentance constitutes a religious/legal obligation. It will not be possible here to comment on all the significant dimensions of repentance as it is discussed in these sources. Still, I hope that the reader will study the sources that follow, keeping in mind the many ways in which creation, revelation, and redemption shape Jewish ethics in general and repentance in particular.

Each of the sources in this chapter is introduced with some historical and/or biographical information and is followed by a brief commentary designed to highlight the way in which it approaches issues of repentance. Those interested in more extensive information about these sources and the history of Jewish ethics in general should consult the Notes and Suggestions for Further Reading.

BIBLE

The Hebrew Scriptures, which Jews call **Tanakh** or *mikra* and Christians call the Old Testament, constitute the foundation of all Jewish life and thought. From the standpoint of traditional Jews, this entire corpus of material was understood as God's word, divine instruction whose validity was eternal and unquestioned. The Pentateuch, or first five books of the Bible (Hebrew, *chumash*), was believed to have been revealed by God directly to Moses atop Mt. Sinai. The remaining books—the prophets (Isaiah, Jeremiah, Ezekiel, and the twelve "minor" prophets), the historical books (Joshua, Judges, Samuel, Kings, and Chronicles), the wisdom literature (Ecclesiastes, Proverbs, Song of Songs, Job), and other narrative and/or poetic works (Esther, Ruth, Psalms, Lamentations, etc.)—were all attributed to human authors inspired by God. Set readings from the Pentateuch (paired with thematically related readings from the Prophets) are included in traditional Sabbath and holiday worship services; indeed, the chanting of these Scriptural passages comprises the largest segment of these services. In addition, substantial portions of biblical text were incorporated into the traditional liturgy, and certain books are read in their entirety on special occasions (e.g., Ecclesiastes is read on Tabernacles, Song of Songs on Passover, Ruth on Pentecost, Lamentations on the ninth day of the Hebrew month of Av,[2] and Esther on Purim).

Modern biblical scholars have determined that most books of the Bible include materials written by more than one author and that, in some instances, a single book includes materials deriving from very different time periods and reflecting diverse viewpoints. Thus, Genesis combines the narratives of the J author (who lived in the 10th century B.C.E.), the E author (who lived in the 9th century B.C.E.), and the P author (who lived in the 5th century B.C.E.)[3]; the book of Isaiah includes the work of at least two separate prophets (and/or their disciples), some of whom lived before and some after the destruction of Jerusalem in 587 B.C.E. Literary analysis of biblical texts, comparative studies of biblical and other ancient Near Eastern literature, and archeological evidence enable scholars to date the various literary strands that comprise the Bible. These scholarly investigations, of course, challenge the more traditional view of biblical authorship by placing these books in their historical context. Rather than timeless expressions of God's will, these biblical writings represent the expressions of diverse interest groups within ancient Israelite society and betray the influence of many non-Israelite sources as well.

Both traditionalists and historical-critical scholars will readily concede that the Bible as a whole incorporates a wide range of views on all the major issues of Jewish theology and ethics, including the nature of God, the covenant between God and Israel, the relationship between Israel and the nations of the world, and what God requires of Israel and/or humanity. Those who see the Bible as God's word will, of course, strive to reconcile and harmonize the inconsistencies among these sources, for all derive from one God and so ultimately reflect a single, indivisible truth. Those, on the other hand, who adopt a more historical perspective (and this includes many contemporary Jewish ethicists whose work will be discussed later in this book) will see these inconsistencies as diverse and perhaps irreconcilable perspectives of different people living in different times and places. The task then is to discern the dominant or majority view on a given subject and to trace the influence of different strands within the biblical tradition on subsequent Jewish thought.

The passages that follow are drawn from each of the major sections of the Hebrew Bible (Torah, Prophets, Writings)[4] and reflect an ongoing preoccupation with the issue of sin and repentance as aspects of the relationship between God and Israel.

1. Leviticus 16:29–30
And this shall be to you a law for all time: In the seventh month, on the tenth day of the month, you shall practice self-denial; and you shall do no manner of work, neither the citizen nor the alien who resides among you.

For on this day atonement shall be made for you to cleanse you of all your
sins; you shall be clean before the Lord.

2. Deuteronomy 30:8–10

You, however, will again heed the Lord and obey all His commandments
which I enjoin upon you this day. And the Lord your God will grant you
abounding prosperity in all your undertakings, in the issue of your womb,
the offspring of your cattle, and the produce of your soil. For the Lord
will again delight in your well-being, as He did in that of your fathers,
since you will be heeding the Lord your God and keeping His commandments and laws that are recorded in this book of the Teaching—once you
return to the Lord your God with all your heart and soul.

3. Jeremiah 31:18–20

I can hear Ephraim lamenting:
You have chastised me, and I am chastised
Like a calf that has not been broken.
Receive me back, let me return,
For you, O Lord, are my God.
Now that I have turned back, I am filled with remorse;
Now that I am made aware, I strike my thigh.
I am ashamed and humiliated,
For I bear the disgrace of my youth.
Truly, Ephraim is a dear son to Me,
A child that is dandled!
Whenever I have turned against him,
My thoughts would dwell on him still.
That is why My heart yearns for him:
I will receive him back in love—declares the Lord.

4. Ezekiel 18:21–23, 30–32

Moreover, if the wicked man repents of all the sins that he committed and
keeps all My laws and does what is just and right, he shall live; he shall
not die. None of the transgressions he committed shall be remembered
against him; because of the righteousness he has practiced, he shall live.
Is it my desire that a wicked man shall die?—says the Lord God. It is
rather that he shall turn back from his ways and live.

Be assured, O House of Israel, I will judge each one of you according to
his ways—declares the Lord God. Repent and turn back from your transgressions; let them not be a stumbling block of guilt for you. Cast away
all the transgressions by which you have offended, and get yourselves a
new heart and a new spirit, that you may not die, O House of Israel. For
it is not my desire that anyone shall die—declares the Lord God. Repent,
therefore, and live!

5. Hosea 14:2–3
Return, O Israel, to the Lord your God,
For you have fallen because of your sin.
Take words with you
And return to the Lord.
Say to Him:
'Forgive all guilt
And accept what is good;
Instead of bulls we will pay
[The offering of] our lips.

6. Lamentations 5:21
Take us back, O Lord, to Yourself,
And let us come back;
Renew our days as of old!

Biblical writers of all periods and persuasions assumed that Israel sins when it disobeys God's directives and that Israel's sins, especially its moral misdeeds, have a deleterious effect on its relationship with God. The central question underlying all these texts is how Israel can be reconciled to God after it has strayed from the proper path. The priestly author of Leviticus refers to a set Day of Atonement (*Yom Kippur*) by means of which God each year cleanses the people of its sins and so gives them a "clean slate." The priests perform an elaborate expiation ritual (Leviticus 16) on behalf of the people while the people themselves fast as a sign of contrition (Leviticus 23:27). The salient point is that God provides a ritualized mechanism for absolving the people of their sins on an annual basis. The very need for such a Day of Atonement testifies both to the fact that sin potentially undermines the bond between God and Israel and to the possibility, indeed the assurance, of reconciliation.

The Deuteronomic author introduces the concept of "return" to God with one's "heart and soul." Now reconciliation with God, and the divine blessings that follow from it, depend on the genuine reorientation of the people to God's law. The idea that "turning" or "returning" is the essence of repentance and the only avenue for reconciliation of the sinner with God becomes a dominant theme in Jewish ethics and a rich source of reflection throughout Jewish tradition. The prophetic authors augment this concept of repentance by emphasizing God's readiness to accept those who repent. In contrast to the oft-repeated claims that Israel's God is stern and harsh to sinners, these biblical authors insist that God is infinitely loving, akin to a parent always ready to forgive one's child. The sinner, then, should never despair of being reconciled to God, provided only that he or she is willing to return, bringing "words [of remorse]," as Hosea emphasizes.

The brief passage from Lamentations, which occupies a central place in Jewish liturgy, appears to assume that the human capacity to move toward God is both essential to reconciliation and insufficient in itself to accomplish this goal. The process of returning itself requires divine assistance and so Israel invokes God's own help in turning away from sin and back toward God.

MISHNAH

The **Mishnah** is the first postbiblical Jewish code of law and practice, dating from approximately 200 C.E. It records the views of the *tannaim,* those rabbis and teachers who were active in approximately the first two centuries of the Common Era.[5] Divided into six "orders" (agriculture [literally, "seeds"], festivals, women, damages, holy things, and purities), the Mishnah discusses a wide array of topics from domestic law to civil and criminal law, the proper treatment of produce grown in the Land of Israel, the order of established prayer, and the order of sacrificial offerings in the Temple. These large categories encompass individual treatises or "tractates" (sixty-three in all), which are further subdivided into chapters and paragraphs. The systematic arrangement of the collected views of the early generations of rabbis is traditionally ascribed to Rabbi Judah the Prince (often referred to simply as "Rabbi") who lived in the Land of Israel at the beginning of the third century C.E.

Mishnaic law greatly expands on biblical law in many areas. Certain topics that receive only the briefest treatment in the Bible (e.g., divorce) are the subject of an entire tractate in the Mishnah. Clearly, in the centuries since the biblical law was written, a great deal of oral tradition had developed about how to interpret the provisions of that law. Moreover, new situations not envisioned by the biblical authors arose and needed to be addressed. Thus, often the Mishnah provides whole chapters of law with no explicit basis in biblical law whatsoever, yet the authors of the Mishnah throughout assume familiarity with the biblical text and its teachings; without a thorough understanding of the latter, many mishnaic teachings would be entirely unintelligible.

Apart from its organization, perhaps the most salient feature of the Mishnah is the frequency with which it records disputes among the tannaim. Thus it is common to find the articulation of a particular legal issue followed by "Rabbi Eliezer says x . . . Rabbi Joshua says y. . . . Sages say z . . ." Not only are these disputes left unresolved, but even the legal reasoning behind the divergent views is often left unexplained. In a sense, then, the Mishnah is less a law code in the modern sense than a compilation of legal views, many of which are given anonymously. Precisely how the Mishnah came to be written and organized in this way has been the subject of intense scholarly investigation.[6]

For the purposes of this introduction two other points are especially significant. First, the Mishnah does not represent the sum total of the views of the tannaim. A second collection of contemporaneous materials, the **Tosefta** (Aramaic, "addendum"), is organized in the same fashion and incorporates alternate versions of many mishnaic teachings, as well as other materials that augment and/or contradict the Mishnah. The Tosefta thus provides more information about the views of the tannaim and serves, as its name implies, as a supplement to the Mishnah. Second, neither Mishnah nor Tosefta is organized as a commentary to the Bible, though, of course, it takes up and develops much biblical law. In that sense, the Mishnah is a free-standing document designed to be studied in its own right. The first of the passages that follows is taken from the mishnaic tractate Yoma ("The Day"), devoted to the Day of Atonement; the second is from a collection of tannaitic aphorisms known as Avot ("Fathers") or Pirke Avot ("Chapters of the Fathers"). Because many of these aphorisms have an ethical thrust, they are often cited in discussions of Jewish ethics.[7]

1. Yoma 8:8–9
A sin offering and an unconditional guilt offering atone.
Death and the Day of Atonement atone in conjunction with repentance.
Repentance atones for minor transgressions of positive and negative commandments.
But concerning serious transgressions, [repentance] suspends [the punishment] until the Day of Atonement arrives and atones.
One who says, 'I shall sin and repent, sin and repent'—they give such a person no means by which to repent.
[One who says,] 'I will sin and the day of Atonement will atone,'—the Day of Atonement does not atone.
For transgressions between an individual and the Omnipresent, the Day of Atonement atones.
For transgressions between one individual and another, the Day of Atonement does not atone, until the one [who transgressed] appeases the other. . . .

2. Avot 4:17
[Rabbi Jacob] used to say: Better one hour spent in repentance and good deeds in this world than the whole life in the world-to-come; and better one hour of pleasure in the world-to-come than the whole life in this world.

Mishnah Yoma 8:8–9 attempts to sort out the differences between different media through which atonement can be effected. Plainly, the Bible indicates that both (1) atonement for sins, or expiation, is achieved both through the sacrificial cult and through the Day of Atonement and (2) repentance is necessary for reconciliation with God. The problem is to determine how repentance contributes to divine forgiveness without undercutting the efficacy of sacrifice and the Day of Atonement. A series of distinctions is introduced (between minor and major transgressions, between transgressions against God and those against other people) designed to demonstrate both the power and the limitations of repentance. On the one hand, even the Day of Atonement will not erase sins committed against others unless the offender first repents and achieves reconciliation with the offended party. On the other hand, in the case of major transgressions, repentance will not erase the sin but only postpone punishment for it until the Day of Atonement effects complete expiation. Note that the person who casually sins counting on either repentance or the Day of Atonement to set things right is instructed that expiation is not possible in this way. What emerges from this discussion is less a coherent theory about how sacrifice, death, repentance, and the Day of Atonement constitute vehicles for expiation than an insistence that each plays a role, although none plays the decisive role in all cases.

The passage from Avot emphasizes the significance of repentance through its juxtaposition of this world and the afterlife. Rabbi Jacob's point would appear to be that there is no way to quantify the value of even one hour spent in repentance and good deeds. Just as nothing in this life can compare to the bliss of the life beyond, so too nothing in eternity can match (or, presumably, compensate for lack of) genuine contrition and acts of lovingkindness performed during our lifetimes.

Note that neither of these mishnaic passages articulates the assumptions behind or the theory underlying these rabbinic pronouncements. Here, as throughout the Mishnah, the text is extraordinarily terse and even opaque. As you shall see, the rabbis who undertook a systematic explication of the Mishnah in the two to three centuries following its promulgation attempted to fill in the silences of the mishnaic text.

TALMUD

The Talmud is a monumental collection of halakhah (Jewish law) and **aggadah** (folklore and anecdotes), as well as history and science, prayer and parable; in a word, it constitutes the most comprehensive expression of rabbinic Judaism. It is difficult to exaggerate the significance of the Talmud for the history of Judaism, since, quite apart from the immense body of learning contained within its several thousand pages, it has spawned new commentaries and supercommentaries in every generation since it was written. Indeed, for the past fifteen centuries, study of the Talmud has been virtually synonymous with the study of Judaism itself. To appreciate why the Talmud has been so influential and why it has necessitated such a long tradition of commentary, readers must consider its scope, the style in which it is written, and the conceptual world that it reflects.

Although people frequently refer to "the Talmud," there are in fact two Talmuds, one produced in the Land of Israel (known in Hebrew as the "Jerusalem Talmud," also referred to sometimes as the "Palestinian Talmud") about 400 C.E., and another produced in Babylonia about a century later. The latter, being far larger and more complex, is more frequently studied and quoted. (In fact, whenever "the Talmud" is referred to without qualification, the Babylonian Talmud is meant.) The basic framework of both works, however, is the same. Each is organized as a commentary to the tractates of the Mishnah and includes primarily the debates of the *amoraim* (rabbis who lived from the third to the sixth centuries C.E.) about the meaning of the Mishnah's rulings. Thus, on a typical page of Talmud, one finds a paragraph of Mishnah followed by the amoraic commentary, called **gemara** (Aramaic, "study"), which frequently extends for several pages until the next paragraph of Mishnah is cited, followed by its gemara.[8] In effect, then, to study either of the Talmuds is to follow the discussions of the Mishnah because these were carried on in the ancient rabbinic academies and subsequently edited and organized into their present form.

The conversational quality of the gemara is among its most salient features. Although scholars do not assume that the Talmud preserves verbatim conversations within the academies of Babylonia and Israel, they recognize its distinctly dialectical quality. By way of example, frequently one rabbi's opinion (A) is challenged by another (B) who may cite yet another (C) in support of his argument. This, in turn, may be countered by yet another rabbi (D) who insists the B's use of C is incorrect, and so B's challenge to A fails. In its place, D may suggest that the view of yet another sage (E) does properly challenge A's view. Often the participants to a debate will cite anecdotes about a certain rabbi whose behavior is presumed to indicate his position on a certain matter, a move that almost invariably prompts others to challenge the veracity of the anecdote or its relevance to the matter at hand. So the debate unfolds, often incorporating the views (and reported practices) of multiple rabbinic authorities living in different generations. Given this dialectical quality, it is little wonder that the Aramaic name for a talmudic tractate is *massechet* ("loom"), for the voices of the rabbis are woven together in a complex cross-generational conversation.

Although the Talmud is primarily organized as a commentary to the Mishnah, it is considerably more than this. As commentators, the amoraim take up the many questions left unanswered in the Mishnah. These include probing the rationales behind the opposing views cited in the Mishnah, exploring the circumstances that surround a particular Mishnaic ruling, and comparing a given Mishnaic sage's views on multiple topics (the amoraim were invariably concerned to explain apparent contradictions or inconsistencies within the Mishnah). In the course of these investigations, however, the gemara often drifts into tangential (and even wholly unrelated) topics. Sometimes the mention of a certain rabbi will prompt a long digression including biographical information about him or about the place where a certain incident occurred. At other times, a particular rabbi's view on one topic will be compared with his view on another, which then takes center stage and may give way to yet another tangentially related matter. Not infrequently, these long talmudic discussions are inconclusive in that central legal questions raised about the Mishnah at the outset are left unanswered, or are answered by different authorities in different ways.

The dialectical and wide-ranging quality of talmudic discourse would make it complex and difficult to follow even if it were written in clear, crisp prose. To the contrary, the language of the Talmud is frequently sparse and cryptic. A single word often stands in for an entire phrase, a plethora of rhetorical key words and abbreviations are employed, allusions to pertinent biblical and rabbinic concepts and laws are left unexplained; in short, the Talmud speaks in a peculiar idiom that the reader must master in order to follow its logic. In many respects, studying Talmud is like deciphering a telegram in which a minimum of words is used to convey the message but whose message can be an extraordinarily complex mixture of legal analysis, debate, and narrative.

These stylistic and conceptual difficulties account for the long tradition of talmudic commentaries. The linear commentary of Rabbi Solomon ben Isaac ("Rashi") has been an indispensable aid to students of the Babylonian Talmud since it was written in the eleventh century. Frequently, Rashi's comments guide the reader through the ins and outs of the talmudic debate; occasionally, he proposes corrections to the text of the gemara itself, thereby resolving an obscure passage. His grandsons composed a second, much more selective commentary to the gemara (*Tosafot*) in which they often challenge Rashi's reading of the text, as well as raising secondary issues that extend beyond the plain meaning of the talmudic debate. Since 1520, when the first printed edition of the Talmud appeared in Venice, the commentaries of Rashi and Tosafot have been printed in the margins of each page. Numerous additional commentaries have been composed by talmudic scholars in each generation, many of which are now included at the end of standard editions of the Talmud. When one considers the sheer volume of material contained within the Talmuds, together with the voluminous commentaries on them that have accumulated over the centuries, it is possible to appreciate the intellectual challenge of talmudic study as well as the achievement of those who have mastered this encyclopedic compendium of law and lore.

Standard citations of the Babylonian Talmud include the name of the tractate followed by the number of the folio page and either *a* or *b*, to indicate the side of the folio on which the passage appears. Citations to the Jerusalem Talmud generally provide the chapter and paragraph numbers of the Mishnah passage preceding the gemara in question.[9] In general, references to talmudic tractates are preceded by a *B* or *Y* to indicate whether it is to the Babylonian or Yerushalmi (Jerusalem) Talmud. The following passages are all drawn from tractates of the Babylonian Talmud.

> **1. Berakhot 34b**
> **Rabbi Hiyya bar Abba said in the name of Rabbi Yohanan: All the prophets prophesied only concerning penitents, but concerning the wholly righteous, "No eye has seen [them], O God, but You," (Isaiah 64:3). But Rabbi Abbahu differed, for Rabbi Abbahu said, "In the place where the penitents stand, even the wholly righteous are not permitted to stand, as it is said, 'It shall be well, well with the far and the near' (Isaiah 57:19)—firstly to one who has been far, and only afterward to one who has been near all along."**

This passage considers the question of who is greater and more beloved by God, the one who is wholly righteous or the one who has sinned but repented. Hiyya quotes Yohanan as saying that God reserves a special, unrevealed reward for the wholly righteous people, and that the (more modest) blessings spoken of by the prophets are only for those who repent. Abbahu counters with another biblical verse that he interprets to mean that those who have sinned but returned to God hold an even higher place in God's scheme than those who have not sinned. Those who have returned from far away are especially beloved insofar as they have extricated themselves from their sinful behavior and found their way back to God.

2. Shabbat 153a
When Rabbi Eliezer said, "Repent, [even if only] one day before your death," his disciples asked him, "But does anyone know the day of one's death?" He said to them, "That is all the more reason that one should repent today. For if one dies tomorrow, one's entire life will have been spent in repentance." In his wisdom, Solomon also intimated [the need to repent] when he said, "Let your clothes always be freshly washed, and your head never lack ointment" (Ecclesiastes 9:8).

The notion that a person should repent before death occurs in many places in Jewish tradition along with the recognition that this necessitates being in a state of continual repentance. The possibility that a person might die at any time without having availed himself or herself of the opportunities in this lifetime for repentance should motivate people to reflect every day on their deeds and perpetually to set themselves in proper relationship to God.

3. Yoma 86a-b, 87a (excerpts)
We have been taught that Rabbi Eliezer said: It would seem to be impossible to say, "will clear the guilty" (Exodus 34:7), when Scripture is about to say, "will not clear the guilty" (ibid.).[10] Nor would it seem to be possible to say, "will not clear the guilty," having just said, "will clear the guilty." How is the inconsistency explained? That God clears the guilty who repent, but does not clear the guilty who do not repent.

Rabbi Matia ben Heresh asked Rabbi Eleazar ben Azariah in Rome: Have you heard about the four categories of those who atone for sin that Rabbi Ishmael has set forth? Rabbi Eleazar answered: They are actually three, and in each category repentance is required. When a man transgresses a positive commandment and vows penitence, forgiveness is granted him even before he stirs from the place where he is, as it is said, "Turn back, O rebellious children, I will heal your afflictions!" (Jeremiah 3:22). If he has transgressed a negative commandment and vowed repentance, his penitence suspends punishment and the Day of Atonement procures atonement, as it is said, "For on this day atonement shall be made for you to cleanse you of all your sins" (Leviticus 16:30). If he has committed [a sin punishable by] excision or by any of the deaths decreed by the High Court and has vowed repentance, his repentance and the Day of Atonement suspend punishment, and his suffering completes the atonement, as it is said, "I will punish their transgression with the rod, their iniquity with plagues" (Psalms 89:33). But if the man was guilty of profanation of the Name, repentance has no power to suspend punishment, nor can the Day of Atonement procure atonement, nor will suffering

complete it; but all of them together suspend the punishment, and only death completes atonement, as it is said, "Then the Lord of hosts revealed Himself to my ears: This iniquity shall never be forgiven you until you die" (Isaiah 22:14).

Rabbi Hama son of Rabbi Hanina said: Great is penitence, for it brings healing to the world, as it is said, "I will heal their affliction, generously will I take them back in love" (Hosea 14:5). Rabbi Hama son of Rabbi Hanina pointed out a contradiction: It is written, "Turn back, rebellious children" (Jeremiah 3:14), that is, you who were formerly backsliding, and it is written, "I will heal their affliction" (Ibid.)? [It seems that the verse from Jeremiah implies that those who repent are "children," i.e., pure, while the word "heal" in the verse from Hosea implies some remaining taint of sin.] This is no difficulty: in the one case the reference is where they repent out of love, in the other, out of fear.

Rabbi Levi said: Great is repentance, for it reaches up to the throne of glory, as it is said, "Return, O Israel, [all the way] to the Lord thy God" (Hosea 14:2) Rabbi Jonathan said: Great is repentance, because it brings about redemption, as it is said, "God shall come as redeemer to Zion, to those in Jacob who turn back from sin," (Isaiah 59:20) that is, why will a redeemer come to Zion? Because of those that turn from transgression in Jacob. Resh Lakish said: Great is penitence, because it reduces one's deliberate sins to mere errors. But did not Resh Lakish say at another time: Great is penitence, because it transforms one's deliberate sins into merits? The latter statement refers to penitence out of love; the former, to penitence out of fear. Rabbi Samuel bar Nahmani said in the name of Rabbi Jonathan: Great is penitence, because it prolongs one's days and years, as it is said, "And when a wicked man turns back from his wickedness and does what is just and right, it is he who shall live by virtue of these things" (Ezekiel 33:19). Rabbi Isaac said: In the west [the Land of Israel], the sages said in the name of Rabbah bar Mari: Come and see that the conduct of flesh and blood is not at all like the conduct of the Holy One. The conduct of flesh and blood: when a man angers his friend with words, it is questionable whether or not the friend will agree to be pacified by him. And even if you suppose the friend is willing to be pacified, it is questionable whether he will be pacified by mere words or will have to be pacified by compensation. But with the Holy One, there is no question. When a man commits a sin in secret, He is pacified with mere words, as it is said, "Take words with you, and return to the Lord" (Hosea 14:3). More: He even accounts it to him as a good deed, as it is said, "And accept what is good" (Hosea 14:3). Still more: Scripture accounts it for him as though he had offered up bullocks, as it is said, "Instead of bulls we will pay [the offering of] our lips" (Ibid.) Lest you suppose that Scripture refers here to obligatory bullocks, it is said, "I will love the voluntary offerings [of bullocks]"[11] (Hosea 14:5).

**We have been taught that Rabbi Meir used to say: Great is penitence, for
on account of one individual who vows penitence, pardon is given to him
as well as to the entire world, to all of it, as it is said, "I will heal their
affliction, generously will I take them back in love; for my anger has
turned away from him" (Hosea 14:5). Hosea does not say, "From them,"
but, "From him."**

**"How is one to tell whether a penitent is genuine? Rabbi Judah said: When
the penitent has the opportunity to commit the same sin once and once
again, and he refrains from committing it. Rabbi Judah said, "with the
same woman, at the same time, in the same place."**

**When a man causes many to earn merit, no sin will come through him;
when a man causes many to sin, the opportunity to repent will not be
given him. "When a man causes many to earn merit, no sin will come
through him"—so that he will not have to be in Gehenna [the under-
world] while his disciples are in the Garden of Eden. "When a man
causes many to sin, the opportunity to repent will not be given him"—so
that he will not manage to get to the Garden of Eden while his disciples
are in Gehenna.**

This long passage from Yoma consists of excerpts from the full discussion of Mishnah
Yoma 8:8–9 cited earlier. Indeed, this entire passage reads like a compendium of
short teachings on repentance, some of which are related to issues raised in the mishnah and many of which are not. Throughout, in characteristic fashion, the amoraim
attempt to sort out a series of apparent contradictions or inconsistencies in the biblical and earlier rabbinic teachings about repentance. How can God "clear the guilty"
and yet hold them accountable for their deeds? How does the power of repentance
square with the power of the Day of Atonement, of punishment, or of death to bring
about the reconciliation of the sinner with God? Answers to these questions are
teased from biblical texts, many of which have no direct relation to the issue at hand.

The question of how a person recognizes genuine repentance is more important than it might at first appear. Given that repentance is required by the law of the
Mishnah, it is essential that people be able to determine who has fulfilled their obligation and who has not. The suggestion that a person has only truly repented when he
or she faces the opportunity to commit the same sin again and declines to do so may
contain a profound insight into the nature of repentance: It can be tested only in the
real world of human affairs where temptation is constant and where proper behavior
can be observed and judged. This view, as you shall see, is picked up by Maimonides
and others in the tradition and so becomes the standard definition of repentance.

4. Taanit 16a

**Rabbi Adda bar Ahavah said: One who committed a transgression, con-
fesses, but does not change his way—what does such a person resemble?
One who persists in holding a dead reptile in his hand [which is considered defiling]—even if such a person immerses in all the waters of the**

**world, one's immersion will be ineffectual. But once one casts off the
reptile and immerses oneself in no more than forty *seah* of water, [the
amount required for ritual purification] the immersion is effective, as it
is said, "One who confesses and gives them [their sins] up will find
mercy" (Proverbs 28:13) and, "Let us lift up our hearts with our hands
to God in heaven" (Lamentations 3:41).**

The lesson here relies on the absurdity of holding a dead reptile, which is defiling, while an individual immerses herself in a pool, which purifies her from the effects of defilement; the immersion cannot do its work so long as she continues to hold the defiling object. By the same token, the person who confesses but does not change his ways cannot overcome the effects of that transgression. Once again, the rabbis express their insistence that repentance and forgiveness of sins come only with genuine transformation of one's behavior.

COMPILATIONS OF RABBINIC MIDRASH

Midrash, which means "investigation" or "seeking," refers to a whole genre of literature that interprets the meaning of biblical texts. In the world of late antiquity, midrash was created by the Dead Sea community to validate its own existence by the New Testament writers to demonstrate that Jesus was the messiah predicted by the ancient Israelite prophets and by the rabbis to explore a vast range of issues. Within the study of Jewish ethics, of course, it is the tradition of rabbinic midrash that is most pertinent, though creating midrash is by no means distinctively rabbinic. Indeed, insofar as all religious traditions seek to expound the meaning of their sacred literature, they engage in the creation of midrash.

Midrash is often referred to as part of the *aggadah* ("narrative") component of rabbinic literature, as distinct from the other major component, *halakhah* ("law"). Indeed, the vast majority of midrash is narrative in the very general sense that it relates stories (parables, events in the lives of rabbis, imaginary dialogues among biblical characters, or between God and angels, etc.) that have no legal implications whatsoever. Scholars of rabbinic literature have long viewed aggadah as a window into the rabbinic imagination, for through midrash the narrative impulse is given free rein. On the other hand, there is halakhic midrash, consisting of interpretations that link rabbinic legal rules to specific biblical passages. The legal passages in Exodus, Leviticus, Numbers, and Deuteronomy in particular gave rise to midrash that explains the rabbinic laws related to these scriptural texts. Still, in common parlance the word "midrash" by itself refers to the means by which the rabbis explored a wide range of theological topics: creation, good and evil, reward and punishment, the course of Israel's history, human nature, the messiah, the world to come, and, most important for our purposes, ethics.

While midrash is the name of a particular activity, it is also used to designate specific literary works (of which there are hundreds) that contain these biblical interpretations. Many of these volumes of midrash are devoted to a single biblical book, such as Genesis Rabbah, Sifre on Deuteronomy, or Midrash on Psalms. Others, such as Tanhuma or Pirke d'Rabbi Eliezer, include midrash on selections from several biblical books. Apart from these differentiations, scholars often divide midrashic works into two subcategories, exegetical and homiletical. The former are more systematic expositions of a text, such as Genesis, in which the midrashic writers move verse by verse through the book providing their explications. The latter are more free-form in that only selected verses are subjected to midrashic interpretation, often the first verses in each chapter or the first verses in the portions of Scripture designated for liturgical use on a given holiday.

Midrash was created and utilized in various contexts. Some midrash has the character of a sermon or homily delivered to a congregation, presumably following the reading of the assigned scriptural passage for that day. This provided an occasion for the midrashist to enlighten those assembled about the deeper meaning of a biblical text, much as preachers in many traditions do to this day. Some midrash, however, was undoubtedly created in academic circles devoted to the close study of the biblical text and was intended for a more exclusive audience. In the late medieval period, a number of anthologies of midrash that gleaned materials from a range of earlier midrashic sources were created.

Quite apart from these differences among midrashim, rabbinic midrash is characterized throughout by certain distinctive methods or interpretive strategies. Often the explication of a biblical verse (e.g., in Genesis) opens with a biblical verse, called a *proem,* drawn from a remote place (e.g., Lamentations). Through a series of associations and inferences, the midrash proceeds to link the proem to the primary verse being explicated. This technique appears to have served a double purpose, to demonstrate the unity of Scripture by connecting seemingly unrelated verses and to pique the audience's curiosity by opening the homily with a verse having no apparent connection to the text at hand. Other classical rabbinic midrashic techniques include taking individual verses or words out of their original context and relating them to a different context, revocalizing the consonants of the Hebrew text of Scripture to yield new words with different meanings, and the use of *gematria,* an interpretive technique in which each letter of the Hebrew alphabet is assigned a numeric value (e.g., A = 1, B = 2) so that whole words and phrases can be interpreted in relation to their numeric values (or in relation to other words with equivalent numeric values). Rabbinic midrash is also full of parables that explore the relationship between God and Israel (often using domestic analogies), inferences drawn from the juxtaposition of otherwise unrelated phrases within a text (or drawn from the use of the same word in two quite unrelated texts), dialogues between biblical characters meant to fill in lacunae, or gaps, in the biblical text, and free-form reflections on any theme or topic prompted by the scriptural text or even loosely related to it.

Midrashic literature is notoriously difficult to date with precision. The material itself includes scant references to historical events. Moreover, the same passage sometimes appears in more than one collection of midrash (as well as in the Babylonian or Jerusalem Talmud), making it difficult to ascertain which version or context is primary. To complicate matters more, often later midrashim were ascribed to earlier authorities as a way of giving them greater weight. In all, collections of classical rabbinic midrash date from the fourth to the eleventh centuries C.E.

The importance of midrash for the study of Jewish ethics lies in the fact that it represents a vast repository of reflections on matters that often bear on ethical values and moral responsibilities, human psychology, and the human condition. Because these reflections are extremely imaginative and unsystematic in character, we find within rabbinic midrash a wide range of views on almost every topic. Little wonder, then, that Jewish preachers and ethicists down to the present have turned to midrashic materials as a resource for their own reflections on moral matters. The following passages will give readers a taste of the many ways in which the biblical text provides a springboard for the midrashic imagination.

1. Midrash Psalms 90:12; Genesis Rabbah 1:4
R. Abbahu bar Ze'era said: Great is repentance, for it preceded the creation of the world, as it is said, "Before the mountains came into being. . . . You return people to contrition" (Psalm 90:2-3).

2. Midrash Psalms 45:3
It depends upon yourselves. As the lily blooms and her heart is turned upward, so if you repent and your heart is turned upward, in that very hour I will bring the Redeemer.

3. Exodus Rabbah 19:4
"No sojourner spent the night in the open; I opened my doors to the road." (Job 31:32). The Holy One declares no creature unfit—God receives all. The gates [of repentance] are always open, and all who wish to enter may enter.

4. Song of Songs Rabbah 5:3
"Let me in, my own." (Song of Songs 5:2) According to Rabbi Yose, the Holy One said to Israel: My children, open to Me in penitence an opening as small as the eye of a needle, and I shall make an opening in Me for you so wide that wagons and coaches could enter through it.

5. Ecclesiastes Rabbah 7:32
As long as people live, the Holy One expects them to repent. But once they are dead, the hope that they will repent is gone. As it is said, "At death the hopes of the wicked are doomed" (Proverbs 11:7). The matter may be illustrated by the parable of a band of robbers confined in a prison. What did they do? One of them dug an opening and they fled. One alone remained behind—he did not flee. When the warden came, he began beating the prisoner with a stick, saying to him, "Unfortunate and hapless fellow! There was an opening before you, and you did not escape!" So, too, in the time-to-come, the Holy One will say to the wicked, "Repentance was before you, and you did not repent!"

6. Pesikta Rabbati 184a

Beloved is repentance before God, for God cancels his own words for its sake. For it says in the Law, "A man takes a wife and possesses her. She fails to please him because he finds something obnoxious about her, and he writes her a bill of divorcement, hands it to her, and sends her away from his house; she leaves his household and becomes the wife of another man; then this latter man rejects her, writes her a bill of divorcement, hands it to her, and sends her away from his house; or the man who married her last dies. Then the first husband who divorced her shall not take her to wife again, since she has been defiled" (Deuteronomy 24:1–4). But God does not act thus. Even though the Israelites have forsaken him [their husband] and served other gods, God says "Repent, draw near to me, and I will receive you." (Jeremiah 3:1).[12]

7. Lamentations Rabbah 3:35

Rabbi Helbo asked Rabbi Samuel bar Nahman: Since I have heard of you as a master of *aggadah* [tell me] what is meant by the verse "You have screened Yourself off with a cloud, that no prayer may pass through" (Lamentations 3:44). Rabbi Samuel answered: Prayer is likened to an immersion pool, but repentance is likened to the sea. Just as an immersion pool is at times open and at other times locked, so the gates of prayer are at times open and at other times locked. But the sea is always open, even as the gates of repentance are always open.

The central theme of these midrashic reflections is that repentance is freely available to all at all times. By contrast to prayer, which must be offered at set times and in specified ways, repentance offers a means of drawing closer to God that is unlimited in time. Similarly, sinners should not despair of the possibility of reconciliation with God, for God desires repentance from all, regardless of their past behavior. Moreover, sinners need not return to God "all the way"; the smallest opening of their part will be met with unbounded grace on God's side. In all, these midrashim portray repentance as a joint process in which God and the individual take steps toward one another. The individual sinner must make the first move but can then count on God's love and forgiveness in response.

The greatness of repentance can be illustrated in numerous ways: by the idea that it preceded creation, by the notion that in accepting penitents God overrides the usual provisions of the law, and by the belief that redemption depends on Israel's repentance. Indeed, taken together, these passages link repentance with creation, revelation, and redemption. The world that God created could not continue to exist were it not for the possibility of repentance, for human sinfulness would forever alienate us from God. In anticipation of that very problem, God created repentance at the very outset of creation, thereby giving humans the necessary means to transcend the effects of their misdeeds. Revelation, represented by the law of divorce found in Deuteronomy, is supposed to provide the model for ideal behavior that is pleasing to God, yet the midrashist notes that God permits humans through repentance to repair the divine-human relationship in a way entirely inconsistent with the rules governing the relationship between husband and wife. God's love supercedes God's own instructions in the Torah with respect to reconciliation. The idea that repentance will bring redemption is consistent with the view that redemption depends on human action. Specifically, if people acknowledge their moral misdeeds and strive through repentance to reconnect with God—the source of all life and value—God will bring the redeemer and save the world.

MEDIEVAL ETHICAL TREATISES

During the medieval period, the varieties of Jewish literature expanded greatly as Jewish writers were influenced by the cultures of the many peoples alongside whom they lived in Europe, Asia Minor, and North Africa. Greek philosophical traditions (especially as interpreted by Islamic thinkers), pietistic movements, and mystical schools left their mark on Jewish ethical writing from the seventh century C.E. through the beginning of the Renaissance in the fifteenth century. Although the vast literature created during these centuries differs with respect to literary style, content, and structure, a few broad generalizations can be made. Many of these new ethical works were composed as independent treatises, not as commentaries on the biblical or earlier rabbinic texts (even if they often quoted them). These works were intended to stand on their own and did not assume an audience steeped in rabbinic literature. Also, although some were sophisticated attempts to synthesize Aristotelian and Jewish moral thought, many were written as popular "handbooks" on ethical development and eschewed abstract, theoretical issues in favor of practical and concrete advice. Moreover, much of this literature is concerned less with halakhic, or legal, issues than with questions of the general principles of the moral life, how to overcome the internal obstacles to living such a life, and the benefits of doing so. It is impossible to provide examples here of all the various streams of medieval Jewish ethical thought, but one prominent work will serve to illustrate the sharp contrast between this literature and the biblical/rabbinic texts discussed earlier.

Bahya ibn Pakuda, an influential Jewish thinker and moralist, lived in Spain in the eleventh century (precise dates unknown). He is known today largely for his work, *Duties of the Heart,* written in Arabic in approximately 1080 and translated into Hebrew by Judah ibn Tibbon in 1161. Bahya's purpose in writing this work, he tells us, is to remedy the gap that exists in Jewish religious literature, most of which deals with the "duties of the limbs," that is, the concrete actions that Jews must perform in service to God. This book, by contrast, deals with the inner life, the way to perfect the soul and so to infuse outward behavior with inner religiosity. Bahya divided the work into ten chapters or "gates," each devoted to a spiritual quality that he regarded as necessary to live a pure moral life: affirming the unity of God, examining the world for evidence of God's workings, divine worship, trust in God, sincerity of purpose, humility, repentance, self-examination, separation from worldly pursuits, and love of God.

In its Hebrew translation, *Duties of the Heart* became one of the most influential works of medieval Jewish thought, despite the fact that Bahya draws on many non-Jewish sources for his views. Indeed, the spiritual orientation of the book became a model for later generations of Jewish pietists who, like Bahya, believed that the essence of the Jewish moral life was devotional, not behavioral, a matter of the proper orientation toward God.

Bahya ibn Pakuda, Hovot Halevavot (Duties of the Heart), Seventh Gate (Repentance), Chapter Three

What must one do to start the process of repentance? I would say that there are seven things of which the penitent should be aware. First, one should be clearly aware of how awful one's deed was. For, if that is not clear to the person or if there is any doubt about it or if what was done was not done on purpose but rather inadvertently, then there can be neither regret nor the seeking of forgiveness [and hence no repentance]. Hence, it is said, "For I recognize my transgressions, and am ever conscious of my sin" (Psalm 51:5).

Second, one should know positively that one's deed was evil and reprehensible. For, if it is not clear that one's action was evil and one's activity not good, one will neither regret having done it nor accept what needs to be done to repent of it. The act will be viewed merely as a mistake and one will find excuses for having done it. Thus it is said, "Who can be aware of errors?" (Psalm 19:13)

Third, one must know positively that one will have to pay for what has been done. Otherwise, one will feel no need to regret having done it. Once it is clear that one will indeed suffer as a result of it, then one will regret the act and seek forgiveness for it. As it is written, "Now that I have turned back, I am filled with remorse . . . now that I am made aware . . . I am ashamed, and humiliated" (Jeremiah 31:19). Also, "My flesh creeps from fear of You. I am in awe of Your rulings" (Psalm 119:120).

Fourth, one should know that one's deed is being watched, that it is being recorded in the book of one's transgressions, a record in which nothing is overlooked, forgotten, or omitted, even as it says, "Lo, I have it all put away, sealed up in My storehouses" (Deuteronomy 32:34). Another verse adds, "a sign on every person's hand, that all people may know God's doings" (Job 37:7). If one thought that no notice was taken and no record was kept of one's sin, and therefore, one need not regret or seek forgiveness for having sinned, all on account of a delay in punishment—hence, it is written, "the fact that the sentence imposed for evil deeds is not executed swiftly, which is why people are emboldened to do evil" (Ecclesiastes 8:11).

Fifth, one should truly know that repentance brings healing to one's character and is the road to recovery from one's evil deeds and reprehensible acts. By it, one corrects one's error and retrieves what one has lost. If this were not clear, one would despair of receiving God's atonement and compassion. One would not seek forgiveness for what he has done in the past, as it says, "This is what you have been saying: Our transgressions and our sins weigh heavily upon us; we are sick at heart about them. How can we survive?" (Ezekiel 33:10). The prophet continues with God's reply: "As I live, declares the Lord God, it is not My desire that the wicked shall die, but that the wicked turn from his [evil] ways and live (Ezekiel 33:11)."

Sixth, one must reflect deeply about all the good things that the Creator has already given to us and how one has rebelled instead of being grateful for them. One should weigh the punishments of sin against its pleasures and the reward of righteousness against the travail in this world and the next, just as the Sages said: "Compute the loss incurred in doing a *mitzvah* against its gain [in the Life to Come] and the gain involved in a transgression against its loss" (Avot 2:1).

Seventh, one must struggle mightily to keep oneself from the evil to which one had become accustomed, resolve to turn away from it in one's heart and mind, as it is written, "Rend your hearts rather than your garments" (Joel 2:13).

When these seven notions are clearly understood by the sinner, then repentance from all one's sins becomes possible.

Bahya's discussion of repentance emphasizes not the requirement to repent or even the means to do so but the internal attitude, the cognitive awareness, that precedes repentance. This inner-oriented approach to the repentance, which we today might call "psychological," is consistent with Bahya's overriding concern to explore the spiritual (as distinct from the physical) dimension of ethical conduct. To repent, people must sincerely regret their actions and be fully cognizant of the severity of their consequences. Only then will they be motivated to undertake repentance and, more to the point, only then will their acts of repentance be infused with genuine contrition. For Bahya, this requires that we reflect deeply on their situation as creatures accountable for our actions before God. It also requires that we pay close attention to the nature of our misdeeds, for people are always capable of deceiving themselves into thinking that what they know to have been wrong was acceptable or that a major offense was only a minor one. Rationalization and self-deception, similar to the preoccupation with self or the belief that there is no ultimate accountability, are major internal impediments to repentance. The Scriptural passages that Bahya cites call Jews to think differently about themselves and their relationship with God. He knows that the road to repentance is filled with obstacles of their own making and that only when they recognize these obstacles can Jews hope to overcome them and that only by overcoming them can they achieve genuine repentance and reconciliation with God.

LAW CODES

During the medieval period, several scholars attempted to codify and organize the expansive body of rabbinic law. As noted, the Talmuds themselves are rambling and unsystematic in their approach to Jewish law, leaving many issues unresolved and shifting unpredictably from one topic to another. Subsequent centuries of talmudic commentators had helped to clarify the lines of argument within the text, making the Talmud somewhat more accessible, but it remained very difficult to locate answers to specific legal questions within this maze of talmudic literature. Codes of Jewish law, then, were created for eminently practical reasons: to make it possible for those without the time or learning necessary to master the Talmud and its commentaries to find readily the halakhic rules on a given topic. The *Arba'ah Turim (Four Rows)*, written by Jacob ben Asher in 1475, together with the *Shulhan Arukh (Set Table)* written by Joseph Caro in 1565 became (and, for many, continue to be) the standard compilations of Jewish law. The first and in many ways most comprehensive and elegantly organized of the codes of Jewish law, however, was completed by Maimonides around 1178.

Moses Maimonides, known in Hebrew as Rambam (acronym for Rabbi Moses ben Maimon), lived from 1135–1204 in Spain and North Africa. Unquestionably one of the most influential thinkers in the history of Judaism, Maimonides was a prodigious legal scholar and philosopher, a renowned physician and the acknowledged leader of the Jewish community in Egypt where he spent the last years of his life. He authored several extremely influential works. His *Commentary to the Mishnah* includes his *Shemoneh Perakim*, a treatise in which he attempts to reconcile Aristotelian and rabbinic ethics, and *Perek Helek*, in which he expounds his famous thirteen principles of Jewish faith. His philosophical magnum opus was his *Guide for the Perplexed*, a complex work designed to answer doubts about the veracity of Scripture engendered by the study of Greek, especially Aristotelian, philosophy. In fact, Maimonides went further than any Jewish philosopher before him in affirming the truth of much Greek philosophy by showing how it agrees with the Bible and Talmuds.

His most important legal work was his *Mishneh Torah*, a masterful summary of the whole of rabbinic law, logically organized and rendered in clear, crisp Hebrew. Because of its comprehensiveness and its organizational clarity, *Mishneh Torah* became a standard halakhic (legal) reference work. Subsequent commentaries to this code direct readers back to the talmudic sources of Maimonides' codification of each law. It was Maimonides' expressed hope that his *Mishneh Torah* would make all prior legal works superfluous, for here the entire body of rabbinic law would be summarized in an easily accessible format.

Ironically, Maimonides' very success in this Herculean undertaking engendered substantial criticism. *Mishneh Torah*, it was claimed, would dissuade people from undertaking the study of the Talmud. Moreover, by not citing the sources of his views, Maimonides was breaking with the venerable tradition that rabbis should transmit the halakhah in the name of those who taught it. Finally, some felt that by cutting through the complex dialectic and interplay of divergent views found throughout the Talmud and recording only the "final opinion," Maimonides was replacing the many voices of talmudic debate with only one, his own. These qualities of his code, together with his philosophical rationalism, made Maimonides and his work the subject of considerable controversy for centuries after his death. Still, history has vindicated his achievements, which are now widely recognized as monumental in scope and of enduring significance.

Moses Maimonides, *Mishneh Torah, Hilkhot Teshuvah* (*Laws of Repentance*), Chapter Two

1. **What is complete repentance? If the repentant individual has the opportunity and the ability to sin and yet refrains because the individual has repented, but not because the individual is afraid or because that person lacks the capacity to sin. How so? Where a man has sinned sexually with a woman, and after a period of time he is alone with her, and still desires her, is physically able to sin again, and is in the same place where he sinned with her, but refrains and he does not transgress—such a person has truly repented. King Solomon referred to this, "Remember your Creator in the days of your youth" (Ecclesiastes 12:1).[13] However, if a person repents in old age at a time when the repetition of the sin would be physically impossible, even though such penitence is not exalted, one is regarded as having done *teshuvah* [repentence]. Were a person to have been a sinner all his life and yet repent on the day of his death, and to have died while still repenting, all his sins would be forgiven. As it is written, "Before sun and light and moon and stars grow dark, and the clouds come back after the rain" (Ecclesiastes 12:2). From this we learn that if one remembered the Creator (Ecclesiastes 12:1) and repented before death, that person is forgiven.**

2. **What is repentance? It is that the sinner should leave sin and turn from (evil) thought and resolve in his heart never to do that sin again, as it says, "Let the wicked give up his ways" (Isaiah 55:7). And so, the individual will feel remorse for transgressing, as it says, "Now that I have turned back, I am filled with remorse" (Jeremiah 31:19). The One that knows the secret things will attest that the individual will never again return to that particular sin, as it says, "Nor ever again will we call our handiwork our god" (Hosea 14:4). And one must confess verbally all these things that one has resolved in one's heart.**

3. **Anyone who confesses verbally but has not resolved internally to leave off [sinning] is like one who immerses oneself in a ritual bath [for purposes of purification] still holding a [contaminating] reptile, for the immersion will not be effective until the person who confesses casts away the reptile. As it is written, "One who confesses and gives them up will find mercy" (Proverbs 28:13). One should confess one's sin in detail, as it says, "Alas, this people is guilty of a great sin in making for themselves a god of gold" (Exodus 32:31).**

4. One of the ways of repentance is for the penitent to cry out weeping and in supplication continually before God and give *tzedakah* [charity] according to one's ability, distancing oneself from that concerning which the person has sinned. One should change one's name as if to say, "I am a different person. I am not the same person who did those things." That person should change all of one's ways for good and for the straight path. That person should go into exile from one's original place, since exile atones for guilt. It causes one to be humble, to become modest and lowly of spirit.

5. It is extremely praiseworthy for the penitent to confess publicly and to announce one's sins to all, to reveal one's transgressions between oneself and others and say to them, "Indeed, I have sinned against so-and-so and I did thus and such. Today, I am penitent and remorseful." Whoever arrogantly hides one's sins and does not make them known will not achieve full repentance, as it says, "The one who hides one's sins will not succeed" (Proverbs 38:13). To what do these words refer? To those transgressions between person and person. However, with regard to transgressions between persons and God, one need not publicize them. It would be arrogant indeed to reveal them. Rather let such a person repent before God and detail the sins before God. One offers a simple undetailed public confession, for it is better that one not reveal one's transgression [in detail], as it says, "Happy is the one whose transgression is forgiven, whose sin is covered over" (Psalm 32:1). . . .

9. *Teshuvah* and Yom Kippur bring atonement only for transgressions between individuals and God, for example, one who ate something forbidden or engaged in forbidden sexual relations and similar matters. However, concerning transgressions between individuals, for example, one who injured one's neighbor or who cursed one's neighbor or who robbed that person and similar matters, one is not forgiven until one restores [whatever is necessary] to the injured party and appeases that person. Even though one paid back the money owed to another, that person would still have to appease the other and ask for forgiveness. Even if one provoked another only with words, such a person would still have to appease the other, approaching him until ready to forgive. If the other were not willing to forgive, then the one [asking for forgiveness] should bring three individuals to entreat and to request the other person to forgive. If that person (the injured party) remains unappeased, then the person asking for forgiveness should bring a second and a third group of people. If the person still refuses, then the person asking for forgiveness should leave and go on his way. The one who would not forgive is now the sinner! If, however, the affronted party were the other individual's teacher, then the student must come and go even a thousand times until forgiven.

10. It is forbidden for a person to be cruel and unwilling to be appeased; rather one should be easy to appease and hard to provoke. When the sinner

asks to be forgiven, it should be done with a whole heart and with a willing spirit. Even if one has provoked and sinned against another repeatedly, the individual should not be vengeful or carry a grudge. This is the way of the descendents of Israel whose heart is proper. It is different for idolaters, those uncircumcised of heart, who hold a grudge forever. Thus Scripture describes the Gibeonites, who, because they did not forgive or become appeased, "were not of Israelite stock" (II Samuel 21:2).

11. The one who sins against a person who dies before one can ask forgiveness should bring a *minyan* [ten adult male members of the community] to that person's grave and say in their presence, "I have sinned against the Lord, God of Israel, and against this person, in doing thus and so." If the individual were obligated to pay money to the deceased, it should be paid to that person's heirs. If the individual does not know who the heirs are, the individual should leave that money with the court and confess.

As noted earlier and as this passage amply illustrates, Maimonides' genius lay in his ability to systematize and clarify the halakhah as it had developed to that point. In many instances, he simply summarizes or paraphrases points encountered in earlier sources: the definition of repentance as refusing to repeat one's sinful behavior, the distinction between offenses committed against God and those against other people, and the inefficacy of confession if the offender continues sinning (analogized to clutching a defiling animal while purifying oneself in a ritual bath). Yet, he also provides a number of important illustrations and elaborations of earlier rules: how to deal with a case in which the offended person has died (and when his or her heirs cannot be found), how it is a sin for an offended person not to grant forgiveness to those who seek it sincerely, and where in the Yom Kippur liturgy confessional prayers are added. Overall, it is the clarity of his formulations and the straightforward logic of his exposition that have made *Mishneh Torah* an invaluable resource for the study of halakhah.

RESPONSA

The tradition of sending written queries on legal matters to distant scholars who, in turn, wrote back letters articulating their legal opinion dates back to early post-talmudic times. These "questions and answers" (Hebrew, *she'elot ut'shuvot*), known as responsa literature (singular, "responsum"), arose when local authorities were unable to answer the questions themselves (especially when the situations presented were unprecedented) and when disputes between communities (or factions within the same community) needed to be referred to outside authorities. Eventually these responsa were collected (sometimes organized by topic, sometimes by their author) and became legal sources available for others to consult and ultimately incorporate within later codes of Jewish law. Over the centuries the responsa literature has grown to encompasses thousands of volumes, a portion of which deals with moral (as distinct from ritual and political) issues. Contemporary rabbinic authorities continue to write responsa and consult the responsa literature of earlier generations of scholars.[14]

Rabbi Meir of Rothenberg (c. 1215–1293 C.E.) was born into a prominent rabbinic family and became a leading legal authority of his time. The author of more than one thousand responsa in addition to commentaries on many talmudic tractates, he was consulted in particular when intercommunal disputes arose and on business and political matters. He received queries from across Europe, and his responsa, collected in four volumes, were held in high esteem. The following is a brief excerpt from one of his responsa, written in reply to someone inquiring about whether a man who has had intercourse with a married woman can repent and be forgiven.[15]

Responsum of Meir of Rothenberg, Volume 4 (Prague edition), 1:23
"The Ways of Repentance"

This is the penance of one who has had sexual relations with a married woman: he should sit naked in the winter in ice and snow up to his navel once or twice or three times a day, until he is able to read the first paragraph of the Sh'ma with full attention. He should do this daily all the days of winter for as long as he lives, except on the Sabbath and holidays, and thus afflict himself all his days. He should wear sack-cloth close to his skin and not eat meat or drink wine or liquor, except on the Sabbath and holidays. And if he is not able to afflict himself every day, he shall do so on Mondays and Thursdays [the days on which special penitential prayers are said]. So shall he do, and he shall confess his sins twice every day in tears. . . . And in the summer he should sit naked twice a day among biting ants . . . until he is able to read the paragraph of the Sh'ma with full attention three times a day. He should not eat meat or drink wine or liquor, except on the Sabbath and holidays. He should afflict himself every day and wear sack-cloth close to his skin and confess his sins twice a day, and they flog him and he should remain downcast. And if he receives rebuke, he should remain silent. He should not experience joy all his days, nor should he wear colorful clothing, so that perhaps the One who spread out the heavens like a curtain will have mercy upon him. . . .

Anyone who has committed a sin and is embarrassed to repent should exchange [his sinful deed] for a good deed by repenting and being forgiven. An analogy: it is like the case of one who has bundles of bad coins who goes and gives them to a shopkeeper and receives the increase when he [the shopkeeper] exchanges them for good coins. So, too, one who possesses bad deeds should repent and exchange the bad deeds for good ones and be forgiven. Beware lest one say, "My sin is too great. How can I repent? I am afraid that the Holy One who is blessed will not receive my repentance." Thus it says, "forgiving iniquity and remitting transgression" (Micah 7:18).

Great is repentance, for on account of one person who repents, the entire world is forgiven. As it says, "[I will heal their affliction, generously will

I take them back in love,] for my anger has turned away from them" (Hosea 14:5). Who is a God like you, who forgives the sin of the wicked and receives them, as it says, "Return, O Israel, to the Lord." (Hosea 14:2) [which means] when God is given over to the quality of compassion, when God no longer judges you by strict justice. Great is the power of repentance, for even sinners who betray their Creator are received like the smell of the incense, as it says, "[You love righteousness and hate wickedness; rightly has God, your God, chosen to anoint you with oil of gladness over all your peers.] All your robes [are fragrant] with myrrh and aloes and cassia" (Psalm 45:8-9). There are three things that reverse a divine decree concerning an individual: repentance, prayer and charity. Why is it written, "he shall wear righteousness like armor" (Isaiah 59:17)?[16] Just as armor is composed of layer upon layer which join together to create armor, so too each and every small coin that one gives to charity adds up to a great sum. . . .

With respect to all the commandments in the Torah, whether positive or negative, if one violates one of them, whether intentionally or unintentionally, when one repents and turns from his or her sin, one is obligated to confess before the Holy One who is blessed, as it says, "When a man or woman commits any wrong toward a fellow person . . . one shall confess the wrong that one has done." (Numbers 5:6-7): this is confession. How does one confess? One says, "O God, I have sinned, transgressed and committed iniquity before you in doing such and such. Behold I regret and am ashamed by what I did and I will never again do this thing." This is the essence of the confession. And everyone who is expansive in confessing is to be praised.

"Anyone who does something and regrets it, the Holy One who is blessed forgives him or her, as it says, '[I will act as a relentless accuser against] those who have no fear of Me' (Malachi 3:5)—but those who do revere Me are forgiven" (Yalkut Malachi, 589). And what is complete repentance? One who comes upon the situation in which he had sinned and controls his impulse. Such is the case of one who once had sexual relations with a woman and afterwards encounters her again but does not sin. Even someone who sinned throughout his life and then repented and died in a state of repentance, his sins are forgiven, as it says, "before sun and light and moon and stars grows dark" (Ecclesiastes 12:2).

For the character of the Holy One who is blessed is not like that of flesh and blood. With respect to flesh and blood, if one brings a gift to a king, it is questionable whether or not he will receive it. If the king hates him, he will turn to others to help him to appease the king so that he loves him. But the Holy One who is blessed is not this way. For when a person returns from his or her evil deed and gives charity, the Holy One who is blessed accepts him. And the Holy One who is blessed says, "Return

yourself to me and I will accept your repentance," as it says [in the High Holiday prayerbook], "For your right hand is extended to receive those who return."

And a person should not say, "I will go and commit this transgression, since the Holy One who is blessed cannot see me. Why? Because the Holy One is in heaven and I am on earth." For that reason it says, "For a person's ways are before the eyes of God" (Proverbs 5:21). If a person is on the way to doing a *mitzvah* [commandment], it is accounted to him as if he had done that commandment; if one is on the way to committing a sin, it is accounted to him as if he had done that sin.

In this particular responsum, the author does not so much offer a new theory of repentance as he assembles a range of sources reinforcing the view that no sin, including adultery, is unforgivable if the sinner genuinely repents. The lengthy ordeal prescribed at the outset seems to be a way for the sinner to demonstrate his sincere remorse. By making himself suffer in these ways, he humbles himself, perhaps even shows that he despises himself as a sinner. In doing so, he will presumably be moved to submit to God's will and rededicate himself to God's commandments. These severe self-punishments are similar to those prescribed in Christian pietistic literature of the same period.

This chapter has offered an overview of the many sources of Jewish ethics. Even such a selective and cursory introduction is sufficient to highlight a number of points that should be remembered as you proceed in your study of Jewish ethics. First, Jewish ethical literature is extremely varied in form. The genres represented within the Hebrew Bible itself (law, narrative, prophecy, poetry, wisdom literature) are greatly augmented by those in the rabbinic materials. To study Jewish ethics in an historically sensitive way, a person must attend to the various idioms in which Jewish authorities have expressed themselves, for sometimes the message is conveyed through the form as much as through the content of the literature. Second, Jewish literature builds on itself; an idea first appearing in a piece of midrash may also be included in the Talmud, be cited by Maimonides in his code, and appear yet again in later responsa, not always in precisely the same formulation. Finding the original formulation, then, often requires some investigation into earlier sources. In any case, a reader cannot assume that any particular passage is original to the context in which it is first encountered. Third, taken as a whole, this literature is not very systematic and sometimes not even internally consistent. With the exception of law codes such as that of Maimonides, the rabbis tended not to organize their exposition of a topic in a straightforward, logical fashion. Moreover, given the expansiveness of this literature, you should not be surprised to discover a wide range of views and, in the usual case, some sources that attempt to reconcile those differences. This has profound implications for the work of contemporary Jewish ethicists who wish to draw on this tradition in their efforts to offer "Jewish perspectives" on modern moral issues, as you will see in the final section of this book.

KEY POINTS

- Traditional Judaism assumes that truth is to be found primarily in sacred texts, beginning with the Bible, and so the study of these texts is the primary means of finding moral guidance.

- Rabbinic authorities tended to record their own insights by writing commentaries to previous texts; notwithstanding exceptions to this generalization (such as Maimonides' *Mishneh Torah*), commentaries tended to spawn further commentaries as successive generations of scholars added their voices to those of their predecessors.

- Within this vast body of literature is a multiplicity of styles and viewpoints; indeed, the tradition as a whole values debate about both foundational principles and their practical application. The inconclusiveness of many talmudic discussions is intended, in part, as a way to invite the reader to join in this open-ended discourse.

- Judaism's textual tradition comprises a vast interconnected resource of laws, values, philosophies, and stories (together with multiple reflections on these) on which later generations draw freely as they develop moral views on the issues of their day.

QUESTIONS TO CONSIDER

1. What difference does it make that Jewish ethics is text based? How might Jewish ethics be different if the tradition located truth, for example, in personal religious experience or in the dictates of conscience?

2. It has often been noted that (in contrast to traditions such as Roman Catholicism) authority in rabbinic Judaism is markedly decentralized and nonhierarchical. How does the textual tradition reflect this?

3. Given the value that Judaism places on debate and preserving diverse views on virtually any question that arises, how can such a tradition provide definitive guidance about moral matters?

4. From the rabbis' standpoint, the entire textual tradition represented "Torah," the gradual unfolding of the truth contained in God's original revelation. To what extent, then, is moral authority vested in *God*? in the classical *texts* of the tradition? in the *rabbis* who wrote those texts and who continued to interpret them for successive generations of Jews?

5. Given the peculiar idiom in which much rabbinic literature is written, what specific challenges do you face in trying to read and understand these sources? What reading strategies can you develop to help you make sense of these materials?

Chapter Four

The Contours
of Jewish Moral Life

Summary

This chapter explores some characteristics of Jewish moral living by examining a single value (justice), virtue (humility), and rule or obligation (honoring parents). The chapter stresses the religious roots of each of these forms of Jewish morality.

◆ ─────────────────────────────────────

"Do what is right and good in the sight of the Lord." (Deuteronomy 6:18)

This refers to compromise and conduct beyond the requirements of the law. The intent of this is that initially God had said that you should observe the laws and statutes that He had commanded you. Now God says that, with respect to what He has not commanded, you should likewise take heed to do the right and the good in His eyes, for He loves the good and the right. This is a great matter, for it is impossible to mention in the Torah all of a person's actions toward his neighbors and acquaintances, all of his commercial activity, and all social and political institutions. So, after God had mentioned many of them . . . He continues to say generally that one should do 'the right and the good' in all matters through compromise and conduct beyond the requirements of the law.[1]

The focus turns now from the very general features of Jewish ethics as described in Chapter Two to a more substantive description of Jewish moral life. Living morally encompasses a great many actions and attitudes and expresses itself in so many aspects of daily life that it would be impossible to offer a complete account of

84

what it means to live a moral life, Jewish or otherwise. Nonetheless, it is possible to sketch the contours of such a life, to indicate the types of moral demands and goals that characterize a particular system of ethics. In the case of Judaism, it is possible also to explore the ways in which certain characteristic moral attitudes and actions relate to religious beliefs that Jews have held rather consistently across the centuries. Focusing on just a few salient features of Jewish morality makes it possible to see, if only in broad outline, the Jewish moral landscape. With these points of orientation, the reader will be able to understand and contextualize all other aspects of Jewish moral living—what Nachmanides in the preceding quote considered under the heading of "doing the right and the good."

Scholars of ethics have long understood that morality takes many forms and expresses itself in many idioms. Three forms in particular have been identified: values, virtues, and obligations (or rules). Although not every system of ethics contains moral teachings in each of these forms (and certainly not always in equal measure), most systems of ethics offer some combination of values, virtues, and obligations. This introduction to Jewish moral life will therefore explore briefly the distinctions among these categories of moral teachings, as well as the ways in which they intersect.

Moral values are statements of broad principles or moral ideals. They express goals for interpersonal behavior or for society as a whole without necessarily spelling out specific steps that could or should be taken to achieve them. Examples of values include the dictum "Equal Justice under Law" inscribed over the entrance to the United States Supreme Court Building in Washington, D.C., as well as many statements in the Bible (such as "Love your neighbor as yourself" [Leviticus 19:18]) and in rabbinic literature (such as "Be a disciple of Aaron, loving peace and pursuing peace, loving your fellow creatures and drawing them near to Torah" [Avot 1:12]). Broad moral principles of this type are useful in indicating lofty ideals and helping focus attention on the goals of moral living. Of course, their very generality leaves them open to varying interpretations, for example, of the way in which justice should be actualized in particular situations or of the best way to demonstrate love of your neighbor, or of the proper means to pursue peace. Still, values provide in a rather succinct way a general orientation to moral life.

Virtues describe the inner qualities of the moral person, the character traits that he or she should develop to live a proper moral life. Moral systems that focus on virtues understand that moral life depends as much (or more) on inner attitude as on outward behavior. Western moral tradition commonly promotes the virtues of honesty, prudence, courage, and generosity, among others. Classical Judaic statements of virtues include these: "Better a patient spirit than a haughty spirit. Don't let your spirit be quickly vexed, for vexation abides in the breasts of fools" (Ecclesiastes 7:8–9). "Who is wise? Those who learn from everyone. . . . Who is mighty? Those who conquer their evil impulse. . . . Who is rich? Those who are content with their portion. . . . Who is honored? Those who honor all people."[2] Statements of virtue are useful in helping to shape our dispositions and intentions, in focusing on the kind of person we are and not only, or primarily, on the deeds we perform. Because virtues are, in a sense, embodied values, they are often communicated through the stories of heroes and saints. Within Jewish tradition, stories of Abraham's hospitality and Moses' humility, as well as of the compassion and sensitivity of the *tzaddik* (the righteous individual) represent vehicles for the transmission of specific virtues. Of course, virtues, like values, tend to be open ended, difficult to pin down with precision and difficult (if not impossible) to enforce.

Obligations or rules are perhaps the most common form of moral teaching. More specific than values and more easily enforceable than virtues, rules provide detailed directives for how to behave morally in concrete situations (sometimes accompanied by specific sanctions for failing to do so). Jewish tradition is full of moral rules, for much of Jewish ethics falls within the scope of Jewish law. Classical examples of moral rules include, "You shall neither side with the mighty to do wrong. . . . nor shall you show deference to a poor man in his dispute. When you encounter your enemy's ox or ass wandering, you must take it back to him. . . . Do not take bribes. . . . You shall not oppress a stranger, for you know the feelings of the stranger, having yourselves been strangers in the land of Egypt" (Exodus 23:2–9). The power of rules lies in their specificity and in their focus on what can be observed publicly and so regulated. By the same token, their usefulness is limited because no finite set of rules can provide guidance in every situation that demands moral discernment.

Within any moral system, values, virtues, and rules may overlap. What is expressed in one text as a rule may be reformulated in another as a principle or value and in yet another as a virtue. The case of justice illustrates the point. Although some Jewish sources make broad pronouncements about justice (value statements), others offer stories about the traits of a just person (virtue), and still others provide specific directives about how justice should be administered (rules). So you should not be misled into thinking that values, virtues, and rules are mutually exclusive categories of moral teaching. Rather, the point is to observe that ethical systems such as Judaism speak in different idioms and formulate moral teaching in different ways. To appreciate the full scope of the moral life, then, you do well to pay attention to each of these spheres. The remainder of this chapter examines a characteristic Jewish value, virtue, and a rule in the hope that this will enable you to appreciate the scope of Jewish moral life.

A JEWISH VALUE: JUSTICE

> *Rabban Simeon ben Gamaliel said: The world stands on three things—on truth, on justice, and on peace, as it is said, "Execute truth, justice, and peace within your gates." (Zechariah. 8:16)[3]*
> *These three are really one: when justice is done, truth is achieved, and peace is established.[4]*

Understanding the value of justice in Judaism, requires an exploration of two sets of questions. First, how is justice defined? What does it demand of people? How do people distinguish justice from injustice? Second, what role does justice play within the worldview of classical Judaism? What is the significance of dispensing it or failing to do so? What meaning does this moral value hold within this religious community? The first set of questions concerns the *definitive character* of justice, that is, the particular behaviors that constitute a just society; the second concerns the *theology* or *significance* of justice, that is, the beliefs that underlie this concept and the broader context in which they have meaning. In Judaism, the practice of justice cannot be divorced from its theology, for every moral concept is defined and concretized in ways that reflect its conceptual underpinnings and deeper meaning. This brief explication of justice as a Jewish value will be clearer if practice is discussed separately from theory, that is, the substantive definition of justice from the role it plays in Judaism's theological system.

Moral philosophers have differentiated several different senses of justice. *Distributive justice* concerns the distribution of goods within a society. The gap between the rich and the poor or unequal distributions of power among groups raise questions of distributive justice. *Retributive justice* concerns the ways in which society responds to behavior that threatens its well-being or stability. Thus, the sanctions imposed on those who commit felonies or misdemeanors (and even the way in which those categories are defined) are issues of retributive justice. Finally, *procedural justice* concerns the systems established for dispensing either distributive or retributive justice. In both the Jewish and U.S. systems of government, courts are the primary vehicles of procedural justice. The rules governing the operation of those courts, including the criteria employed for selecting judges, are part of a system of procedural justice. In the discussion that follows, I consider all three dimensions of justice in their classical Jewish expressions.

Judaism has a great deal to say about each of these aspects of justice, and here it will be possible to provide only an overview with some representative examples of classical Jewish views. Before discussing each of these three aspects of justice, I begin with a summary of some general perspectives on justice that remain central to Jewish tradition throughout most of its history and that reflect distinctively Jewish religious beliefs and values.[5]

Justice is part of a family of concepts that includes peace, mercy, compassion, and righteousness (*tzedakah*) as well as law (*mishpat, din*). In many texts, the terms for righteousness and law are used interchangeably, and either might be equated with justice. At other times, sources distinguish between the law proper and a more expansive sense of justice (which might be called "equity") or between justice and mercy (as when God is portrayed as moving from the throne of justice to that of mercy).[6] Some of these distinctions will be taken up in the following chapter, which investigates certain theoretical issues within Jewish ethics. For now, it is sufficient to note simply that, within Judaism, justice is a complex concept with connections to several related concepts and with deep religious roots.

The Anatomy of Justice

The essence of justice lies in distinguishing between right and wrong, in giving people what they deserve, and in treating all similar cases similarly. It is about discriminating between behavior that is positive and negative, desirable and undesirable, and responding accordingly. This is evident even in the early stories of Genesis, as when Abraham confronts God about the decision to destroy the cities of Sodom and Gomorrah:

> Far be it from You to do such a thing, to bring death upon the innocent as well as the guilty, so that innocent and guilty fare alike. Far be it from You! Shall not the Judge of all the earth deal justly? (Genesis 18:25)

This passage is formulated as an indictment of God, yet on a deeper level it assumes that justice represents a common ground on which humans and God stand together. Like God, people have the capacity to differentiate those deserving of punishment from those who are innocent. Justice establishes a set of standards to which God is subject, just as humans are. Indeed, earlier in the same story, the biblical text refers to Abraham and his descendants being chosen "to keep the way of the Lord by doing what is just and right" (Genesis 18:19). However the particular demands of justice are defined, it is clear at least that justice is essential to the identity of both God and the Jewish people.

Distributive Justice.   Within the Hebrew Bible the most prevalent and best known principle of distributive justice (the fair distribution of power and resources in society) is the demand to show special concern for the disadvantaged within society: the stranger, orphan, widow, and poor. The reason consistently offered for this striking principle is that "you were strangers in land of Egypt" (Exodus 22:20, 23:9; Leviticus 19:34; Deuteronomy 10:19). For the biblical authors (and arguably for the rabbis of later generations), this is the most important social lesson to be drawn from the Israelites' experience of slavery. Having once been marginalized and disenfranchised within another society, they understood the moral imperative of supporting those within their own society who lacked power and status.

More than historical experience is behind the demand to care for the marginalized, however. Just as God was on the side of the Israelites in their liberation from Egyptian slavery, God will surely support others' struggle for freedom and dignity. As contemporary Latin American liberation theologians have rightly observed, God is on the side of the oppressed.[7] The biblical text (Deuteronomy 10:17–19) is explicit about this:

> For the Lord your God is God supreme and Lord supreme, the great, the mighty, and the awesome God, who shows no favor and takes no bribe, but upholds the cause of the fatherless and the widow, and befriends the stranger, providing him with food and clothing. You too must befriend the stranger, for you were strangers in the land of Egypt.

God takes special concern for those in the world who are at the bottom of the social hierarchy. So, in modeling our behavior on God's, people also must reach out to assist those who are disadvantaged. This is what underlies the specific rule that on the Sabbath, which is observed in remembrance of the exodus from Egypt (Deuteronomy 5:15), all members of the household must rest, including aliens and slaves. On the day devoted to acknowledging God's dominion over all creation, all people must be treated equally, independent of their social status.

This same concern to rectify social and economic inequalities is reflected in the biblical legislation about the Sabbatical and jubilee years.

> When you enter the land that I assign to you, the land shall observe a Sabbath of the Lord. Six years you may sow your field and six years you may prune your vineyard and gather in the yield. But in the seventh year the land shall have a Sabbath of complete rest, a Sabbath of the Lord: you shall not sow your field or prune your vineyard. . . . But you may eat whatever the land during its Sabbath will produce—you, your male and female slaves, the hired and bound laborers who live with you and your cattle and the beasts in your land may eat all its yield . . . (Leviticus 25:2–4, 6–7).
>
> [In the fiftieth year] you shall proclaim release throughout the land for all its inhabitants. It shall be a jubilee for you: each of you shall return to his holding and each of you shall return to his family. . . But the land must not be sold beyond reclaim, for the land is Mine; you are but strangers resident with Me. Throughout the land that you hold, you must provide for the redemption of the land (Leviticus 25:10–11, 23–24).
>
> Every seventh year you shall practice remission of debts. This shall be the nature of the remission: every creditor shall remit the due that he claims from his fellow; he shall not dun his fellow or kinsman, for the remission proclaimed is of the Lord. You may dun the foreigner; but you must remit whatever is due you from your kinsmen (Deuteronomy 15:1–3).

These sweeping social rules prevent economic disparities from becoming permanent features of Israelite society. To the biblical authors, the fact that such disparities arise may be inevitable; nonetheless, they must be remedied. There can be no permanent underclass, for every seventh year, those burdened by debt and those who have sold themselves into slavery are released. Similarly, the land, which was the major source of wealth in ancient Israelite society, could be bought and sold only temporarily, not held by anyone in perpetuity.

Just as the seventh day marks a time when all are freed from the burden of work, the seventh year marks a time when all are freed from the burden of poverty. All that people do and all that they own ultimately derives from God and belongs to them only provisionally. When people act on this principle by redistributing wealth and privilege within society, they make it plain that the social order in this world must reflect the reality that people are all equally God's creatures, all equally strangers on God's earth. The power that they exercise over one another must be restricted, or it would betray the power that God exercises over all of them equally.

If this principle were extended, it would prohibit private ownership of property entirely,[8] but neither biblical nor rabbinic sources demand such a radical renunciation of human prerogative. The underlying principle would seem to be that it is natural and proper for people to own the fruit of their own labor. But this ownership is never absolute, for everything of value ultimately derives from God. What people own, then, must be used as God intends, and it is God's intention that the world be a place in which no group can use its power, either political or economic, to oppress another. God intends people to use what they have to free the captives, feed the poor, clothe the naked, and care for those disadvantaged members of society who do not yet share in God's wealth.

Retributive Justice. The most characteristic feature of retributive justice (the principles governing punishment for those who violate social norms) within the biblical corpus is the *lex taliones,* which establishes the principle of parity between crime and punishment (Leviticus 24:19–20; see also Exodus 21:23–5, Deuteronomy 19:21):

> If anyone maims his fellow, as he has done so shall it be done to him: fracture for fracture, eye for eye, tooth for tooth. The injury he inflicted on another shall be inflicted on him.

By contemporary standards, the rule may seem harsh, even barbaric, but within the biblical world, it represented a major advance over existing penal codes.[9] In particular, it established that the punishment cannot be more severe than the original crime (which is to say, there are no punitive damages in cases involving bodily injury). Moreover, the social status of the victim and of the perpetrator is irrelevant for purposes of punishment. The eye of the nobleman and that of the slave are equally valuable, and those who inflict injury, no matter who they are, receive the same punishment.

Behind these rules is the principle that people bear ultimate responsibility for the harm they do to others. Violence cannot go unpunished, for this would only encourage criminals to prey on innocent victims. Thus, while it is sometimes claimed that the biblical law of retribution multiplies violence within a society, its intent is precisely the opposite. When acts of violence are met with proportional, fair, and swift punishment, further acts of violence are discouraged. In fact, the *lex taliones* is nothing other than the essential principle of retributive justice spelled out in graphic detail.

Still, the rabbis of a later time, obviously bothered by the ethic of responding to violence with violence, reinterpreted the rule to apply only to monetary compensation. The point, they said, was that the person who is blinded in one eye is entitled to compensation for the value of that eye, and so too for all similar injuries. This, of course, shifts the emphasis away from inflicting physical punishment and toward making the victim "whole," monetarily, if not bodily.

The biblical view of retributive justice is exemplified most powerfully in the law of capital punishment, which is prescribed not only for murder but also for kidnapping and even striking or cursing a parent (Exodus 21:12–17). On a practical level, these rules aim to deter socially unacceptable behavior. On a more theoretical level, however, they reflect a view that antisocial behavior threatens the holiness of Israelite society. Throughout the Deuteronomic legislation are stipulations of capital punishment followed by the refrain, "thus you will sweep out evil from your midst" (Deuteronomy 13:6, 17:7, 19:19, 21:21, 22:21–24, 24:7). The holy community must not harbor or tolerate those who flagrantly violate basic communal norms, especially those who would divert people from God's commandments. Because such people defile the holiness of this community, they threaten the very essence of Israel's relationship with God. Seen from this perspective, capital punishment is a form of social purification, a way of ensuring that God's people remains morally pure and holy.

Again, the rabbis significantly modified the law regarding capital punishment. They placed numerous procedural restrictions on capital cases, especially with respect to the testimony of the two witnesses, which had to agree even in the smallest detail in order to obtain a conviction.[10] The practical effect of these rules was to make carrying out the death sentence virtually impossible. Yet, even as they implicitly expressed their reservations about capital punishment, the rabbis affirmed the principle that those who violate certain basic norms forfeit their right to life. For lesser crimes, compensation must be paid, even if retribution would not take place, for retributive justice to be realized.

Procedural Justice. The most basic expression of procedural justice (the procedures governing the proper administration of justice) within the Torah concerns the principle of impartiality: "You shall not render an unfair decision: do not favor the poor or show defence to the rich; judge your neighbor fairly" (Leviticus 19:15). At first glance, this rule appears to stand in striking contrast to the principle of distributive justice that we must give special consideration to the needs of the poor, noted earlier. On closer examination, though, a common concern for equality underlies both sets of rules. Equality of treatment is essential to a just society. The law must not be bent to favor any group within society, for doing so would compromise the sense of impartiality that is the very essence of procedural justice. The very same idea lies behind the symbol of a blindfolded woman holding the scales of justice; if justice is not blind, it is not justice. The very same concern for equality, when applied to the distribution of wealth, requires that that those with a disproportionate share of society's goods share them with those at the bottom of the social scale.

Procedural justice can be threatened in a number of ways, but particularly when the judge's self-interest compromises his or her objectivity. The biblical authors had this in mind when they forbade absolutely the accepting of bribes, "for bribes blind the eyes of the discerning and upset the plea of the just" (Deuteronomy 16:19). Judges cannot dispense justice if they permit anything to bias their assessment of the evidence before them. The very role of the judge demands subordinating self-interest to the interest of producing a just result. This is especially so since, as I discuss later, justice is a divine quality, the judge serving in the role of God's surrogate on earth. To permit, much less encourage, miscarriages of justice is to subvert God's own work in the world.

Theology of Justice

Thus far I have examined the requirements of justice—concern for the socially disadvantaged, punishment that is proportional to the offense, and impartiality. I turn now to the underlying meaning and purpose of justice. Why is it so important to pursue justice? What is gained, according to Jewish tradition, when justice is achieved? The answers to these questions lie in basic theological beliefs that animate all Jewish reflection on justice.

The fundamental belief that human beings are created in God's image implies both that each individual has intrinsic value and that all human life is of equal value to God. As the eighteenth-century philosopher Immanuel Kant was to argue, human beings must always be treated as ends in themselves, never as means to the ends of others.[11] In Jewish thought, the rationale for this principle is theological: treating people as means to an end violates their intrinsic nature as creatures of God. Conversely, treating people with respect, as justice demands, is tantamount to honoring the divine image within all human beings. One tannaitic rabbi expressed this principle in declaring that the most important verse in the Torah is Genesis 5:1: "This is the record of Adam's line—When God created man, God made him in the likeness of God." To mistreat another is to mistreat the image of God.[12] This elevates justice from a social good, something necessary for the smooth functioning of society, to a matter of divine significance.

Insofar as law is essential to the pursuit of justice, justice is a divine good in another sense. Throughout Jewish tradition, law is understood as the primary expression of God's will, revealed to Israel at Mt. Sinai. To observe God's laws—including those related to creating and sustaining a just world—is to make God's presence manifest in the world. As the rabbis put it,

> Every time a judge issues a judgment of true veracity, this causes the Divine Presence to abide in Israel, as it is said, "God stands in the congregation of God when judgment is determined in awareness of God." (Psalm 82:1),[13] and
>
> The Holy One said to Israel: My children, as you live, I am exalted because of your intense concern for justice, "The Lord of hosts is exalted by judgment." (Isaiah 5:16)[14]

Doing justice is nothing less than bringing God's presence into the world; failing to do so, conversely, drives God's presence from the world. To pursue justice is to pursue a closer relationship with God, for observing God's law is a form, perhaps the most important form, of communion with God.

Moreover, doing justice is a matter of doing as God does, not only doing what God says. God is frequently depicted as a righteous judge and a model of perfect justice. This is especially evident in the following passages from Psalms:

> But the Lord abides forever; God has set up His throne for judgment; it is God who judges the world with righteousness, rules the peoples with equity. (Psalm 9:8-9)
>
> Mighty king, who loves justice, it was You who established equity, You who worked righteous judgment in Jacob. (Psalm 99:4)

Modern readers may find much in God's behavior as portrayed in the Bible that is morally objectionable, such as God's hardening of Pharaoh's heart (Exodus 7:13,22; 8:15; 9:35; 10:20; 14:4), God's command that the Israelites dispossess the Canaanites of their land (Exodus 23:27–30), and that they eradicate the Amalekites

(Deuteronomy 25:17–19). The rabbis were confident, however, that God's primary traits were justice and compassion. In reflecting on the verse "Follow none but the Lord your God" (Deuteronomy 13:5), they comment,

> What does this mean? Is it possible for a mortal to follow God's presence? The verse means to teach us that we should follow the attributes of the Holy One, praised be God. As God clothes the naked, you should clothe the naked. The Bible teaches that the Holy One visited the sick; you should visit the sick. The Holy One comforted those who mourned; you should comfort those who mourn. The Holy One buried the dead; you should bury the dead.[15]

Acting justly, then, is a matter of emulating God, not only making the world conform more closely to God's will, but each person making himself or herself more fully god-like.

Finally, justice is deeply imbedded in a vision of the messianic culmination of history, that idyllic time when God and, hence, justice reigns. The biblical prophets were especially eloquent in expressing this vision:

> I will restore your magistrates as of old, and your counselors as of yore. After that you shall be called city of Righteousness, Faithful City. Zion shall be saved in the judgment; her repentant ones, in the retribution. (Isaiah 1:26–27)
>
> . . .at this time I have turned and planned to do good to Jerusalem and to the House of Judah. Have no fear! These are the things you are to do: Speak the truth to one another, render true and perfect justice in your gates. And do not contrive evil against one another, and do not love perjury, because all those are things that I hate, declares the Lord. (Zechariah 8:15–17)
>
> I will espouse you forever: I will espouse you with righteousness and justice, and with goodness and mercy, and I will espouse you with faithfulness; then you shall be devoted to the Lord. (Hosea 2:21–22)

Because the goal of human history is to reach that time when God will reign supreme, and since humans know that God is the paradigm of justice, it follows that that time will be one of complete justice on earth. When people execute justice, therefore, they bring the world closer to the fulfillment of that messianic vision.

In conclusion, to fully appreciate the religious significance of justice one need only consider the many ways in which God enters the world: through creation (especially of humankind), through revelation, and through redemptive acts in history. Justice is central to each of these modes of divine influence. Because God created all people, all are entitled to equal respect; moreover, treating people justly is simultaneously honoring the image of God. Because God's greatest gift to Israel is the law, by obeying the law, Jews bring themselves and the world closer to God. The fact that God's redemption of Israel from Egypt is the model of all God's action in history means that God champions the cause of the disenfranchised and marginalized in society. And the final act of redemption, the coming of the messiah, will be, above all, a time of justice for all nations under God's rule.

In the last analysis, Judaism affirms that people and their institutions are meant to actualize God's presence in the world and that executing justice is central to this task. As Rabban Simeon ben Gamaliel indicated, truth, justice, and peace are corollaries of one another, for truth is affirmed and peace is established only when justice is done. Pursuing justice, then, is a necessary part of emulating God and bringing God's presence into the world. It is nothing less than the means by which we help create the kingdom of God on earth.

A JEWISH VIRTUE: HUMILITY

> Rabbi Joshua ben Levi said: Humility is greater than all other virtues, for it is said, "The spirit of the Lord God is upon me; because the Lord has anointed me; God has sent me as a herald of joy to the humble" (Isaiah 61:1)—not "to the saintly," but "to the humble." From this you learn that humility is greater than all other virtues. [16]

Joshua ben Levi's teaching is intriguing, in part because it raises as many questions as it answers. What does humility consist of? How can it be recognized in others? How can it be cultivated within ourselves? Why is humility a virtue at all, much less the most important virtue? Answering these questions requires exploring other teachings about humility, paying special attention to the religious roots of this character trait as Judaism construes it. First, though, it is helpful to consider the nature of humility in general.

We should begin by noting that humility encompasses two quite different but related attitudes. The humble person may (1) think little of himself, believe himself to be of little worth or (2) think of herself not at all, believing that paying attention to herself at all is evidence of a moral failing. [17] A certain tension exists between these two ways of conceiving humility. Those who are humble in the first sense will minimize their own achievements or talents and believe themselves to be flawed in some basic respects, perhaps particularly in their moral character. They will focus attention on their shortcomings and will adopt a (hyper-) critical attitude toward themselves, insisting on the importance of carefully monitoring their own character. By contrast, those who are humble in the second sense will attempt to become invisible to themselves, believing that excessive focus on the self (in extreme cases, any focus on the self at all) is misguided, a distraction from the proper object of one's attention. Here the goal is not to pay more attention to the self and its shortcomings but to ignore the self as much as possible. Jewish authorities have advocated both types of humility over the centuries.

Moreover, those who are humble in the first sense may adopt this attitude in either a general or a specifically moral way. One could be humble about one's natural abilities and accomplishments (for example, a person's artistic talents or athletic prowess or intellectual achievements). To be humble in the moral sphere, on the other hand, would entail minimizing the person's moral worth or righteousness while perhaps accentuating his or her moral failings and misdeeds. It is possible to exhibit humility in one sphere of life but not in another (or in both, or in neither). Jewish sources consider the value of humility in general, as well as in the moral sphere particularly, although the latter receives the greater share of the rabbis' attention.

Finally, although at first glance they may appear to be similar, humility as these sources describe it should be distinguished from what contemporary psychologists would regard as "low self-esteem." A person's tendency to think little of herself or to hold herself in low esteem may represent a psychological disorder: the lack of a healthy self-image or ego, suggesting a dysfunctional personality. As discussed in Jewish sources, however, humility has little in common with a pathological condition of this sort. Those who exhibit humility do so not primarily because they believe themselves to be less worthy of honor than others but because they believe that this is the appropriate posture for *all* people. They do not suffer from a damaged sense of self; rather, they possess a different sense of what a "self" is or ought to be for themselves and others.

With these preliminary observations about humility, I return to the original questions. Why is humility, in any or all of the senses just delineated, a desirable trait to cultivate? What, after all, is objectionable about being proud of one's accomplishments, including moral deeds? What is the value of minimizing (or ignoring) a person's self-worth and so emphasizing the person's lowliness and shortcomings? What makes humility a virtue, let alone the most important virtue, as ben Levi would have it?

The Roots of Humility

The answers to these questions lie in the particular religious perspective of the self and its place in the world that Judaism offers. The central issue is the nature and source of the individual's value and worth. Pride in oneself[18] is based on two assumptions: (1) a person's traits (e.g., generosity), talents (e.g., athletic ability) or accomplishments (e.g., success in business) add to her importance or worth and (2) a person can take credit for possessing or achieving these things. Jewish moralists have generally challenged one or both of these assumptions on religious grounds.

Consider the following teaching:

> Our masters taught: Adam was created on the eve of the Sabbath [the last of all created beings]. Why? So that if one should become excessively proud, [God might] say, "The gnat preceded you in the order of creation."19

The rabbis here recognize the intrinsic connection between the way humans think of themselves and the place they believe they occupy in the universe. The antidote to pride, these sages suggest, is to remember one's humble place in the created order. Pondering the end of human life as well as its beginning likewise reinforces an attitude of humility. "Rabbi L'vitas of Yavneh said: Be exceedingly humble, for a person's hope is the worm [i.e., the grave]."20 Remembering that life ends in oblivion and that bodies decompose in the earth naturally gives a more realistic and humble appraisal of a person's own significance.

Many centuries later the moralist Bahya ibn Pakuda elaborated on this point: knowing humans' humble beginnings and considering their even more humble destiny should temper any tendency to overestimate their ultimate worth:

> The root of one's existence and one's beginnings is in semen and blood after these have become corrupt and foul smelling. Afterwards one is nourished by unclean blood as long as one is in the mother's womb, and then one emerges weak and infirm in body and members. Later one grows by stages until reaching maturity, growing older and older until reaching the end of one's days. . . .When one reflects on the end of one's days, and the speed with which death comes, when all one's hopes and wishes will cease and all one's possessions will be abandoned, when one despairs of retaining any of them for oneself, or benefiting from them when in the grave, one's face darkened, his visage blackened and bringing forth worms, stench and putrefaction, the signs of one's bodily beauty all gone, while the stench grows stronger as if one had never washed or cleaned or smelled good; when one meditates upon this and similar things, one becomes humble and contrite, not proud or arrogant or self-aggrandizing. As it says, "Oh, cease to glorify man, who has only a breath in his nostrils! For by what does he merit esteem?" (Isaiah 2:22).[21]

This perspective can be extended further. The whole of human life, not only a human's place in the order of creation or his or her ultimate dissolution, bespeaks vulnerability and lowliness. Humans are essentially weak creatures, unable to control many of the perils that beset human life. To recognize this is to see that the many talents and accomplishments of which people are often proud in fact amount to very little. Samuel David Luzzatto, the nineteenth-century Italian commentator, makes this point vividly:

> Let one consider the vicissitudes of life. The rich man often becomes poor, the ruler subservient, and the man of eminence sinks into obscurity. Since a man is thus liable to find himself occupying a station in life that he now looks upon with contempt, how shall he be proud because of the good fortune which he can never be sure will last? How many are the discards to which one is liable, rendering a man so helpless that he begs to be relieved? . . . Daily do we witness these occurrences. They should be sufficient to banish pride from our hearts and to imbue us with humility.[22]

From this perspective, humans ought not to be proud of their moral deeds and not even of their natural talents or worldly accomplishments. In the end, all of this comes to naught, and even in a human's lifetime, much of it results from forces outside her control. Hence, people do well to adopt an attitude of humility with respect to all that they are and all that they do.

Many rabbis regard pride as grounded in a false sense of human importance, in the tendency to misconstrue (or forget) humans' true nature and the fact of our creatureliness. They also insist that pride is tantamount to a theological mistake, for it presupposes forgetting that God is the proper object of devotion:

> Rabbi Yohanan said in the name of Rabbi Simeon ben Yohai: A man who has haughtiness within him is as though he had worshiped an idol, for Scripture says,

"Every haughty person is an abomination to the Lord" (Proverbs 16:5), and else-where it says, "You must not bring an abhorrent thing into your house" (Deuteronomy 7:26). On his own authority Rabbi Yohanan said: [One who is guilty of haughtiness] is tantamount to denying the essential principle [of God's existence], as it is said, "When your heart was haughty, you forgot the Lord your God." (Deuteronomy 8:14)[23]

Pride is closely associated with idolatry because both entail the same mistake—namely, believing that something or someone other than God is the source of life and of all value. To believe that people have a right to take credit for their talents and accomplishments is to ignore their true source in God.

For the rabbis there is a psychological, as well as a logical, connection between pride and the failure to remain focused on God. Those who think too highly of themselves will simply push God further from view. This lesson is reinforced in a number of other rabbinic teachings about the intimate connection between pride and distance from God.

Rabbi Hisda (according to some, Mar Ukba), said: Of one who is haughty the Holy One says, "I and he cannot dwell together in the world." As it says, "Whoever is haughty of eye and proud of heart, him I cannot endure" (Psalm 101:5).[24] Read not "him" (oto), but "together with him" (itto).[25]

One who walks even four cubits with a haughty bearing is tantamount to pushing aside the feet of the Divine Presence, as it is written, "The Lord of Hosts! God's presence fills all the earth!" (Isaiah 6:3)[26]

The proper religious attitude, these sources suggest, is simply incompatible with arrogance, for being aware of God's presence and power necessarily results in diminishing the focus on human importance and power. More than a thousand years after these talmudic sages taught these values, a Hasidic master affirmed the same lesson: excessive emphasis on a person's ego precludes proper awareness of and devotion to God.

Concerning the verse in the Scriptures: "I stood between the Lord and you," (Deuteronomy 5:5) Rabbi Mikhal of Zlotchov said: The "I" stands between God and us. When a man says "I" and encroaches upon the word of his Maker, he puts a wall between himself and God. But he who offers his "I"—there is nothing between him and his Maker.[27]

These considerations led the rabbis to declare that fear of God and humility are integrally related and that both are associated with wisdom or moral discernment. The rabbis claim: "The following three are of equal importance: wisdom, fear [of God] and humility,"[28] and "The fear of the Lord is the highest manifestation of wisdom, even as it is the basis of true humility."[29] To be wise a person must see things in their proper perspective doing so will manifest itself in both fear of God and an attitude of humility.

This point has been repeated by many authorities over the centuries. Maimonides notes that fear of God is grounded in the awareness of God's greatness and, correspondingly, of human finitude.

What is the way to loving and fearing God? As soon as one reflects on God's won-
drous deeds and creations, and comes to see God's wisdom as beyond all value
and infinite, then one immediately loves, praises, exalts [God] and longs in-
tensely to know God's Name. As David said, "My soul thirsts for God, the living
God" (Psalm 42:3). And when one considers these things themselves, one immediately is taken aback and is afraid, for one knows that one is a small, lowly and
obscure creature who stands, possessing only the most minimal knowledge, before the Omniscient One. As David said, "When I behold Your heavens, the work
of Your fingers . . . what is man that you have been mindful of him? . . ." (Psalm
8:4–5)[30]

Many voices within the tradition also insist that humility and pride both bring
in their wake appropriate consequences. Because God is just, ultimately the proud
will be humbled and the humble will be rewarded, if not in this life then surely in the
life after death.

The one who humbles himself, the Holy One exalts; and the one who exalts himself, the Holy One humbles.[31]
    Rabbi Eleazar said: Anyone in whom there is haughtiness of spirit will not
have his dust stirred [at the resurrection], for it is said, "Awake and shout for joy,
you who dwell with the dust" (Isaiah 26:19).[32] It is not said, "You who dwell *in* the
dust," but, "You who dwell *with* the dust"—one who in life becomes as a neighbor
to dust [i.e., lives humbly].[33]
    Rabbi Eleazar ha-Kappar said: Be not like the upper lintel, which no one's
hand can touch; but be like the threshold below, upon which everyone steps—in
the end, when the entire structure is demolished, it still remains.[34]
    Rabbi Avira expounded: He in whom there is haughtiness of spirit will
ultimately be diminished, as it said, "Exalted for a while, let them be gone"
(Job 24:24).[35]

These rabbinic teachers share a belief that, as Jesus taught, "Blessed are the
meek, for they shall inherit the earth" (Matthew 5:5). Any appearances to the contrary notwithstanding, God has so constituted the world that those who are lowly and
humble will endure while those who are not, will not. Indeed, this is God's own way,
as is known from that fact that God appeared to Moses in a lowly thorn bush and
revealed the Torah on lowly Mt. Sinai.[36]
    Overall, Jewish tradition affirms the importance of humility because it insists
that when humans recognize their true place in the universe—their rank in the order
of creation, their mortality, their limited knowledge, and their vulnerability, especially
in contrast to God's power and majesty—they will be led inexorably to minimize their
sense of importance and surely to avoid any hint of arrogance. Humility, as Jewish
tradition presents it, is a matter of living, as the philosophers would put it, *sub specie
aeternitatis,* under the aspect of eternity. But how is humility taught? Where and how
does Judaism inculcate the perspectives on life that foster humility?

The Cultivation of Humility

The "training ground" of humility can be found most clearly within traditional Jewish liturgy. In the daily worship service and especially in the liturgy for the Day of Atonement, Jews are reminded of their place within the universe, of their dependence on God, and of their moral failings. In most cases, these prayers do not deduce from these beliefs the moral conclusion that it is necessary to strive to be humble. There is no need to; the moral message is immediately obvious.

Among the prayers to be recited every day on first waking are these:

> I am grateful to You, living, enduring King, for restoring my soul to me in compassion. You are faithful beyond measure.
>
> The soul which you, my God, have given me is pure. You created it, You formed it, You breathed it into me; You keep body and soul together. One day You will take my soul from me, to restore it to me in life eternal. So long as this soul is within me I acknowledge You, Lord my God, my ancestors' God, Master of all creation, sovereign of all souls. Praised are You, Lord who restores the soul to the lifeless, exhausted body.

There could scarcely be a more direct statement of the view that life utterly depends on God's grace. To begin each day with this expression of God's power over life and with gratitude for another day of life is implicitly to negate the view that humans are the masters of their fate, that their lives and fortunes are within their control. These same messages are repeated countless times within the daily liturgy, especially in the Amidah, which is recited three times each day by traditional Jews:

> We are grateful to You, for You are the Lord our God and God of our ancestors throughout all time. You are the Rock of our lives, the Shield of our salvation in every generation. We thank You and praise You morning, noon, and night for Your miracles which daily attend us and for Your wondrous kindnesses. Our lives are in Your hand; our souls are in Your charge. You are good, with everlasting mercy; You are compassionate, with enduring lovingkindness. We have always placed our hope in You.

Interestingly, the Amidah concludes with the following meditation:

> My God, keep my tongue from evil and my lips from speaking slander. To those who slander me, let me be silent and may I be as the dust before everyone. . . .[37]

As creatures whose very existence depends entirely on God's providence, humans do well not to inflate their sense of self-worth. Instead, they must adopt an attitude of modesty and moral circumspection, for only in this way will their attitudes toward themselves and others reflect the reality of the human condition. People are extremely vulnerable and deeply flawed creatures, subject to all manner of ailments and prone to sin. To know this is to know that they must be humble.

These messages play an especially prominent role in the liturgy for the High Holidays when self-scrutiny and penitence take center stage. Among the prayers that worshippers repeat several times during the course of these "Days of Awe" is the *Avinu Malkeinu,* "Our Father, our King."

Our Father, our King, we have no King but You . . .

Our Father, our King, forgive and pardon all our sins.

Our Father, our King, ignore the record of our transgressions . . .

Our Father, our King, remember that we are dust.

Our Father, our King, have pity for us and for our children . . .

Our Father, our King, answer us though we have no deeds to plead our
cause; save us with mercy and lovingkindness.

This, coupled with the central prayer in which the congregation collectively confesses
its sins (Hebrew: *vidui*), reinforces the image of God's power in contrast to human
weakness, God's goodness in contrast to human sinfulness. As the congregation
repeatedly pleads for God's forgiveness, individual worshippers are reminded of just
how little justification they have to be arrogant, smug, or self-satisfied.

This entire way of viewing the world is summed up in the following prayer,
which appears in the preliminary service recited on both weekdays and holidays:

Master of all worlds! Not upon our merit do we rely in our supplication, but upon
Your limitless love. What are we? What is our life? What is our piety? What is our
righteousness? What is our attainment, our power, our might? What can we say,
Lord our God and God of our ancestors? Compared to You, all the mighty are
nothing, the famous nonexistent, the wise lack wisdom, the clever lack reason.
For most of their actions are meaningless, the days of their lives emptiness.
Human preeminence over beasts is an illusion when all is seen as futility.

Humility is simply the natural outcome of such a worldview.[38] To adopt any other
moral attitude would be radically out of step with the understanding of reality that
these traditional sources present. The more a person internalizes the message of the
liturgy, the more that person is drawn to realize that humility is not the *best* way to
live so much as it is the *only* way that makes any sense.

The fruits of humility, its expression in everyday behavior, are not difficult to
discern. Humility expresses itself potentially in a whole range of behaviors that significantly affect the moral relationships that people have with those around them.

In the first place, those who are humble will feel driven to scrutinize their
moral behavior and to engage in regular soul-searching (Hebrew: *heshbon ha-nefesh*).
In the ordinary course of things, this will lead them to pay close attention to the ways
in which their behavior has negative consequences on those around them and to
repent when they fail to live up to the highest ideals. Because they do not have an
inflated sense of their own moral worth, they will seek to improve themselves and
their relationships with others. Because pride does not stand in their way, they will
readily apologize for their misdeeds and seek forgiveness from those whom they have
harmed. Humility provides a strong impetus for *teshuvah*, repentance, as it was
described in the previous chapter.[39]

Moreover, those who cultivate humility will refrain from judging others harshly,
precisely because they are not inclined to assume an attitude of superiority to others.
They will try to be patient with others' failings and to forgive readily, especially the
small slights that they experience in the course of daily living.

Insofar as humility presupposes seeing all human achievements and acquisitions as relatively insignificant, the humble will tend to be "satisfied with their portion." They will not be strongly motivated to seek fame or fortune, to amass material possessions, or to seek accolades for the good deeds that they do. To be humble does not necessitate an attitude of complete passivity or resignation, but it does seem to preclude its opposite, striving to maximize personal power, especially power over others.

In all, cultivating humility will significantly alter a person's relationships with others, for it is grounded in a different way of thinking about moral worth, the person's own and that of everyone else. In that sense, the statement attributed to Rabbi Joshua ben Levi quoted at the beginning of this section makes sense. Humility may be the most fundamental of the virtues both because it is so deeply rooted in basic beliefs about the nature of human existence and because it affects interactions with others in such profound ways. As Ronald Green rightly notes in his discussion of humility in Judaism, "humility is demanded of men if they are to develop all the other attributes and dispositions necessary for the moral life."[40]

A JEWISH MORAL OBLIGATION: HONORING PARENTS

> *When Rabbi Joseph heard the sound of his mother's footsteps, he would say, "I must rise before the Presence, which is approaching."[41]*

Most of us are familiar with the fifth of the Ten Commandments, "Honor your father and your mother" (Exodus 20:12, Deuteronomy 5:16), but it is seldom noticed that the rule as it stands is ambiguous. What does honoring parents entail? What specific behaviors does this require? And what happens when this rule conflicts with other responsibilities, to God or to society? The biblical text never provides the rationale for this commandment. It says only, "that you may long endure on the land that the Lord your God is giving you," which explains the reason for following the rule but not why honoring parents is a rule in the first place.

Not surprisingly, the ancient rabbis went to some length in answering these questions. Their embellishments indicate both the extent of this obligation and its deeper purpose as they understood it. Jewish tradition has a very expansive sense of what honoring parents requires, for it sees this rule as the exemplification of a fundamental religious principle.

How to Honor and Revere Parents

The rabbis note that there are two biblical injunctions regarding parents, the one in the Ten Commandments and the one in Leviticus 19:3, "You shall each revere his mother and his father." Always concerned to explicate verses that appear to be redundant, the rabbis suggest that these two passages enjoin different behaviors.

> Our rabbis taught: What is reverence and what is honor? Reverence means that
> one must neither stand nor sit in one's parent's place, nor contradict her words,
> nor weigh in against him [in a dispute]. Honor means that one must give her
> food and drink, clothe and cover him, and lead her in and out.[42]

Honoring parents requires caring for their physical needs,[43] and revering them
requires showing them respect and deference. Whether or not the biblical terms
employed here can sustain the distinction that the rabbis draw, the point is clear
enough: Rabbinic authorities assume that the parent-child relationship encompasses
both material and psychological dimensions; hence, total concern must incorporate
regard for both the person and the status of parents.

Reverence might also be thought of as an internal attitude, and honor relates
to external behaviors. The rabbis were well aware that one could take care of one's
parents, hence *honoring* them, without genuinely caring for them. This is undoubtedly the concern that animates the following passage from Rabbi Israel ben Joseph
Alnakawa (d.1391):

> A son must not dishonor his father in his speech. How so? For example, when the
> father is old and wants to eat early in the morning, as old men do because they
> are weak, . . . and the son says, "The sun is not yet up, and you're already up and
> eating!"
>
> Or when the father says, "My son, how much did you pay for this coat?" And the
> son says, "What do you bother yourself for? I bought it and I have paid for it, it is
> no business of yours to ask about it!"
>
> Or when he thinks to himself, saying, "When will this old man die and I shall be
> free of what he costs me?"[44]

Caretaking alone, in the absence of genuine reverence, fails to fulfill one's obligation
to one's parents.[45]

With respect to honoring parents, one of the primary obligations is to provide
financial support. Noting the parallel, but also the contrast, between the verses
"Honor your father and your mother" and "Honor the Lord with your wealth"
(Proverbs 3:9), the rabbis comment:

> [With respect to honoring God] if you have the means, you are obliged to do all
> this, if you do not have the means, you are not. But with "Honor your father and
> your mother" it is not so; whether you have the means or you do not, "Honor
> your father and mother," even if you must become a beggar at the door.[46]

In a more straightforward explication of the same verses, another rabbi offers the following lesson:

> It is stated, "Honor your father and your mother." And it is also stated, "Honor
> the Lord with your wealth." Just as the one demands economic sacrifice, so does
> the other demand economic sacrifice.[47]

While all seemed to be in agreement that honoring parents required financial sacrifice, the exact nature of this sacrifice was a matter of dispute among later talmudic
sages. Some assume that filial responsibility encompasses direct monetary payments
to meet the parents' needs. Others assume that the parents must be maintained out

of their own financial resources and that the "economic sacrifice" spoken of refers to the loss of income that the children incur when they provide personal services to their parents. On this latter view, indigent parents must be cared for, not because of the commandment to honor parents but based on the general obligation to give charity to the poor. Leaving aside the complexities of the talmudic debates on this point, it is apparent that children must be prepared to suffer some form of financial loss in the support of their parents.

Beyond financial support, just how extensive is the obligation to honor and revere parents, as the rabbis understood it? The biblical text itself includes some extraordinarily severe punishments for what would seem to be minor infractions of one's filial obligations.

> He who strikes his father or his mother shall be put to death. (Exodus 21:15)
>
> He who insults his father or his mother shall be put to death. (Exodus 21:17)
>
> Cursed be he that insults his father or his mother. (Deuteronomy 27:16)

The rabbis extend these strictures on filial responsibility, offering numerous anecdotes about the extent to which the honor and reverence of parents can and should be taken. In one instance, they commend as exemplary the behavior of a certain gentile who declined to sell jewels for a fabulous sum of money because doing so would have required waking his sleeping father. The same individual is also said to have restrained himself from reprimanding his mother even when she humiliated him in public.[48] The following frequently quoted anecdote indicates the extent to which some rabbis supposedly took their filial obligations.

> The mother of Rabbi Tarfon went walking in the courtyard one Sabbath day, and her shoe tore and came off. Rabbi Tarfon came and placed his hands under her feet, and she walked in this manner until she reached her couch. Once when he fell ill and the sages came to visit him, his mother said to them, "Pray for my son Rabbi Tarfon, for he serves me with excessive honor." They said to her, "What did he do for you?" She told them what had happened. They responded, "Were he to do that a thousand times, he has not yet bestowed even half the honor demanded by the Torah."[49]

Though the final rejoinder here is no doubt hyperbolic, the idea that virtually no act of honoring parents is excessive here receives clear expression.

With his characteristic clarity, Maimonides summarized the law of honoring and revering parents as follows:

> How far must one go to honor one's father and mother? Even if they took one's wallet full of gold pieces and threw it into the sea before one's very eyes, one must not shame them, show pain before them, or display anger to them; but one must accept the decree of Scripture and remain silent.
>
> And how far must one go in their reverence? Even if one is dressed in precious clothes and is sitting in an honored place before the congregation, and one's parents come and tear one's clothes, striking one's head and spitting in one's face, one may not shame them, but he must remain silent, and be in awe and fear of the King of Kings who commanded thus. For if a king of flesh and blood had

decreed that one do something more painful than this, one could not hesitate in its performance. All the more so, then, when one is commanded by the One who spoke and created the world![50]

Against this background, you can appreciate the statement of Rabbi Simeon bar Yohai that "the most difficult of all commandments is 'Honor your father and your mother,'"[51] and that of Rabbi Yohanan that "Blessed is the one who never set eyes on his parents" for, as Rashi comments, "it is impossible to honor them adequately."[52]

Given such an expansive definition of honoring parents, it could be expected that this obligation would trump all conflicting responsibilities. This is not universally so, however; indeed, the rabbis debated at some length the problems that arise when one's obligations to parents conflict with other religious duties. Two such instances deserve special note: conflicts with duties to God, such as observance of the Sabbath, and conflicts with duties to one's spouse or to the maintenance of domestic harmony.

What is the child to do if parents wish him or her to violate a religious law, such as observing the Sabbath? Honoring parents would seem to necessitate complying with their request while honoring the Torah would necessitate the opposite. An early rabbinic source resolves this conflict directly:

> "You shall each revere his father and his mother, and keep My Sabbaths: I the Lord am your God" (Leviticus 19:3); "You shall each revere. . .": perhaps I might think that one is obliged to obey even if one's father or mother desired that one violate a commandment—therefore the Torah says, ". . . and keep My Sabbaths. . .": you are all required to honor Me.[53]

The underlying theory seems to be that parents cannot require their children to violate God's law, to which both they and their children are obligated.

The case is slightly more complicated when the issue concerns not the direct transgression of a commandment but rather attention to a competing positive duty, such as reciting one's prayers or returning a lost article to its owner. Here there is some disagreement among authorities.

> Elazar ben Matya said, "If my father says, 'Give me a drink of water,' and I am simultaneously presented with an opportunity to perform another divinely commanded act, I must waive the honoring of my parent and perform the other commandment, for both I and my father are obliged to perform the commandment."
>
> Issi ben Judah said, "If the commandment can be performed by others, let it be done by others, and one must must attend to one's father's honor."
>
> Rabbi Matnah said, "The law follows the opinion of Issi ben Judah."[54]

The sages disagree here about how to resolve the conflict between two responsibilities. Elazar, following the logic of the last source cited, argues that divine commandments, which obligate both father and child, must take precedence over honoring parents. Issi agrees, but only in the case where the requirements of the law cannot be met by anyone else. On this view, reciting one's prayers at the proper time takes precedence over caring for a parent, for one's obligation to pray cannot be fulfilled by anyone else. On the other hand, if a lost object can be returned by someone else, this must not be allowed to keep the child from the obligation at that moment to care for his or her parent. Although it appears that Rabbi Matnah resolves that disagreement, note that a number of medieval authorities ruled that the performance of a divine commandment (e.g., to emigrate to the Land of Israel or even to study with a certain esteemed teacher) takes precedence over honoring parents.[55]

Another sort of problem entirely arises when honoring parents conflicts with one's duties to one's spouse, in cases where the spouse and in-laws do not get along.[56] Can a man neglect his duties to his parents if his marriage is at stake? Can a man force his parents to leave his home if they make their daughter-in-law's life miserable?

In such cases, many authorities ruled that the wife's well-being took precedence, perhaps relying on the biblical comment that "a man leaves his father and his mother and cleaves to his wife" (Genesis 2:24). Honoring parents, it seems, cannot be permitted to undermine the sanctity of marital life, especially if, as many sources appear to assume, it is the parents themselves who generate the discord. As Rabbi Solomon ibn Adret, the prominent thirteenth-century Spanish scholar, opined,

> A wife can certainly tell her husband, "I refuse to live with people who pain me," for if her husband may not pain her, she certainly need not live among others who pain her and occasion quarrels between herself and her husband.[57]

Note that other authorities are not so quick to relieve a man of his filial responsibilities in deference to his wife. An example of the attempt to find a delicate balance between these conflicting responsibilities can be seen in the following passage from the twelfth-century *Sefer Hasidim:*

> Parents who command their son not to marry so that he might serve them make an inadmissible request; let him marry and live near them. But if he cannot find a wife in the town in which his parents live, and his parents are aged and need him to support them, let him not leave the town. And if he can earn only enough to support his parents, and would be forced should he marry to end this support, let him obey his parents. But if the son is wealthy and can have someone else serve his parents, he may then go to another town to take a wife.[58]

The array of views taken by authorities over the centuries in such cases cannot readily be summarized, but it is fair to conclude that, at least, filial responsibilities may be limited when they conflict with a man's obligation to marry and/or to care for his wife.[59]

The Religious Basis of the Obligation to Honor Parents

It is not difficult to explain the obligation to honor parents on purely secular grounds. Those who give people gifts and bestow benefits upon them that they have no right to expect are entitled to their gratitude. When people fail to acknowledge the generosity of others—either in word or deed—they are guilty of taking others for granted by mistaking gifts for entitlements. To receive without giving in return is an act of selfishness, a moral failing. If this is true of even routine benefits that come to people, it is certainly true with respect to their parents, who give them life and make many sacrifices on their behalf over a period of many years. Following this logic, some Jewish authorities do, in fact, see a basic principle of gratitude in the commandment to honor parents and so regard this as a universal commandment.[60]

The rabbis more consistently ground this obligation in the religious realm, however, in the relationship to God, as the following rabbinic text relates:

> It is stated, "Honor your father and your mother" (Exodus 20:12), and it is also stated, "Honor the Lord with your wealth" (Proverbs 3:9). Scripture equates the honoring of parents with the honoring of the Omnipresent.
>
> It is stated, "You shall each revere his mother and his father" (Leviticus 19:3), and it is also stated, "Revere only the Lord your God" (Deuteronomy 6:13). Scripture equates the reverence of parents with the reverence of the Omnipresent.
>
> It is stated, "One who curses his father or mother shall be put to death" (Exodus 21:17), and it is also stated, "Anyone who blasphemes his God shall bear his guilt; if he also pronounces the name Lord, he shall be put to death" (Leviticus 24:15–16). Scripture equates cursing of parents with blasphemy against the Lord.
>
> The rabbis taught: Three are partners in [the creation of] a person—God, father and mother.
>
> When one honors one's father and mother, the Lord says, "I reckon it as though I abided with them and they honored me." . . . When a man pains his parents, the Lord says, "I have done wisely not to abide with them, for if I did, they would pain me."[61]

This teaching is richly suggestive of the many ways in which honoring parents is both rooted in and reinforcing of honoring God.

First, the rabbis wished to stress that both human and divine energies are necessary for the creation of a person; neither alone is sufficient. In some versions of the preceding text, the rabbis spell out the various contributions that the human and divine partners make to the forming of a person.

> The white matter is of the man—from that are formed the brain, the bones, and the veins; the red matter is of the woman—from that comes the skin, the flesh, and the blood; life, and the spirit, and the soul are of God. . . .
>
> When a person's time comes to depart from the world, God takes back his share, and leaves the share of the parents before them."[62]

Given this way of understanding human generation, there is a parity between father, mother, and God, for each contributes something essential to the creation process. As was stressed earlier in this chapter, just as human beings owe their very lives to God, it is no less true that they owe their lives to their parents.

It follows that honoring God and honoring parents are analogous, for in both cases one acknowledges gratitude for one's very existence. The rabbis make this point astutely by noting the precise parallels between the biblical verses about honoring, fearing, and cursing God/parents.

This leads directly to the idea that honoring parents is not only parallel to honoring God but is also in fact an instance of it. When we show respect for parents as the source of our life, we simultaneously acknowledge the divine Source of life. Indeed, the two are so closely related that it is assumed (by God!) that people who do not honor their parents cannot be counted on to honor God either.

The connection between God and parents extends beyond their partnership in creation, however. The following series of biblical verses makes it evident that God has many other qualities in common with human parents, as well.

> Do you thus requite the Lord, O dull and witless people? Is not God the Father who created you, fashioned you and made you endure! (Deuteronomy 32:6)
>
> You, O Lord, are our father, from of old, Your name is "Our Redeemer." (Isaiah 63:16)
>
> Truly, Ephraim is a dear son to Me, a child that is dandled!
> Whenever I have turned against him, my thoughts would dwell on him still.
> That is why My heart yearns for him; I will receive him back in love, declares the Lord. (Jeremiah 31:20)
>
> As a father has compassion for his children, so the Lord has compassion for those who fear God. (Psalm 103:13)

Even this small sample of biblical verses is sufficient to indicate the richness of the parental metaphor as applied to God. Like a father, God is protective, the source of security and an abiding source of love and mercy. In using the imagery of God as father, the biblical authors were no doubt attempting to express the closeness and intimacy that they experienced (at least sometimes) in their relationship with God. The same imagery works in the opposite direction, making the human father a mirror-image of the divine. The parent, perhaps especially the father,[63] embodies the very same qualities attributed to God; this has the dual effect of humanizing God as well as investing the human father with divine significance. Honoring a human father, then, is merely an extension of honoring the divine father.

Against this background, we can understand the rabbinic comment that the commandment to "honor your father and your mother" is really a duty to God. Nahmanides makes this clear in his commentary on this commandment:

> [The commandments concerning our obligations to others] begin with the father who, in relation to his offspring, is like a creator, involved in their formation. For God is our first Father, who creates our natural father. For this reason [God] says just as I have commanded you concerning My honor, so I command you to honor My partner with Me in your creation. . . .
>
> Of the Ten Commandments, five deal with honor due the Creator and five deal with the good of man. For "honor your father" is the honor of the Lord; it is for the honor of the Creator that He commanded that one honor one's father who participated in one's creation. Five commandments thus remain for the welfare of human beings.[64]

As Nahmanides sees it, the fifth commandment of the Decalogue, along with the first four, concerns honoring God, while the final five commandments concern duties to others. Honoring parents is, in fact, a way of honoring God, for it is a matter of acknowledging what parents and God have in common.

So even the respect humans owe their parents is understood by Jewish tradition as a duty to God, and this is so in two distinct senses. First, it is a rule (like all others in the Torah) commanded by God, and, second, it is a rule whose proper object is God. Once again, Judaism transforms a human, interpersonal responsibility into a matter of maintaining a proper relationship with God. Here, too, the moral life is infused with divine significance.

Stepping back and reflecting on this brief overview of Jewish moral life, you will notice that the values, virtues, and rules that define Jewish morality are thoroughly shaped by religious perspectives on the world. As noted in Chapter One, religion intersects with morality on a number of levels. Sometimes it provides a divine model for moral behavior, as when human justice is patterned on God's attributes of justice and mercy. Sometimes it offers a perspective on a person's place in the world that fosters certain characteristic moral postures, as when it emphasizes human fraility and the virtue of humility. Sometimes it transforms moral relationships between human beings into extensions of their relationship to God, as in the case of the duty to honor parents. Frequently, it does all these simultaneously, and more.

Finally, you should note that the religious dimension of Jewish ethics is pervasive and operates not only on the rational, philosophical level but on a subtle, psychological level as well. The traditional Jew who regularly recites the words of Jewish liturgy, engages in Jewish ritual, and lives within a Jewish community infused with a sense of religious purpose simply absorbs certain moral ideas, ideals, attitudes, and behaviors. Moral lessons for everyday life are encoded within the religious patterns of the community and are learned intuitively, even when they are not being preached explicitly. The moral life is part and parcel of the religious life, not something separable from it, and at times not even distinguishable from it.[65] Jewish ethics, then, is religious through and through, for moral values, virtues, and rules are woven into the fabric of religious life.

It is time to turn from the concrete to the abstract, from the patterns of moral life to the theory of morality. Over the centuries, Jews have not only reflected on how to live a moral life in the practical sense, but also have pondered the concept of morality, the nature of moral obligation in general, and the theoretical foundations of ethics. Although such concerns may seem to be of interest only to philosophers and professional ethicists, in fact they are integral to a fuller understanding even of Jewish ethics. The following chapter attends to these theoretical questions about ethics as Jewish authorities have historically understood it.

KEY POINTS

- Within Judaism, values, virtues, and obligations (rules) are interwoven into a comprehensive moral life.
- Jewish authorities have explored in great detail the practical requirements of living morally as well as the religious basis of this moral life and the meaning or benefits of following it.
- The value (justice), virtue (humility), and obligation (honoring parents) examined here are infused with religious significance. They illustrate the ways in which Jewish moral life is grounded in beliefs about being created in God's image, the importance of imitating God's own behavior, the transitory nature of human life as God created it, the fact that human owe their lives to God (and to their parents), and the importance of bringing God's presence into the world by executing justice in all of their affairs.
- Jewish moral living is part and parcel of the larger structure of Jewish religious life. Morality is thus embedded within and reinforced by patterns of religious life, including prayer, ritual, and studying sacred texts.

QUESTIONS TO CONSIDER

1. How do Jewish views of justice, humility, and honoring parents compare to views found within secular systems of ethics? Do Jewish teachings affect the substance of these aspects of morality or only the ways in which they are justified?

2. Try to extrapolate from these few specific teachings—about justice, humility, and honoring parents—to other values, virtues, and rules. Given the principles and values evident here, what positions would you expect Jewish authorities to take on affirmative action, organ donation, and surrogate parenthood?

3. Chapter Two presented creation, revelation, and redemption as the central beliefs that shaped Jewish ethics. Can all of what Judaism teaches about justice, humility, and honoring parents be captured under these rubrics? What other beliefs or values, if any, come into play?

4. As you begin to enter more fully into the "world of Jewish ethics," which aspects of this religious-moral system make sense to you? Which are still opaque or confusing? To what extent can you imagine what it would be like to live the sort of moral life described by these sources?

Chapter Five

Foundations of Jewish Moral Obligation

Summary

What makes a particular action right or wrong, good or bad? How do people come to know their moral obligations? This chapter considers the ways in which Judaism has addressed these questions first with respect to the moral duties of Jews in particular, and then in relation to the (far more restricted) moral duties that are incumbent on all people. The final section explores the ways in which some Jewish thinkers have attempted to relate the universal and the particular components of Jewish ethics.

◆ ————————————————————————————

> *Myth is less likely to dictate specific moral directives than it is to inscribe the general—and normative—contours for moral life. It can point to the nature and locus of the good, to the cosmic context of moral behavior, to the nature of moral agency, and to the significance of moral community. At the same time, the myth may indicate the threats to the moral life as well as the consequences of immoral conduct.*[1]

The last chapter considered questions of a practical nature, such as the virtue of humility and the duty to honor parents, the substance of day-to-day moral living. In addition to providing moral guidance, every system of ethics must justify its moral norms, which requires attending to certain basic theoretical questions. In particular, it must account for what the nature of moral obligation is, what distinguishes right from wrong, and how people come to know what morality requires of them in particular situations. Any ethical system that fails to provide even minimal answers to these questions will quickly collapse into a set of arbitrary moral rules with no apparent rationale behind it. Ethical theory constitutes the intellectual foundation of a moral life, for it explains how to *define* morality and provides a basis for claims to *know* what is moral or immoral.

Of course, a great many people live extremely moral lives without ever developing an ethical theory or even confronting these theoretical issues. Indeed, many people are content to leave these questions to professional philosophers, theologians, and ethicists. If you have ever discussed or debated your moral views with others, however, you have almost certainly touched on questions of ethical theory. Whenever people challenge someone's moral views or attempt to defend their own, they quickly discover that the source of their differences often lies in how they understand what makes something moral or immoral in the first place, or perhaps in how (or whether) they can know what morality requires of them. Certainly, none of the ethical systems that have survived for centuries has failed to address these theoretical questions.

Over the centuries, Judaism has considered these questions, although not always in a form that contemporary ethicists would recognize as moral theory. As noted, classical Jewish sources speak in a peculiar idiom and only rarely offer extended analyses of theoretical questions.[2] As a result, this attempt to summarize major trends in Jewish moral theory will necessarily rely on inferences drawn from many nontheoretical texts, any one of which could be (and has been) interpreted in diverse ways. Moreover, as you will have come to expect by now, Jewish authorities have not always agreed with one another about these matters. The following discussion outlines multiple ways of answering these theoretical questions, which rely on diverse ways of reading the pertinent traditional sources.

This discussion of Jewish moral theory explores two central and widely discussed questions. First, *how do people define* what is right and wrong, good and bad? What makes one action morally commendable and another morally reprehensible? Second, *how do people come to know* what their moral obligations are in any given situation? Is moral knowledge intuitive or rational? Is it innate or acquired, does it grow out of human experience, or is it communicated by God? These questions, of course, do not exhaust the theoretical questions that can be raised about moral systems, but they represent two central issues in ethical theory that have far-reaching implications for how people understand the moral life.

To understand how Jewish thinkers have approached these questions of moral theory, I must begin by returning to an observation made in Chapter Two. Classical Jewish ethics concerns primarily the moral obligations of the Jewish people, who have understood themselves to stand in a special relationship to God. Nonetheless, Jewish tradition has long acknowledged that non-Jews also have moral obligations (albeit of a more limited nature) and that their moral lives are also of concern to God. Accordingly, Jewish moral theory operates in two distinct spheres: in relation first to those particular moral duties that are incumbent on Jews alone and second to those universal moral duties that are incumbent on all. Later this chapter turns to the problem of relating these two distinct, but overlapping, sets of moral obligations.

JEWISH ETHICS

It should be clear now that Jewish ethics is fundamentally covenantal, a matter of living a holy life as set forth in the Torah that God revealed to Israel. So it appears that the theoretical underpinnings of this ethical system are straightforward. What makes any particular action morally right or wrong is simply that God has commanded or proscribed it.[3] Moreover, if morality is defined simply as God's command communicated through the Torah, then the epistemological question is equally easy to answer: Jews know their moral duties through study of Torah. Indeed, from this perspective, you can understand the enormous authority vested in the rabbis, for their deep knowledge of Torah gives them access to divinely ordained moral rules that they alone are qualified to interpret for the community. Classical Judaism, then, exemplifies a "divine command morality," a moral system that has its authority and sanction in God's revelation of moral rules and principles.

The situation is not nearly as simple as this quick summary would suggest, however. It is correct to say that the revelation of God's will to Israel established an exclusive covenant, the terms of which are preserved in Torah, yet revelation, covenant, and Torah are complex concepts, subject to quite diverse interpretations. Does the text of the Torah fully exhaust God's revelation? Do its laws specify fully the terms of the covenant or merely provide an outline of those terms? Does Torah specify Israel's covenantal duties fully or only minimally? The answers to these questions will determine to a large extent how to answer the theoretical questions posed earlier about the nature of Jewish ethics.

Sometimes Scripture describes the covenant in a legalistic way, suggesting that the totality of God's revelation is contained in the Torah's many rules. The language of Deuteronomy 4:44–45 is typical: "This is the Teaching that Moses set before the Israelites: these are the exhortations, laws, and rules that Moses addressed to the people of Israel, after they had left Egypt." Similarly, Deuteronomy, Chapter 28, which contains a lengthy list of blessings for those who "observe faithfully all God's commandments" together with a list of curses for those who do not, concludes with the words, "These are the terms of the covenant which the Lord commanded Moses to conclude with the Israelites in the land of Moab, in addition to the covenant which God had made with them at Horeb" (verse 69). On this view, the Torah constitutes a written contract.[4] The terms of God's relationship with Israel are finite, encompassed fully by the detailed laws found in Scripture.[5] Yet other biblical passages suggest a more holistic view of covenant:

> And now, O Israel, what does the Lord your God demand of you? Only this: to revere the Lord your God, to walk only in His paths, to love Him, and to serve the Lord your God with all your heart and soul, keeping the Lord's commandments and laws, which I enjoin upon you today, for your good. (Deuteronomy 10:12–13)

> Do what is right and good in the sight of the Lord, that it may go well with you and that you may be able to possess the good land that the Lord your God promised on oath to your fathers. (Deuteronomy 6:18)[6]

He has told you, O man, what is good, and what the Lord requires of you: Only
to do justice and to love goodness and to walk modestly with your God. (Micah
6:9)

Doing "what is right and good in the sight of the Lord" and "walking modestly with
God" are metaphors that suggest a more fluid, less static, definition of moral duty.
The moral life, in this view, is not, perhaps cannot be, contained fully within the pre-
scriptions and proscriptions of the written law. In this view, observing the laws enu-
merated in the text is only part of what God demands. For one thing, those who
scrupulously observe the law might nonetheless lack true reverence or love of God.
The covenant demands that Israelites not only conform to a set regimen but also
inwardly possess the proper attitude toward God. Moreover, loving and serving God
wholeheartedly might take any number of forms. The specific laws that God enjoins,
while indispensable, might be suggestive rather than exhaustive, a bare minimum
rather than a thorough compendium. From this perspective, it seems, the covenantal relationship is too fluid to be reduced to a legal formula.[7] Or, put another way,
obeying God's will is not synonymous with observing all the moral rules contained in
the Torah.

Insofar as this covenant between God and Israel is a legal contract, its
demands are finite and reducible to writing. The text of Torah spells out the terms of
the relationship, and what is not stated explicitly can be inferred from its words.
Insofar as the covenant is a holistic relationship, however, it is, like all human relationships, dynamic. The demands that it makes cannot be fixed in advance or set in
stone once and for all time. Israel's duties, from this perspective, are potentially infinite; they arise not from the text of Torah or even from the interpretations of that
text but from living in relationship with God.[8] "Keeping God's commandments,
statutes and ordinances" is in the realm of covenant as contract; "walking modestly
with God" is in the realm of covenant as interpersonal relationship. These two views
of covenant point to divergent ways of understanding the scope and meaning of
God's revelation to Israel in Torah, and the Jews' vision of revelation and Torah has
everything to do with the way they understand Jewish ethics, especially in relationship to Jewish law.

In their own way, the ancient rabbis continued this discussion of whether God's
ethical demands of Israel are fully exhausted by the law or whether, conversely,
Judaism has an extralegal ethic. Those within the tradition who argue for the existence of moral norms independent of the law point to a number of concepts and
texts. The most often cited example of a so called "extralegal" morality in Judaism is
the concept of acting *lifnim mishurat hadin*, "beyond the line of the law."[9] The tradition frequently praises those who go "above and beyond" their legal duty when this
will benefit another party. In cases of *lifnim mishurat hadin*, then, one does more than
the law requires (or, what amounts to the same thing, presses one's rights less strictly
than the law permits). One source even states that it was the Israelites' failure to act
lifnim mishurat hadin that was responsible for the destruction of Jerusalem,[10] which
suggests just how important such an extralegal ethic might be. Other terms of moral

praise within rabbinic sources appear to denote upholding a moral standard more demanding than the law. At times the rabbis refer to *middat ḥasidut*, "the trait or quality of piety," which signifies a level of moral behavior characteristic or expected of certain exemplary individuals but more exacting than the standard to which others are held.[11] Likewise, in many instances it is noted that "the sages are pleased" with the individual who helps others, even when the law does not require him or her to do so.[12] All this strongly suggests that some moral actions, even if "extralegal" in some sense, are nonetheless part of what God expects of Israel.

In addition to these sources are texts suggesting that moral considerations sometimes entered into the development of the law itself. In other words, at times the sages appear to construe legal duty in a particular way precisely because this accords with their moral judgments. Perhaps the classic example of this is the rabbinic understanding of Exodus 21:24, "an eye for an eye and a tooth for a tooth."[13] The sages interpret this to mean that one must pay monetary compensation to the victim equal to the value of an eye or a tooth, not that one should engage in physical retribution.[14] The plain meaning of the Biblical rule presumably became objectionable in light of the moral standards of a later age. As a result, the application of the law had to be changed to accord with accepted principles of ethical conduct. Similarly, it is argued that sometimes the rabbis, when faced with a conflict between a biblical law and their moral principles, would limit the application of the law so severely that it became effectively inoperative. For example, in their treatment of the biblical laws regarding capital punishment, the rabbis introduced extraordinarily stringent conditions that had to be met before a person could be convicted of a capital offense. Given that the rabbis could not directly abrogate a biblical law, their strategy apparently was to interpret it out of existence. In doing so, they clearly, if indirectly, expressed their moral condemnation of capital punishment as the Torah prescribed it.[15]

These sources have been variously interpreted by rabbis who have attempted to explain the nature of Jewish ethics.[16] Some have argued that Judaism acknowledges a realm of ethics quite independent of the written law. On this view, ethics is dynamic and open ended as distinct from the written law, which is static and unchangeable. Broad ethical principles—such as compassion for the marginalized in society, freedom for the oppressed, equal justice for all—must guide the interpretation of the law, for without constant reinterpretation in light of these moral principles, the written law would quickly become archaic and inapplicable to the moral realities of contemporary Jews. In some instances, it would even yield immoral results. Hence, if the Torah's statutes about slavery or capital punishment appear to violate one of these basic moral principles, those rules must be reinterpreted. To use a more recent example, if the halakhah places women at a legal disadvantage, it must be reinterpreted in light of Jews' moral understanding about the essential equality of men and women. The moral principles so invoked may themselves be grounded in Torah and Jewish tradition, although they may (as in the case of feminism) also be prompted and shaped by secular and non-Jewish moral systems. The point is that this theory of Jewish ethics construes ethics as separate (in both content and origin) from law and not fully contained within Torah, though intertwined with it. Theologically speaking, God imbues Jews with wisdom and moral insight, gained in part through the words of revelation, but also in part through the experience of living in relationship with God and with one another. Jews' moral experience in this broad sense both tutors their interpretation of the Torah's moral rules and enables them to navigate the situations that those rules do not explicitly address.

Other people have insisted that the sources reviewed here, which appear to differentiate between legal and extralegal Jewish ethics, mark "a distinction without a difference." In this view, the Torah provides detailed moral instruction in the form of laws together with more general principles of ethics that are meant to fill in the inevitable gaps in the legal system. Jewish morality, then, is two-tiered: One dimension is captured in the law, another in the situational, extralegal dimensions of the tradition, but both dimensions derive from God, and both have their source in Torah. Indeed, it is this second dimension of ethics that the Torah intends when it prescribes "you shall do the right and the good in the eyes of the Lord" (Deuteronomy 6:18). As one contemporary scholar puts it, "traditional halakhic Judaism demands of the Jew both adherence to Halakhah and commitment to an ethical moment that, although different from Halakhah, is nevertheless of a piece with it and in its own way fully imperative."[17] This theory of Jewish ethics presumes that ethics derives from the same source as law and that the content of ethics, although not identical with law, is fully consistent with it. Thus, ethics and law are never in tension with one another, but are fully complementary. In theological terms, God's will as revealed in Torah provides both concrete rules for living a moral life and points Jews toward a model of righteousness significantly more extensive than those rules alone.

Still others have insisted, based on their reading of the very same sources, that there can be no distinction whatsoever between law and ethics in Judaism. As they note, the rabbis never explicitly criticized any biblical law as immoral, and they frequently blurred the distinctions mentioned earlier by insisting that these "extralegal" standards of morality were, in fact, backed by the full force of the law. To suppose that the law is in need of "reinterpretation" or even "supplementation" by ethics is to imply that the law itself is less than perfect, that is, that it is not fully divine. From one perspective, this is heretical for, as the Psalmist says, "the teaching [or law] of the Lord is perfect" (Psalm 19:8). In this view, the principles employed in legal interpretation are internal to the legal system; they do not reside in a realm of ethics separate from the law. Whatever the rabbis meant by their use of the terms *lifnim mishurat hadin* and *middat hasidut*, they surely did not mean to imply that God's law is less than perfectly moral or that the person who obeys the law scrupulously is in need of moral instruction from any other source. The theological perspective underlying this position is simply that God's revelation in Torah is complete and perfect, that the law as written in Torah and interpreted by the rabbis is the sum and substance of Jewish ethics. It follows that if the law as stated is patently immoral, we human beings must have misinterpreted it.

Even this brief overview of the debates about the relationship of law and ethics in Judaism should help you to understand why it is so difficult to answer definitively the basic questions of moral theory with which we began: How do we define morality and how do we know our moral obligations? Depending on the interpretation of the ambiguous evidence found in classical Jewish texts, we might answer that ethics is (1) separable from revelation and Torah and constitutes an independent (or semi-independent) realm of obligation, (2) part and parcel of God's revelation, contained in Torah next to law and fully consistent with it, or (3) simply synonymous with the law contained in the Torah. These different ways of understanding the nature of Jewish ethics, of course, lead inevitably to different ways of answering the epistemological question of how Jews come to discover their moral duties.

Those who define Jewish ethics in terms of law will be inclined to adopt a formalist approach to moral reasoning. After all, if the content of God's revelation is essentially legal, it must be interpreted accordingly. Matters of consistency, predictability, and logical coherence must be considered. Moral authority will be vested in legal experts, rabbis, whose moral discernment will rely on the creation and application of rules and principles, the search for precedents, and the use of analogies. As Elliot Dorff has written, "The Covenant model . . . provides the basis for Jewish legal development, for God not only commands but enters into a legal relationship through the Covenant. Therefore such legal techniques as interpretation, usage, and recourse to course of dealings became appropriate legal techniques to give meaning to the parties' original relationship."[18] Of course, Jewish authorities over the centuries have produced a voluminous and complex legal literature precisely because they have understood the covenant and its terms as fundamentally legal. To this day, many rabbis and Jewish ethicists continue to offer ethical guidance by combing this literature for precedents and drawing out their implications for contemporary situations.

Those who have understood the scope of the covenant in more holistic terms have adopted a less formalistic and systematic approach to moral reasoning. They have placed less emphasis on interpreting the *words* of the text (whether biblical or rabbinic) than on intuiting and appropriating the *spirit* of divine instruction. They focus less on defining a uniform system of ethical behavior than on exploring the inner motivations and intentionality that is expressed through moral acts and that, for them, is the essence of the moral life. Through the use of stories and the examples of extraordinarily pious individuals (*tzaddikim*), these ethicists have sought to inspire a type of moral life that cannot be defined by adherence to rules alone. Because they understand the covenantal relationship between God and Israel in more interpersonal terms, their style of moral reasoning is fluid and suggestive rather than concrete and definitive. This sort of pietistic moral literature was especially popular in the medieval period, the best known example being Bahya ibn Pakuda's *Duties of the Heart*, but it was revitalized in the **musar** movement[19] and in hasidic[20] circles. It continues to exert an influence on modern Jewish thinkers such as Martin Buber and, more recently, Eugene Borowitz, who writes that his own brand of liberal Jewish ethics consists less "in obedient observance than in authentically living in Covenant."[21]

This review of Jewish moral theory is necessarily inconclusive for, as you have seen, the sources are consistent with several divergent ways of understanding the nature of morality and Jews' knowledge of it. However, broad general areas of agreement exist within the tradition that should be noted. Invariably, Jews define their moral duties within the context of their covenantal relationship with God. That implies that morality is defined in relationship to God's will as expressed (at least partly) in Torah and as interpreted by rabbis (however that interpretive process is understood). Because morality is invariably defined in the context of that covenant, it is always discovered in the context of the community and its collective traditions. The notion that something such as individual conscience is the ultimate moral authority is nowhere to be found in the classical sources, for this would suggest that the individual is a higher moral authority than is the community or that moral truths could be discovered without reference to the Torah and its interpreters. Classical Judaism is hospitable to several ways of understanding the underpinnings of the moral life, but it cannot imagine such a life divorced from the Jewish community and its historic relationship with God or from Torah in its broadest sense. Torah is the primary (if not necessarily exhaustive or exclusive) source of truth and so points Jews to a life of holiness.

UNIVERSAL ETHICS

The evidence of a universal morality within Judaism is widespread. From the very beginning, the Hebrew Bible has portrayed human beings as moral creatures who have been placed in a world fraught with moral challenges. As the opening stories in Genesis amply attest, God created human beings as moral agents, creatures with specific cognitive capacities that enable them to make moral decisions. The central theme of the second creation story (Genesis 2–4) is that human beings possess free will either to obey or disobey God's commands. In her dialogue with the serpent, Eve clearly indicates that she understands that eating this fruit is wrong (Genesis 3:2–3). Moreover, both she and Adam display shame and guilt when God discovers that they have eaten the forbidden fruit (Genesis 3:8–13). The fact that God punishes them further reinforces the view that the biblical writers imagined human beings as inherently moral agents, capable of distinguishing right from wrong and of freely choosing a course of action for which they must be held accountable. Subsequently, when Cain murders his brother Abel, God reprimands Cain with the words, "What have you done? Hark, your brother's blood cries out to Me from the ground" (Genesis 4:10). Clearly, without having received any prior moral instruction, the exchange (and Cain's subsequent punishment) assumes that Cain should have known that his behavior was immoral. The same perspective informs the flood story, in which God sees the wickedness of humankind and so resolves to destroy the world but saves Noah, for he is "a righteous man; he was blameless in his age" (Genesis 6:9). Here again we see that the biblical authors conceived of God as establishing a moral relationship with humanity and of human beings as creatures capable of moral discernment long before God established a specific covenantal relationship with Israel.[22]

Moreover, even after the Sinaitic covenant, God continues to have a moral relationship with non-Jews. This is especially evident in the prophetic writings, in which God excoriates the non-Jewish peoples for their immorality and warns them of the consequences of their behavior:

> "For three transgressions of Damascus, for four, I will not revoke it [their punishment.]" (Amos 1:3; the same prophetic oracle is pronounced against Tyre, Edom, the Ammonites, Moab, and finally the Israelites themselves)
>
> "Now the word of the Lord came to Jonah son of Amitai: Go at once to Nineveh, that great city, and proclaim judgment upon it; for their wickedness has come before me." (Jonah 1:1–2)

The view that God judges all nations for their transgressions is also reflected in the Psalms:

> the fields and everything in them exult; then shall all the trees of the forest shout for joy at the presence of the Lord, for God is coming, for God is coming to rule the earth; God will rule the world justly and its peoples in faithfulness." (Psalm 96:12–13; also Psalm 98:8–9)

Although the Bible is clear that non-Jews have moral duties and that God calls them to account for their moral behavior, it remains unclear just what these moral duties are and how non-Jews are assumed to know them. In fact, no biblical text directly explores the theoretical foundations of this universal morality. The answers to these questions can only be inferred from the biblical sources through a process of reflection on the theological assumptions implicit in these biblical stories about the moral responsibilities of non-Jews. Two ways of construing the foundation of universal moral duties present themselves; both are equally plausible on the basis of the biblical evidence. The difference between them depends, as you shall see, on divergent ways of understanding the implications of creation.

Creation (particularly in contrast to revelation) is the theological category through which God is related to humanity as a whole. For just this reason, it is God's creation of humankind that provides the context in which a Jewish theory of universal morality takes shape. After all, everything of moral significance about humans—their moral natures, the ways in which they interact with others and the very conditions of their existence—derives from the fact that God creates and sustains human life. The question, then, is what God's creation of the world and humankind says about universal morality.

On the one hand, it may be that certain moral laws are "natural," simply embedded in the structure of the social world just as certain laws of physics are embedded in the structure of the natural world. In this view, God created the conditions of human life in a way that automatically gives authority to certain moral values. Because human life is inherently social, those attitudes and behaviors that contribute to smooth social relationships, such as respect for the life and property of others, are universally "good," and the converse attitudes are "bad." Because cooperation between human beings is necessary for survival, actions that facilitate cooperation are "naturally" moral, and actions that inhibit it are immoral. Because society would quickly disintegrate if murder and theft were rampant, these things are innately wrong. In short, the biblical authors may have assumed that God established certain basic moral standards simply by creating human life in this particular way. Morality is simply part of the fabric of human social life as God created it.

This view is reflected in a talmudic comment on Leviticus 18:5 ("You shall keep my laws and my rules") in which the rabbis distinguish biblical "laws" from moral "rules": "This [rules] refers to those commands which, had they not been written, should rightly have been written. These include the prohibition of idolatry, adultery, bloodshed, and blasphemy."[23] The rabbis recognized that some moral rules were obvious and so could be known independent of their being commanded in Scripture, indeed, independent from any knowledge of God at all. For human beings to live peacefully with one another, certain moral constraints must be observed. Thus, morality is universal, for it is embedded in unchanging features of human life. Knowing what morality demands requires no theological knowledge whatever, only an awareness of the human condition and the constraints that it places upon human beings.

On the other hand, universal morality may be grounded in the view that God created human beings "in God's image" (Genesis 1:27). The text of Genesis never specifies just what being created in the divine image means, but the point may be that implanted within us is something essentially divine and that this is what gives human life its value and moral direction. Because every person shares equally in this divine quality, each person is equally valuable and deserving of respect. Moreover, being created in God's image may imply something about the goal, as well as the origin, of human life. If humans are in some respect like God, then arguably their purpose is to actualize that divine potential within them. The more closely humans imitate God's qualities, such as righteousness and compassion, the more fully they fulfill their purpose, which is to make human life godly.

This view is reflected in the one explicit moral commandment that God gives to all humanity in the early chapters of Genesis.

> But for your own life-blood I will require a reckoning: I will require it of every beast; of man, too, will I require a reckoning for human life, of every man for that of his fellow man. Whoever sheds the blood of man, by man shall his blood be shed; for in God's image did God make man. (Genesis 9:5–6)

Human life is valuable, indeed sacred, because it is divine in character. To willfully take another innocent human life is to defile the image of God. Later rabbinic authorities similarly saw the creation of human life in God's image as a central moral principle.

> 'Love your neighbor as yourself.' (Leviticus 19:18) Rabbi Akiva said: This is a great principle of the Torah. Ben Azzai said: The verse "This is the record of Adam's line. When God created man, God made him in the likeness of God" (Genesis 5:1) is an even greater principle. For you must not say, "Since I have

been humiliated, let my fellow also be humiliated; since I have been cursed, let my neighbor also be cursed." For, as Rabbi Tanhuma said, if you act thus, know whom it is that you are willing to humiliate—"one whom God made in His likeness."[24]

In this view, then, morality is defined in terms of being created in God's image, which dictates the ways in which we must respect the divine spark within human life.

These two views provide contrasting theories of what makes a particular action morally right or wrong. In the first view, murder is wrong because it undermines society, which in turn is necessary for human life. In the language of moral philosophers, this perspective is "teleological" insofar as it defines morality in terms of the consequences of people's acts. The primary good is human flourishing, which requires social cooperation; morality is defined in terms of that which facilitates or impedes this goal. In the second view, murder is wrong because it constitutes an assault on God's image in the world and because it fails to recognize the divine value of each human life. This perspective is "deontological," for it defines morality in terms of the intrinsic quality of certain acts. Acts that respect the divine character of human life (or, as some would put it, that reflect God's attributes) are moral, quite apart from their consequences. On both accounts, it should be noted, God is the source of morality, but in different ways. In the first account, morality is defined as what puts humans in sync with the natural conditions of human life as God created them. In the second account, morality is defined as what links humans to God, or what is consistent with respect for the godly part of human beings.

These two views have different implications for the answer to the epistemological question asked earlier: How do humans come to know their moral responsibilities? If universal morality is understood as "natural," it seems that people need no special instruction in morality, for awareness of these universal moral rules is either (1) programmed into human consciousness or (2) immediately discernable through the use of human reason. Again, the biblical authors never speculate on this directly, for they may have assumed that, insofar as all human beings are conscious of their sociality, they are aware of the moral rules that flow from it. Moral knowledge, in this view, is an innate part of human consciousness no less than the capacity for imagination or for cognition in general. Non-Jews no less than Jews have knowledge of certain basic moral rules because God created them either with this knowledge or with the capacity to discover it.

This way of thinking about universal morality accords nicely with an oft-quoted rabbinic text: "If Torah had not been given, we could have learned modesty from the cat, aversion to robbery from the ant, chastity from the dove and sexual mores from the rooster."[25] Insofar as some moral knowledge does not depend on special revelation (we would know it "even if Torah had not been given"), it is accessible in principle to all people through their observations of the way the world works.

Later Jewish thinkers tend to attribute this universal moral knowledge to the exercise of human reason. This view had perhaps its clearest expression in the work of Babylonian sage, Saadia Gaon (882–942 C.E.), who distinguished between rational and ritual commandments. The former include the requirements of gratitude and reverence and the prohibition against aggression toward others. All of these, in Saadia's words, are dictated or "required by reason" (Hebrew, *ha-sekhel mehayyeb*). When Saadia discusses the prohibition against bloodshed in particular, he adduces the following reasoning:

> Wisdom lays down that bloodshed must be prevented among human beings, for if it were allowed people would annihilate each other. That would mean, apart from the pain suffered, a frustration of the purpose which the Wise (God) intended to achieve through them. Homicide cuts them off from the attainment of any purpose He created and employs them for.[26]

Wisdom or reason enables all human beings to recognize that certain types of behavior are morally wrong, for they run counter to the very nature and purpose of human life. In short, universal morality is imbedded in the nature of human social life, and its dictates are readily discernable to anyone capable of reflecting on that fact.

The second theory of universal morality, however, points to a different answer to the question of how humans know their moral obligations. If being created in God's image provides the foundation for universal ethics, then this fact must have been communicated to non-Jews in some way. This idea is conveyed in the rabbinic comment that

> humans are beloved, for they were created in the image of God. They are still more beloved, for it was made known to them that they were created in the image of God, as it is written, "For in God's image did God make man." (Genesis 9:6)[27]

Of course, Scripture offers no account of God's "making known" to the pre-Israelite peoples that they were created in God's image. Perhaps, according to this source, human beings have some sort of intuitive knowledge of this fact, or perhaps the point is simply that this information is available to anyone who takes the time to become familiar with Hebrew Scripture. In either case, the central point is that, if non-Jews know that all people are created in God's image, they also can be assumed to know the moral implications of this fact.

Thus far I have explored two ways of understanding the biblical sources about creation and their bearing on the question of universal morality. The rabbis also explored this question through the concept of Noahide law, the belief that all descendants of Noah—that is, all humankind—were obligated to observe seven basic rules.[28] The following passage is in Tosefta Abodah Zarah 8:4:

> Seven commandments were the sons of Noah commanded: concerning adjudication, concerning idolatry, concerning blasphemy, concerning sexual immorality, concerning bloodshed, and concerning robbery and concerning [eating] a limb torn from a living animal.[29]

Curiously, these specific commandments were derived by the rabbis through a complicated and rather far-fetched explication of Genesis 2:16 ("And the Lord God commanded the man saying, 'Of every tree of the garden you are free to eat'"), a commandment given to Adam and Eve actually, not to Noah.[30] While there seems to have been some disagreement among the sages about the precise number and content of the moral laws incumbent upon non-Jews,[31] the "seven commandments of the Noahides" became the way in which the rabbis most frequently referred to the universal moral law.

David Novak, following a tradition that extends back perhaps as far as the Jewish philosopher Philo in the first century C.E., has identified the body of Noahide law with the concept of "natural law," the basic moral rules imbedded in the nature of human life, society, and the natural order. There is some plausibility to this view, for at least four of the seven—the prohibitions against sexual immorality, bloodshed, and robbery, and the admonition to establish courts ("adjudication")—relate directly to the smooth functioning of society and the conditions for human flourishing. As for blasphemy, idolatry, and eating a limb torn from a living animal, Novak argues that these are fundamentally about curbing the tendency toward human violence. Indeed, for Novak, the whole significance of the Noahide law is precisely that it addresses human nature as God created it and so serves as the backdrop and foundation for God's specific revelation of the Torah to Israel.[32]

Despite the plausibility of Novak's thesis, it must be conceded that the rabbis never offer a theory to explain the moral underpinnings of Noahide law. They do not explicitly link these rules to the "natural" conditions of human life or to the creation of humankind in God's image. The only explanation for these rules is that God commanded them. The language consistently used in reference to the Noahide laws is that the gentiles "received" or "accepted" these "commandments," precisely the same language used to describe the Israelites' taking upon themselves all of the divine commandments found in the Torah. Because Scripture never records God's direct revelation of these rules to the peoples of the world (and since the rabbis were surely aware that they themselves had derived them only through exegesis),[33] this immediately poses a problem: How would non-Jews know of their obligations under Noahide law?

The rabbis considered two possibilities: (1) non-Jews actually received this body of divine revelation through Torah and (2) the Noahide law is rational. The first possibility is reflected in the following source, which suggests that the nations of the world actually studied the Torah.

> Rabbi Judah says that they [priests] wrote the Torah on the stones of the altar [of the Temple; an apparent reference to Deuteronomy 27:8]. They [students] said to him [Rabbi Judah], "how did the nations of the world learn the Torah?" He said to them, "God put the desire in their hearts and they sent scribes and they copied the script from the stones in seventy languages." At that time the judgment of the nations of the world was sealed [for they were condemned to] the lowest pit [insofar as they then knew their obligations, but failed to observe them]."[34]

Quite apart from the obviously contrived and fanciful elements of this explanation, it addresses an important theological and moral problem: If Noahide law is supposed to have been revealed to non-Jews by God and if Scripture never records that this happened, the only possibility appears to be that the non-Jews learned of their divine commandments through the Torah's account of them. In this view, there really is only one record of divine revelation—Torah—although some part of Torah was directed to non-Jews and made availabile to them through dissemination of the text.

A second possibility is reflected in the following well-known source from Maimonides.[35]

> Any one [i.e., non-Jew] who accepts the seven commandments and is meticulous in observing them is thereby one of the righteous of the nations of the world, and has a portion in the world to come. This is only the case if one accepts them and observes them because God commanded them in the Torah, and taught us through our teacher, Moses, that the children of Noah were commanded to observe them even before the Torah was given. But if one observes them because they are rationally compelling, such a person is not a resident-alien and is not one of the righteous of the nations of the world, but he is one of their wise men.[36]

The main point of Maimonides' discussion, for the current purpose, is his acknowledgment that the Noahide laws could be observed by non-Jews either because they recognized the divine authority behind the laws (as in the earlier explanation) or on the basis of their own reason. The latter possibility suggests that at least some rabbis understood this Noahide law as grounded in human reason. That is, these seven rules are universal precisely because their wisdom is accessible to everyone through the use of reason, a view in line with the positions of Saadia Gaon and David Novak previously noted. Indeed, Maimonides seems to assume that this is the usual basis for non-Jewish adherence to the Noahide law given that the person who observes these laws because they are divinely ordained is an exceptional individual, "one of the righteous of the nations."[37]

In the last analysis, the rabbinic doctrine of Noahide law recapitulates the views that can be deduced from other biblical and rabbinic sources. Universal morality is defined either in terms of the principles and rules required by the conditions of human life or in relation to the fact that human beings, like the God in whose image they were created, deserve to be treated respectfully. The epistemological question—how non-Jews come to know their moral obligations—can also be answered in a range of ways. Some sources suggest that moral knowledge arises either through reflection (intuitive or rational) on human experience and the way the world works or through acceptance of God's revelation of a specific body of moral rules as contained in Torah.

THE RELATIONSHIP BETWEEN JEWISH AND UNIVERSAL ETHICS

As has been discussed, Judaism recognizes two moral systems, one binding on Jews by virtue of their special covenant with God and another binding on all humankind by virtue of the way God has created us. It might be easiest to visualize these two moralities as two concentric circles, one small circle enclosed within another, far larger one. The small inner circle represents those universal moral obligations—including the prohibitions against homicide and theft—that can be known either intuitively or through human reason; the larger circle, which includes these moral rules together with an extensive system of halakhic ethics, has been communicated to Israel through Torah. On the level of moral content, Jewish ethics encompasses all of universal ethics and a good deal more. Indeed, it is a principle within the tradition that nothing prohibited to gentiles is permitted to Jews while nothing permitted to Jews is prohibited to gentiles.[38]

In turning to issues of moral theory, however, the relationship between Jewish and universal ethics is more difficult to sort out. The issue is most easily expressed with reference to those concentric circles. For Jews, what is the foundation of those universal moral norms represented by the inner circle? In a sense, they are obligatory in two separate ways: first, because they are affirmed by reason, or known by intuition, which is universal, and, second, because the Torah has commanded them. If these norms are obligatory for Jews on account of their "reasonableness" and if Jews (like gentiles) know these obligations in some natural, rational way, then God's commandments in the Torah with respect to these things are entirely superfluous. Surely God did not need to issue special commandments to inform Jews of the moral duties that all people can recognize on their own. On the other hand, if these moral duties are incumbent upon Jews solely by virtue of their being specifically commanded in the Torah, what difference does it make that they are also incumbent by reason of their universality? What role, if any, does reason play in justifying these moral norms if Torah already sanctions them? In short, for Jews, these universal moral norms are "overdetermined," obligatory in two separate senses or for two sets of reasons. How does Judaism explain the relationship between these two theoretical foundations for the same set of moral duties?

Again, this theoretical question is never raised or addressed explicitly by talmudic sources, but the theological perspectives that inform various answers to this dilemma can be found throughout the tradition. Indeed, it will be easiest to grasp the problem of the relationship between universal and Jewish ethics if we bring the theological issues to the fore; as we have already seen, universal ethics is grounded in God's *creation* of humankind, while Jewish ethics is grounded in God's *revelation* of Torah to Israel. To consider the relationship between universal and Jewish ethics is to consider *the relationship between creation and revelation*. The question at hand is this: How is the moral order that God has created naturally and for all of humanity related to the moral order that God has revealed "supernaturally" for Israel alone? At stake, then, is the relationship between the whole moral system that governs gentiles and that which governs Jews.

Within the history of Judaism, the relationship between creation and revelation has sometimes been viewed as sequential and *progressive*. From this perspective, creation is only a prelude to revelation in the history of God's relationship to the world. God's will is only partially revealed to humanity at large but is fully revealed to Israel at Sinai. It follows that the normative order established through covenant and Torah takes precedence over that established through creation. Any universal moral law, then, is but a precursor to Torah and is necessarily subordinated to it.

This view finds expression in midrashic statements that, in God's mind, "the thought of creating Israel preceded all else" and "the world and the fullness thereof were created only for the sake of Torah."[39] God's purpose in creation can be fulfilled only through revelation. In effect, Rashi expresses this view in his famous commentary on Genesis 1:1. The Torah begins with God's creation of the world, he suggests, so that when Israel comes to possess the land and expel the native inhabitants, they can appeal to the fact that God has created the world and can give it to whomever God chooses. For Rashi, the whole purpose of creation is to justify Israel's place in the world. Such a view, of course, places special emphasis on the doctrine of Israel's chosenness. Israel possesses moral truths (and others as well) unknown to the rest of the world, and to this extent the differences between Jews and non-Jews are more significant than the similarities.[40]

On the other hand, the relationship between creation and revelation may be viewed as *correlative* and *complementary*. From this perspective, creation and revelation are separate, but related, modes through which God's will is made known to the world. Creation establishes a normative world that retains its own integrity even after the Torah is given. Thus, God's engagement with the world does not involve a simple progression from creation to revelation, or from humanity as a whole to the chosen people, but operates differently in different spheres and among different peoples. This point of view has been expressed most cogently by David Novak:

> even though the covenant between God and Israel transcends nature, it still accepts nature as a limit (*peras*) and its own precondition. Jews are human beings who have been elected through the covenant, but they are still human beings within the natural order of things. Nature, constituted as the covenant's general background and horizon, is not overcome.[41]

It follows that Jews have a double relationship to God, first as human beings and second as members of the covenanted community. Those who adopt this view of creation and revelation, then, will necessarily be inclined to stress the similarities as well as the differences between Israel and the rest of humanity.

Although this position is not developed explicitly within classical sources, it is consistent with a certain way of reading those early texts in Genesis. You will remember that the biblical text appears to assume some kind of moral knowledge among the earliest generations of humankind. That moral knowledge, whether intuitive or rational, continues to function for Jews even after the Torah has been given. After all, Israelites do not lose their natural, human moral faculties when they enter their covenant with God. It follows that Jews, together with the rest of humanity, know certain moral norms such as the prohibition against bloodshed "naturally" without benefit of the Torah. To just this extent, they inhabit the same moral universe as their gentile neighbors, notwithstanding the fact that they are the recipients of God's revelation as well.

The contrast between these two perspectives is important for an understanding of Jewish moral theory. For those with a sequential view of creation and revelation, both nature and reason are subordinated to Torah and revelation. The natural order as God created it is only the backdrop and prelude to the supernatural order established by God through the revelation of Torah to Israel. Once Torah is given, all prior moral instruction for Jews becomes strictly preliminary. To suggest that natural or universal moral principles could retain an integrity of their own for Jews entails the virtually heretical suggestions that Torah is not the comprehensive expression of God's will and that Israel is not the focal point of God's plan for the world.[42] Similarly, reason as a source of truth (moral or otherwise) is superceded by revelation. Indeed, as many religious thinkers over the centuries have noted, revelation itself seems to imply that whatever we can know of God's will on the basis of our own rational capacity is not sufficient. According to this view, for Jews there can be only one moral truth (Torah), one mode for receiving it (revelation), and one community that is defined by it (Israel). Gentiles, by contrast, remain within the realm of nature and the moral law that is embedded within it. In theological terms, God has established one moral universe for gentiles through the order of nature and another for Jews through the dictates of Torah. The moral order grounded in creation, which is valid for gentiles, is thoroughly superceded by the moral universe that God creates for Jews through revelation.

For those with a correlative and complementary view of creation and revelation, on the other hand, the norms established through God's creation retain their validity even after God reveals a new set of moral norms through Torah. From this perspective, the natural order constitutes a source of moral instruction, a "natural torah," as it were, more limited in scope than the Torah revealed at Sinai but significant nonetheless. And reason functions as a vehicle for discovering these universal moral norms, insofar as God has created all humans (Jews included) with the capacity to understand human nature and the order of existence. Accordingly, there are two parallel sources of moral truth, one universal, determined by nature and discovered by reason, and the other particular, determined by revelation and discovered in the words of Torah. Jews, when they enter the covenant with God, do not "opt out" of the natural order that encompasses all humanity. Jews and gentiles inhabit partly overlapping moral universes, for their common humanity ensures that certain moral truths, grounded in creation and accessible through natural means, are equally binding on all.

These two perspectives do not exhaust the range of theological possibilities, but they do represent fundamental alternatives and perennial options within the tradition for understanding the theoretical underpinnings of the moral life. On the whole, it would seem, Orthodox Jewish thinkers have endorsed the former view, affirming the absoluteness of revelation over against creation. Accordingly, for Jews the moral implications of the created order have been minimized, together with the power of reason. This may account, at least in part, for the fact that historically many Jewish thinkers have regarded the Greek philosophical tradition with its emphasis on universal truths discoverable through reason with significant suspicion. By the same token, notwithstanding the affirmation of a Noahide law, Jewish thinkers have been less concerned to articulate the universal moral law than to expound the law operative within the covenant. God's will, on this view, is ultimately a mystery that we understand, if at all, only by the grace of divine revelation. The fact that human reason affirms some of the commandments is a happy coincidence from our standpoint and an irrelevance from God's.

Yet the alternative view continually reasserts itself. The moral implications of the human condition per se can be minimized, but they cannot be negated entirely. All human beings, including Jews, stand in a moral relationship to God; all have the capacity to discern God's will through the exercise of reason and through the observation of natural processes. If God's concern for humanity has not been channeled entirely through Israel, there must be a universal moral order, however limited. So the meaning and authority of Torah must be affirmed in a way that allows for an independent source of moral truth, one that operates outside of Torah for non-Jews and alongside Torah for Jews. Jewish philosophy continually reasserts itself as a response to this challenge of reconciling faith and reason or, in the present context, synthesizing the universal implications of creation with the particularist implications of revelation. In the pursuit of that goal, the rationality of some of God's laws will be greeted as opening the door to a kind of pluralism but inevitably at the expense of limiting Israel's distinctiveness as a moral community.[43]

This exploration of Jewish moral theory underscores again the importance of theology for Jewish ethics. Theological beliefs play a significant role in determining both the nature of moral obligation and the way we come to know those obligations, both for Jews and for humanity as a whole. By the same token, the way in which the moral obligations of Jews and of gentiles are related is at root a theological question. The fact that Jewish tradition provides no single clear view of these matters should be no more surprising than the fact that it encompasses diverse viewpoints on a whole range of questions in applied ethics. The central theological concepts of creation and revelation are complex and subtle. They do not dictate answers to moral questions on either the practical or theoretical level so much as they provide the context within which such questions are explored.

KEY POINTS

- Two important theoretical questions of ethics are what makes something morally right or wrong, and how do we come to know our moral obligations. Classical Jewish sources rarely address these questions directly, although various views may be gleaned from this literature.
- These questions are addressed within Judaism in two separate spheres, first with respect to the moral obligations of Jews (Jewish ethics) and second with respect to the moral obligations of all human beings (universal ethics).

- Jewish ethics places primary importance on divine revelation as the source of moral obligation and on study of Torah as the way Jews come to know their moral obligations. Still, some texts suggest a source of morality outside of the revealed law. The relationship between this "extralegal" morality and the law remains a matter of dispute among Jewish authorities.
- Universal ethics may be grounded in a belief in a natural moral order or in the idea that all people are created in God's image. Moral obligations could thus be known either through reason, intuition, or knowledge of the Bible's stories about the origins of humankind.
- The relationship between Jewish ethics and universal ethics is a matter of dispute within the tradition. In one model, the moral order established through God's revelation of Torah to Israel (Jewish ethics) *supercedes* the moral order established through God's creation of humankind (universal ethics). In another model, the moral order of creation remains valid for Jews *alongside* the moral order of revelation and Torah. In this view, reason and "natural law" operate within the Torah and exert some influence on the interpretation of Jewish law.

QUESTIONS TO CONSIDER

1. Judaism's teaching that Jews are the recipients of God's direct revelation and so have a special relationship with God means that they also have more numerous and more demanding moral (and ritual) obligations than do non-Jews. How can this be reconciled with the universalist dimensions of the tradition that sees all people as "children of God"?

2. What practical difference does it make if Jews understand their ethics as (a) entirely separate from the law, (b) encompassed within the law, or (c) synonymous with the law?

3. As noted, traditional Judaism endorses what some have called a "divine command" theory of morality. What is appealing about this view of morality? What is problematic about it?

4. "Natural law," the idea that a moral order is embedded in the nature of things as God created them, has some roots in Jewish moral thinking and has a long history within Roman Catholic "moral theology." What might natural law thinkers in these two traditions have in common? Where might they differ?

5. What moral theory makes the most sense to you? If someone asked you to explain what makes an act moral or immoral, and how you come to know what morality demands of you, what would you say?

Chapter Six

Jewish Ethics
in Modern Times

Summary

The chapter reviews the ideological and sociological changes that characterize modernity and outlines their impact on Jewish theology and the structure of Jewish life. It then investigates some of the key challenges for Jewish ethics as it develops in the context of a modern, secular, pluralistic society.

◆ ─────────────────────────────────────

Modernity challenges us to mediate between the Jewish truth we have inherited and cherish, and that which our surrounding culture deems worth embracing.[1]

To this point, you have learned about the character of Jewish ethics as it developed out of the biblical sources and was shaped by rabbinic authorities in ancient and medieval times. The ways in which Jewish ethics, both applied and theoretical, grew to encompass multiple voices and perspectives as it developed over a period of more than two millenia have been highlighted. At the same time, it is important not to overlook the ways in which certain basic aspects of Jewish ethics remained relatively constant throughout this period. First, the authority of God's word as recorded in Scripture and interpreted by the rabbis was never questioned. To live ethically was to live a holy life as defined by the rules and principles that God had ordained. In this context, people could certainly disagree about the details of how an individual should respond ethically in a given situation (and they did), but they did not question the basic proposition that God's moral instruction was revealed to them through the Hebrew Bible and its authoritative interpretation in the writings of the rabbis. Moreover, the notion that God was the creator of the universe and the author of human history, that human life was invested with divine purpose and that human

129

history would one day reach its messianic culmination was assumed to be fundamentally true (though, again, interpretations abounded). In short, the theological triad discussed in Chapter Two, creation-revelation-redemption, remained the unshakable foundation of Jewish thought, just as the basic values and virtues discussed in Chapter Four remained cornerstones of Jewish moral life.

Throughout this period, that is, from about the first until the sixteenth century C.E., the basic sociopolitical situation of the Jews remained relatively constant. Following the destruction of the Temple by the Romans in 70 C.E. and their subsequent exile from the land of Israel, the Jews always lived as "outsiders." This expressed itself most plainly in the fact that Jews were assumed to constitute a foreign element, as indeed they were, wherever they lived. Their legal status was frequently in flux, and so they could be banished from one country or province to another at the whim of local political or religious authorities. A distinct national/ethnic group, they understood themselves, after all, as a people who had been exiled from their own land by God as punishment for their sins and who one day would be returned there to reestablish their ancient commonwealth. They continued to pray and frequently to write their religious literature in Hebrew, the language of their ancestors; they observed their religious festivals in accordance with their ancient lunar calendar rather than the Gregorian calendar used by their Christian neighbors; and they maintained varying degrees of autonomy (depending on the specific time and place), which sometimes included the right to collect taxes from members of the Jewish community and their own system of rabbinic courts, which adjudicated issues among Jews. In all these ways, Jews lived in communities that were highly differentiated from the larger societies in which they lived, although they were by no means insulated or immune from the influence of those societies.

THE CHALLENGES OF MODERNITY

Beginning with the Enlightenment in the sixteenth and seventeenth centuries, all this began to change. The age of exploration expanded the intellectual horizons of Europeans even as it forced them to alter their geographical image of the globe. Copernicus and Galileo challenged the received truths about the place of the earth in the universe, and Newton explored the laws of nature in ways that explained the movement of both heavenly and earthly bodies. Across Europe the "Age of Reason" and the rise of modern science brought with it a whole new set of values. In Christian Europe, the authority of the Church was called into question with the beginning of the Reformation. Religious truths long held sacred were replaced with a spirit of empirical investigation and a corresponding skepticism about any belief that appeared superstitious. More generally, where previous generations had viewed the purpose of human life as serving God and living in accordance with divine guidance, people began to place more trust in the power of human reason and were more inclined to assume that "man is the measure of all things." Free inquiry took precedence over received truths, reason was more reliable than revelation, and the scope of God's power was reduced in proportion as the domain of human power and influence increased. Eighteenth century Deists imagined that God was like a cosmic watchmaker who had created a complex world and then walked away and let it run on its own. Finally, these intellectual changes brought with them a new interest in historical study. Rather than attributing some historical events to divine intervention in human affairs, it was assumed that all events must be explained as products of purely historical causes. This view, often called *historicism,* flew directly in the face of traditional religious beliefs about revelation.

The implications of these changes were far reaching and complex. Individualism and universalism became the hallmarks of modern thought. The concept of individual rights grew from the notion that individuals in a state of nature are free and autonomous and cede authority over their lives to others, if at all, only by an act of free will. Moreover, if humans are distinguished by reason above all else, then all other distinctions (of religious affiliation, national origin, and ultimately of race and gender) must be less important than what human beings share by virtue of their being rational creatures. With this realization grew the concept of universal human rights enshrined in the words of the Declaration of Independence: "We hold these truths to be self-evident, that all men are created equal, endowed by their Creator with certain inalienable rights, that among these rights are life, liberty and the pursuit of happiness." In the realm of politics, this led to the doctrine of the separation of church and state. The state must remain religiously neutral lest it interfere with the right of citizens to worship God in accordance with the dictates of their own conscience (or, if they so choose, not at all). Religious groups must be free of political control, just as the state must be free to pursue the common welfare without religious interference. All of these changes dramatically reshaped the political landscape as one European country after another abandoned traditional monarchical forms of government (or greatly limited their power) in favor of constitutional democracy.

These intellectual currents deeply affected religious thought and practice. The spirit of critical investigation that pervaded the natural sciences was turned toward the study of religious history and literature. Biblical accounts of the origins of humankind were scrutinized in light of contemporary scientific knowledge. The miracles associated with Israelite history (and, for Christians, with Jesus' ministry) were challenged as contrary to the laws of nature and thus deemed fallacious. The claim that Scripture was God's inerrant word was thus also called into question. Indeed, as critical studies of history and literature proceeded in the eighteenth and nineteenth centuries, it became clear to many scholars that the Torah was actually composed of multiple, even contradictory, strands and that these could be teased apart and analyzed. What had once been accepted as the unitary record of God's revelation to Israel upon analysis appeared to reflect the work of several Israelite authors from different periods with different theological viewpoints and different writing styles. With this challenge to the authenticity of Scripture as God's word, the ultimate authority underlying all religious life was called into question.

This represented a major crisis for all Western religious thought that many would argue continues to this day. Secular reason challenged religious faith, the focus on individualism was in tension with the traditional Jewish focus on community, and the value of universalism conflicted with the belief in Israel's chosenness. Even more fundamentally, because the concept of revelation was criticized, the truth claims and values of each religious tradition were also called into question. For Judaism, this meant rethinking the validity of all traditional beliefs: about God's creation, revelation, and redemption, about the nature of religious authority, and about the meaning of religious truth and the basis of religious and moral life. Later this chapter focuses on the implications of these enormous changes for Jewish ethics in particular, but first it is necessary to focus on the ways in which modernity undermined the traditional Jewish community even as it challenged traditional Jewish thought.

The ideological changes just discussed led to dramatic changes in the political and social status of Jews throughout Europe, especially in the eighteenth and nineteenth centuries. The spread of liberal democracy meant that, for the first time in their long history in the diaspora, Jews were welcomed as equals into civil society. Previously there had been many periods in which Jews had been quite comfortable in non-Jewish society, at times respected and even sought out for their contributions, especially in the realm of commerce. However, their underlying legal status remained uncertain and their position in society subject to change without notice as political winds shifted. Full normalization of their status became possible only with the separation of religious and national identity. This idea that political rights were inherent and inalienable meant that they were independent of religious affiliation, which was voluntary. This brought in its wake the relaxation and eventual revocation of legal restrictions on Jews that had existed since the Middle Ages. Such restrictions included the requirement that Jews pay special taxes, as well as prohibitions against Jews owning land, entering certain professions, living in certain regions, holding public office and/or attending certain schools. This "emancipation" of the Jews represented the most dramatic change in their political fortunes since the loss of their homeland to the Romans in the first century.

As these political changes took place and the opportunities open to Jews increased, the social interactions between Jews and non-Jews also became more significant. Jews began to live and work in the larger community to a greater degree, which began to blur the social boundaries that had kept Jews apart. As a result, Jews were exposed to the culture of their non-Jewish compatriots to a much greater degree than before. Many Jews, eager to take advantage of these opportunities, became doctors, lawyers, and government officials. Despite continued popular anti-Semitism in many quarters, Jews became a socially acceptable group to a greater degree than ever before. In response, many Jews felt that full integration into the larger society was more important than maintaining their identity as a separate religious/national community as Jews had done throughout their history. Some even believed that this new openness in society signaled the imminent end of anti-Semitism, even the dawning of the long-awaited messianic age. Soon intermarriage increased, and during this period many Jews simply shed all vestiges of their Jewish identity and assimilated into the larger society.

All of these changes, both ideological and sociological, launched an era of religious reform among certain segments of the Jewish community. It now seemed evident to many that Judaism needed to change in response to the radically new conditions of modernity. Proponents of Reform Judaism argued that the antiquated elements of the religion—anything inconsistent with the findings of modern science or the spirit of modern, liberal society—had to be either jettisoned or revised if Judaism were to survive as a modern religion. Initially, many of the reforms concerned worship: eliminating from the traditional prayers references to the return to Zion, praying in the vernacular (rather than the traditional Hebrew), introducing mixed seating for men and women, and including an organ and choir, as was customary in Protestant services of the day. Reformers rejected the traditional belief that Jews were a "holy people," that is, a national group with an intrinsically religious identity. In its place, they developed the doctrine that Jews were strictly a religious group, that the period of Jewish nationalism ended with the exile from Palestine in the first century, and that Jews were therefore free to embrace the nationality and citizenship of the countries in which they lived. Moreover, many reformers viewed the halakhic tradition as rigid and arcane, a relic of another time. They regarded following the spirit of the law as more important than observing its letter. Serving God had to be done in accord with the dictates of one's conscience, not only (or primarily) in the way dictated by tradition.

Of course, these trends brought in their wake a countermovement of traditionalists who wished to preserve the time-honored forms of Jewish worship and who affirmed the theological beliefs and halakhic norms that characterized the classical tradition. The reformers, in their view, were "selling out," measuring the validity of the tradition in terms of modern ideas and practices. The traditionalists proposed precisely the opposite: Modernity should be judged in terms of the Torah and only those aspects of modernity that were consistent with the Torah should be embraced. In the words of Samson Raphael Hirsch, the leader of the "neo-orthodox" movement in nineteenth century Germany,

> To them [the reformers], progress is the absolute and religion is governed by it; to us, religion is the absolute. For them, religion is valid only to the extent that it does not interfere with progress; for us, progress is valid only to the extent that it does not interfere with religion.[2]

The traditionalists themselves subdivided into those opposed to every innovation of modernity as a threat to the truth of tradition and those who were more "accomodationist," prepared to affirm the value of secular education, for example, provided it did not undermine traditional beliefs and practices.[3] These ideological differences split the modern Jewish community into several distinct factions or movements, which persist to the present.[4] In short, under the impact of modernization, Jews would never again be a single community united by a common self-understanding, a common set of beliefs and practices, or a shared relationship with the larger society in which they lived.

The vast majority of Jews, especially those living in Western countries, have embraced modernity to a very considerable extent and have developed liberal forms of Judaism, as seems to befit this modern world. In the process, they have faced two central questions about the nature of Judaism and about the place of Jews in modern society. With respect to Judaism, the question has often been expressed as one of continuity and change. Modern liberal Jews have wanted to preserve a connection with Jewish tradition, even as they have wanted to significantly reinterpret and revise (in some cases, even abandon) whole aspects of that tradition. Which elements of Jewish tradition are "essential" or "divine" and hence immutable, and which are "inessential" or "merely historical accretions" and hence subject to change in response to changing historical circumstances? By what criteria can Jews distinguish what is essential from what is not? Different groups of modern Jews have answered these questions in different ways, but all have shared a belief that there is some core of Judaism that retains its validity in the modern world.

On the sociological level, the central question for Jews has been one of self-definition. How should Jews define themselves and their relationship to (and role within) the larger non-Jewish societies in which they live—now as full-fledged citizens? How is it possible for them to integrate fully into society, which is the promise and appeal of modernity, yet maintain their identity as a separate group? In the words of Arthur Hertzberg, "For the last two centuries, as Jews have been entering the life of Western society, they have wanted two antithetical things: to be like everybody else, and to be quite different."[5] Those Jews who have continued to identify as Jews (as distinct from those who have assimilated entirely) have needed to define the ways in which they are like everyone else and the ways in which they are different. The ways in which modern Jews have answered these questions to a large extent have shaped the character of modern Jewish ethics.

JEWISH ETHICS AND MODERN JEWISH LIBERALISM

For many modern, liberal Jews, it seemed self-evident that the essence of Judaism was its ethics. Without exception, early reformers identified the "essence" of Judaism as its belief in one God and the corollary belief in the unity of "mankind." It followed that the primary religious obligation for Jews was to embrace a humanistic, universalist ethic and to work toward the realization of the biblical vision of global peace and harmony. Indeed, they regarded this universalist ethic as the message that God had entrusted to the Jewish people and that they were "chosen" to teach the world. This article of liberal Jewish faith received perhaps its most famous and forceful articulation in the Pittsburgh Platform of 1885:

> We recognize, in the modern era of universal culture of heart and intellect, the approaching of the realization of Israel's great messianic hope for the establishment of the kingdom of truth, justice, and peace among all men. . . .

> We acknowledge that the spirit of broad humanity of our age is our ally in the fulfillment of our mission, and therefore, we extend the hand of fellowship to all who operate with us in the establishment of the reign of truth and righteousness among men.[6]

In this formulation of Judaism, Israel's (particular) mission is to spread the (universal) moral teachings that will lead to the fulfillment of the ancient, messianic vision of global peace.

The quintessential expression of this ideal could be found in the prophetic literature. Thus, it is no surprise that the reformers returned again and again to the prophets for prooftexts to support their preferences—first for ethics over ritual and second for universalism over particularism.

> For I desire goodness, not sacrifice; obedience to God, rather than burnt offerings. (Hosea 6:6)
>
> If you offer Me burnt offerings—or your meal offerings—I will not accept them; . . . . But let justice well up like water, righteousness like an unfailing stream. (Amos 5:22,24)
>
> Have we not all one father? Did not one God create us? Why do we break faith with one another, profaning the covenant of our fathers? (Malachi 2:10)

These passages, and others like them, reassured liberal Jewish thinkers of that time that their tradition remained relevant, that even if many elements of Judaism appeared archaic, its religious-moral truth was timeless. By adhering to this vision of a universal, ethical order, modern Jews could live out the meaning of their faith within a secular society.

This view found expression in the work of every liberal Jewish thinker of the nineteenth and early twentieth century. Kaufmann Kohler, among the most influential Jewish theologians of this period, wrote,

> Judaism is nothing less than a message concerning the *One and holy God* and *one, undivided humanity* with a world-uniting *Messianic goal,* a message intrusted by divine revelation to the Jewish people. Thus Israel is its prophetic harbinger and priestly guardian, its witness and defender throughout the ages, who is never to falter in the task of upholding and unfolding its truths until they have become the possession of the whole human race.[7]

Virtually the same thought is expressed a generation later by Leo Baeck, whose work, in turn, influenced a generation of rabbis and thinkers in America:

> Its ethical character, the basic significance which it sees in the moral action, is the primary thing in the religion of Israel. No matter at what date one may fix its origin and no matter how one may view the question of its progress, one thing is certain, that since that Israelitisch, prophetic religion began, which is the true religion of Israel, the moral law has formed its cardinal point. Judaism is not only ethical, but *ethics constitute its principle, its essence and nature.*[8]

Baeck articulates perfectly the longstanding liberal strategy of identifying ethics as the timeless core of Judaism over against other aspects of the tradition, in particular, the ritual law.

This strategy of placing ethics at the center of a reconstructed Jewish religion appeared to resolve both the intellectual and social challenges of modernity. Within the intellectual sphere, Judaism's essence, the one truth it had proclaimed throughout its long history, was in no sense invalidated by the new emphasis on empirical, scientific study or by the extension of this attitude into historical-critical study of religious traditions. To the extent that empiricism cast into doubt the mythological and miraculous aspects of biblical stories, the reformers could readily concede that science was to be trusted more than the Bible in such matters without thereby sacrificing the essence of Judaism's religious truth. Moreover, the reformers could adopt an historical perspective on the tradition, conceding that some elements were products of human creativity alone while insisting that a kernel of divinely inspired or revealed truth was present as well. Finally, and perhaps most important, the universalism propounded by Enlightenment thinkers such as Rousseau and Kant could be embraced as consistent with (or even prefigured by) the prophetic emphasis on "ethical monotheism."

On the social plane, of course, Jews who subscribed to this liberal interpretation of Judaism could in good conscience integrate into the general society and embrace the opportunities it offered them. In fact, they could even justify their doing so as a religious obligation, insofar as their God-given mission was to spread the religious truth at Judaism's core and thereby facilitate the coming of the "Kingdom of God."[9] Thus, the end of the ghettoization of Jews, as well as their self-isolation as a discrete national group, could be viewed as but the next phase in a necessary process leading to a messianic culmination of history.

In the aftermath of World War I and even more so after World War II, the heady idealism that had prevailed in the nineteenth century came to an end. The carnage and genocide produced by those global conflicts were more than enough to dispel any hopes that humankind was on the brink of the messianic era. A sober realism set in, especially among Jews who gradually woke up to the reality that well over 80 percent of European Jews, who represented one-third of the world's Jewish population at the time, had been exterminated by the Nazis and their allies. European countries that only a century earlier had been opening the doors of opportunity to Jews had participated in the genocide. The liberal Jewish belief that, by modernizing their religious practice and embracing a universalist ethic, Jews could integrate fully into European society was no longer plausible. History had definitively demonstrated otherwise. The feeling that Jewish survival was precarious, that perhaps Jews could never really be safe so long as they lived as a minority within non-Jewish societies, fed the enthusiasm for the Zionist goal of establishing an independent Jewish state. The Zionist movement had begun in the nineteenth century and had attracted substantial support, especially among non-religious Jews, for the revival of Jewish national life, but Zionism had always faced opposition from those who felt that modernity called upon Jews to become more integrated into European society, not more isolated from it. In the aftermath of the Holocaust and the collapse of liberal idealism, however, Jewish nationalism gained new momentum.

All of these changes signaled a new attitude among Jews toward modernity and a new approach to Jewish ethics. It no longer seemed obvious, even to liberal Jews, that modernity was the standard against which to measure the relevance of their tradition (and, of course, it had never seemed that way to traditionalists). Since modernity had shown itself capable of turning against Jews on a massive scale and with disastrous consequences, the wiser course was surely to find a more measured balance between adopting the values of the modern world and preserving the values of Jewish tradition. The prophetic universalism that Jews had embraced so enthusiastically in the nineteenth century now seemed less compelling, for Jews recognized that their survival in the modern world, both physically and culturally, depended on their affirming the value of their own particular heritage. The rush to assimilate into the larger society was tempered by a growing desire to rediscover and reaffirm the distinctiveness of Jewish life and thought. Liberal Jews began to reinstitute ritual practices that their parents and grandparents had abandoned, and religious worship likewise took a turn toward tradition as Jews began to reassert their ethnicity in the late twentieth century. Even orthodoxy, once thought to be destined for extinction as modernity advanced, experienced a striking revival, especially among younger Jews. In short, by the last third of the twentieth century, it was no longer clear that Jews would definitively choose modernity over tradition or universalism over particularism.

Three further developments have influenced the shape of Jewish ethics in recent years. The rise of the feminist movement in the 1960s and 1970s challenged Jewish tradition on several levels. First and perhaps most important, it resulted in opening up the rabbinate to women in both the Reform and Conservative movements, thus breaking the traditional monopoly of men on Jewish religious leadership. Feminists also challenged the sexist language of Jewish prayer, calling for more inclusive language for God and insisting that the vocabulary of Jewish life not perpetuate sexist stereotypes. Feminist thinkers such as Judith Plaskow and Rachel Adler began to formulate feminist Jewish theologies, to write rituals designed to mark the events of special significance in women's lives (childbirth, weaning a child, and pregnancy loss, among others), and many others began to compose feminist midrash on classical sources. In all, feminism transformed the face of Judaism, challenging received truths, creating new ritual forms, and greatly expanding the public role of women as teachers in the Jewish community.

At the same time, the explosion of Jewish studies in the academy opened new avenues for research into all aspects of Jewish history and contemporary life. In the 1950s only a handful of universities in the United States offered courses in Judaica; by the end of the twentieth century, virtually every major college and university in the country offered such courses, and many had developed whole programs devoted to Jewish studies. Fed by the general interest in ethnic and crossdisciplinary studies, Jewish studies became an established field within the liberal arts curriculum. More important, the expansion of Jewish studies generated a wealth of new research into Jewish history, sociology, philosophy, and literature, greatly increasing people's awareness of the complexity of Jewish experience across the centuries. As a result, it was no longer imaginable for Jewish scholars to argue, as they had a century earlier, that Judaism is uniform and essentially unchanging or that Jewish ethics can be reduced to a single principle.

Finally, the rise of "postmodern" philosophy and its influence on many Jewish thinkers must be noted. Drawing on certain twentieth century continental thinkers (Jacques Derrida, Jurgen Habermas, Michel Foucault) and especially on Jewish figures within this tradition (Martin Buber, Franz Rosenzweig, and Emmanuel Levinas), many contemporary writers have endorsed an approach to Jewish thought that emphasizes texts, community, and dialogue. In their view, modern thought was unduly abstract, disembodied, universal, and secular, which impoverished modern thinking especially about ethics (and, perhaps, accounts for the inordinate suffering experienced in the twentieth century in the political arena). By contrast, these thinkers, many of whom refer to their approach as "textual reasoning," call for a return to a more classically Jewish, text-based approach to philosophical discourse. This entails a claim that the modern, liberal outlook that so pervaded nineteenth century Jewish thought must be abandoned (or at least modified) to make room for a more authentically Jewish approach to thinking and acting in the world, one that sees the integral relationships between thinking and acting, between self and other, and between textual study and moral reflection.[10]

In the context of all of these changes, contemporary Jewish ethicists attempt to draw on the values and sources of Jewish tradition in addressing the moral problems that all contemporary people face. In doing so, these ethicists have struggled to answer the two central issues posed earlier: how to identify the essential truths within the tradition and how to understand the place of the Jewish community within modern society. The ethicists' efforts rely on a range of strategies for appropriating Jewish tradition and interpreting it. The following chapter surveys a sampling of contemporary Jewish views on specific moral issues. Before doing so, however, it will be useful here to consider the various methods that characterize this body of contemporary Jewish ethical teaching. Doing so will enable you to understand not only the specific views that modern Jewish ethicists adopt but also the different ways in which they approach the whole enterprise of constructing a modern Jewish ethic.

APPROACHES TO MODERN JEWISH ETHICS

A survey of the current literature identifies three distinct approaches to modern Jewish ethics, which may be described as *legal, covenantal,* and *narrative.* It is important to note at the outset that these are not categories that Jewish ethicists typically use to describe themselves; rather, I employ these labels here as a way to distinguish different ways in which Jewish ethicists have approached the task of drawing ethical guidance from Jewish tradition. Ethicists from across the religious spectrum, from liberals to traditionalists, have adopted these approaches. In some cases, elements of more than one approach can be detected in the work of a single writer. These categories, then, do not function as political party affiliations (e.g., Democrat or Republican) or even as descriptions of one's ethical commitments (e.g., liberal or conservative). It is more accurate to think of them as pointing to a writer's underlying orientation to Torah as a source of moral guidance, a philosophy (often implicit rather than explicit) about what aspect of Torah is timeless and how to construct an authentically Jewish ethic in our time.

The Legal Model

Advocates of the legal model analyze questions in Jewish ethics in light of precedents found in traditional legal sources. Given a moral problem, legalists cite classical Jewish legal sources and, through analogical reasoning and other means, attempt to distill the principles behind this line of precedents and apply them to the question at hand. Different authorities articulate these principles and apply them differently, which accounts for the fact that they frequently differ in their opinions (as, of course, did premodern authorities). Their differences arise within a framework of common assumptions, however, specifically that ethical issues are to be approached as questions of halakhah and, accordingly, that the tradition's primary resource for approaching modern ethical problems is the body of legal sources, especially in the Talmud and subsequent codes and responsa.

This legal model should sound familiar, for it represents the contemporary equivalent of the approach to ethics that characterized most traditional Jewish authorities. Indeed, some contemporary legalists, such as J. David Bleich, write legal responsa on issues in contemporary Jewish ethics precisely as their predecessors would have done generations ago. This philosophy is best captured in his own description of his approach to Jewish ethics:

> A person who seeks to find answers within the Jewish tradition [to questions of ethics] can deal with such questions in only one way. He must examine them through the prism of Halakhah for it is in the corpus of Jewish law as elucidated and transmitted from generation to generation that God has made His will known to man.[11]

For Bleich and others, the problems faced by Jewish ethicists change, but the method for dealing with them is constant. The eternal truths of Judaism are embedded in the halakhic tradition and merely need to be applied carefully to provide the moral guidance that contemporary Jews seek.

Others who have employed the legal approach, including Elliot Dorff, David Feldman, and Solomon Freehof, have done so in a more historical-critical way. They still rely almost exclusively on legal precedents, but they are inclined to consider not only the substance of prior rulings but also the historical and sociological context in which they were written, the state of scientific knowledge at that time, and the philosophy that guided those who made earlier rulings. They see the law less as a repository of divine truth than as a record of human reflection, developed in response to changing circumstances. Dorff has articulated this way of working within the legal system:

> To bring new situations under the umbrella of the law, judges in any legal system
> must often stretch precedents to make them relevant to new circumstances. In-
> deed, for a legal system to retain continuity and authority in current decisions,
> this *must* be done. Thus in our case, if a decision is going to be *Jewish* in some rec-
> ognizable way, it *must* invoke the tradition in a serious, not perfunctory, way. One
> can do this without being devious or anachronistic *if one does not pretend that one's
> own interpretation is its originally intended meaning (its* peshat) *or its only possible
> reading.*[12]

Contemporary Jewish ethicists who follow Dorff's view are working within a legal
model, one that sees halakhah as a dynamic system, evolving in response to changing circumstances and ideas rather than as a timeless repository of eternal truths.

A Covenantal Model

The covenantal model of contemporary Jewish ethics sees covenant, rather
than law, as the cornerstone of Jewish ethics. For these writers, the covenant
between God and Israel has historically been expressed through halakhah, but it has
also exerted a profound influence on Jewish thought and life that extends beyond
the corpus of Jewish law. Eugene Borowitz, among the most prolific and influential
contemporary Jewish thinkers, has expressed the covenantal approach to ethics this
way:

> It accepts the liberal notion that a universal ethical sensitivity must be basic to a
> modern Judaism. But it denies the continuing adequacy of the Kantian under-
> standing of the ethics which derives from a conception of the self as fundamen-
> tally a construction of one's reason. Instead it proposes to integrate rationality
> into a more comprehensive, existentialist sense of the self, producing thereby an
> ethics of relationship rather than of rational rule. Likewise, it reinterprets Jewish
> authenticity in relational terms, suggesting that Jewish responsibility derives from
> personally sharing the Jewish people's covenant with God. The *Halakhah* and
> *agadah* may then be the Jew's best guides to authentic obligation—but they must
> now be read in terms of a given individual's present response to God as one of
> God's dedicated ethnic community.[13]

For those such as Borowitz who ground their ethics in covenant, the goal is to live
faithfully in relationship to God and in continuity with earlier generations of Jews
who likewise have attempted to live faithfully in this same relationship. The point is
not to replicate their moral guidance or simply to reinterpret the words of their rulings for our time; it is to stand in authentic relationship with the Source of moral
guidance, who calls Jews to discover their moral bearings in the context of that
covenantal relationship.

This covenantal approach characterizes not only liberals such as Borowitz but
also some contemporary Orthodox thinkers including Irving Greenberg. In an article
on Jewish medical ethics, he develops a covenantal approach to the use of medical
technology. On the one hand, humans' medical power constitutes a "religious calling,"
for it enables us to engage in the task of "repairing the world," curing illnesses and pro-
moting human flourishing. For this purpose God has given people these extraordinary

powers of healing. On the other hand, the Sabbath is a reminder that God has placed limits on the use of human power. Jews are called to respect the natural world as God has created it, not change it for their purposes. As Greenberg puts it,

> Thus there is a dialectic in Judaism: power is affirmed, but respect for that which already exists is also affirmed. Holiness consists of shaping and perfecting the world, of developing all the possibilities in life and eliminating sickness, and ultimately hoping to eliminate death, while at the same time respecting and enhancing the life that is.[14]

This model of Jewish ethics, then, is dialectical. It involves a constant attempt to balance the power that God has given Jews and the goals that God has set for them. God both empowers and restricts the use of that power, encourages creativity, and sets limits on it. Like all intimate relationships, the covenant between God and Israel involves an endless balancing act between the two partners and their needs and goals. Living in covenant demands that Jews remain continually attentive to what their divine partner is asking of them as they approach each new moral dilemma.

Covenantal ethicists, then, find guidance not so much in the substance of the legal tradition as in the character of the covenantal relationship between God and Israel and between God and the world, which for covenantal thinkers is the foundation of that legal tradition. The legal rulings of previous generations are by no means irrelevant. Through them Jews can discern the ways in which earlier sages defined their own obligations under the covenant.[15] In the last analysis, however, Jewish moral obligations are not determined by legal processes but by living in a covenantal relationship with God and attending to the responsibilities that are imposed by the very character of that relationship. Covenantal ethicists differ from one another, then, in the ways they interpret the demands of living ethically in the context of this relationship.

A Narrative Model

Narrative ethics looks to the stories within Jewish tradition for moral guidance. The essence of this approach, as Stanley Hauerwas expresses it for the Christian theologian, is that "being a Christian involves more than just making certain decisions; it is a way of attending to the world. It is learning 'to see' the world under the mode of the divine. . . . A Christian does not simply 'believe' certain propositions about God; he learns to attend to reality through them."[16] Jewish narrative ethicists believe that Jews learn to see the world in a distinctively religious way through stories. The importance of such stories is not only their content, the principles they teach, or points they make, but also the narrative form of the message. The very structure of the story—its characters and plot, its dramatic or tragic or comic qualities—are part and parcel of the message. Hearing these stories again and again, Jews learn to internalize their structure, to project themselves into the world described by the story, indeed, to see the world around them as a continuation of the story. Thus, narrative ethicists say Jews learn to attend to the world and act within it by means of the story.[17]

Among Jewish thinkers, Michael Goldberg and Laurie Zoloth have consciously employed this narrative approach. Goldberg contrasts Jewish and Christian ways of seeing the world through a comparative analysis of their respective "master stories," the exodus and the passion-resurrection. He argues that for Jews the exodus narrative decisively shapes their understanding of the world and their moral responses to it. He writes,

> . . . the Exodus as a master story serves as a model, a guide, for suggesting how we are to go on from here. It thus not only relates some past events in the life of one particular people, but simultaneously holds out a vision of how the life of all peoples may be sustained—and even transformed!—in the future. Hence, in the last analysis, the Exodus master story is quite literally one of *promise,* speaking of our duties and obligations as well as of the world's hopes and dreams.[18]

For Goldberg, then, Jews learn what God expects of them morally by attending to the story of how God brought this people from slavery to freedom, how the Israelites participated in their own redemption, and so forth.

Zoloth has developed an extensive and sophisticated Jewish analysis of access to health care drawing on the moral perspective embedded in the biblical book of Ruth.[19] As Zoloth reads it, the story of Ruth is about how to survive in a situation of scarcity and, ultimately, how to preserve a family in the face of potential extinction. The lessons she draws from the narrative are that Jews are called to be faithful and "cleave" to those who appear to have no future (Ruth's "cleaving" to Naomi) and that Jews must extend themselves and share their resources with those who are in need (Boaz's relationship to Ruth). In all, the book of Ruth teaches that Jews must directly encounter others, pay attention to their needs, and offer them emotional and material support. These lessons can readily be extended to the contemporary debates about the allocation of scarce medical resources and access to state-funded health care.

Like Goldberg, Zoloth eschews legal and philosophical models of ethics in favor of the narrative approach. Narratives, perhaps especially religious narratives, capture moral truths in the very form in which people actually encounter them, for what is a narrative but an account of lived experience unfolding over time? To divorce moral lessons from the narrative contexts in which people discover them and learn to live them out is to rob these lessons of their subtlety, to turn the richness of human moral experience into a "system." Moral wisdom is simply not reducible to moral rules and principles. In contrast to the whole liberal tradition, with its emphasis on the autonomy of the individual and on the moral self as a disembodied, abstract entity stripped of his or her particularities, Zoloth affirms the perspective of many feminist and communitarian theorists. Her emphasis, accordingly, is on the life stories and particular identities of the moral agents, on the ways in which they are inseparable from the communities that nurture and sustain them, and on the sense of responsibility that arises in the real-life encounter with the "other."

Plainly, then, this narrative model is even more open ended than the covenantal one. For Greenberg, Borowitz, and other covenantal theologians, halakhah represents at very least a valuable resource for understanding the history of covenantal responsibility. On the narrative model, by contrast, it appears that turning to the law as a resource for ethical reflection is looking in precisely the wrong place. The moral life is not about applying principles and rules to novel fact patterns; it operates on an entirely different level. Hauerwas expresses this orientation when he writes, "our moral reasoning, especially in cases of moral doubt, is not deductive but analogical . . . . Moral reason is more dependent on imagination than strict logical entailment."[20] Thus, the preoccupation with legal analysis that characterizes both traditional and much of modern Jewish ethics will strike narrative theologians as misguided, both because it looks to the wrong sources and because it appropriates them in the wrong ways.

Notwithstanding the marked differences among these various models for doing Jewish ethics, these models share a few fundamental assumptions that should be noted. In the first place, all would agree that Jewish ethics is distinctive in its method if not also in its content. There is a source of specifically Jewish moral obligations separate from, though not necessarily incompatible with, whatever obligations Jews have in common with other humans. Moreover, this distinctively Jewish ethic, however it may be defined, is inescapably religious in nature. That is, it presupposes that Jews, both individually and in community, stand in relationship to God and derive their moral orientation from that relationship. Thus, modern Jewish ethicists share a commitment to affirming a transcendent source of morality while accepting the legitimacy of some secular modes of thought.

By the same token, each of these models locates the source of transcendent moral truths in Torah, understood in the broadest sense as encompassing both sacred scripture and the rabbinic tradition that builds on it. It follows that all these Jewish ethicists could rightly claim to derive moral guidance by reading and interpreting texts. Given the centrality of the written word to Judaism as a whole, it is hardly surprising that this should be so. Indeed, it is difficult to imagine how anyone could claim authenticity for any Jewish ethic that displayed no relationship to the very body of literature that has been viewed throughout history as the authoritative source of values.

At this point these models begin to diverge, however. For if all agree that doing Jewish ethics necessarily entails reading and interpreting Jewish texts, there is anything but agreement on which texts to read, or how to read them. The differences among these three models can best be appreciated by paying close attention to how the text *functions* within each of these models, that is, what role it plays for the Jewish ethicist. Each model of Jewish ethics just considered offers a distinctive way of relating to Torah, which could be characterized through a series of metaphors.[21]

For legalists, Torah functions as a type of blueprint for building an intricate structure. Like a blueprint, the goal of this text is to instruct the reader in how to produce a certain finished product. The text is utilitarian, serving as a medium for the architect to communicate a design to the builder, who will follow it for the sole purpose of actualizing this particular design. The direction that the blueprint provides is quite explicit and detailed. Reading and following blueprints is not always easy, even if one possesses the requisite skills. It demands strict discipline and extraordinary attention to detail. It also requires that the builder exercise judgment in performing all the tasks that the blueprint does not specify but that are necessary to complete the project.

For legalists, Torah instructs Jews in the construction of a moral life, with certain fixed dimensions and contours. To succeed in its goal, Torah needs fundamentally only to be followed. To be sure, the Torah on this model provides an extremely complex plan that directs Jews not in how to complete a single finite task (like building a house) but in how to perform all their moral tasks throughout their lives. In this view, Jews often find themselves in situations for which the Torah's plan does not provide clear direction. At this point, the legalists will insist that Jews have no choice but to study the text with the greatest care, to try to discern the intentions of the architect, and to carry them out as best they can. Indeed, it may even be that the divine architect intended that the construction of a moral life entail just such ambiguities because they force Jews to study the Torah ever more diligently.

The covenantal model, by contrast, views the Torah not as a blueprint but as a type of marriage contract. Like that document, it establishes an intimate relationship between two parties but offers little in the way of concrete guidance for living in it. To be sure, this relationship requires certain personal qualities, such as trust, faithfulness, and integrity. In the day-to-day business of maintaining a marriage, it helps little to consult the words of the marriage contract. That document provides the foundation for an evolving, dynamic relationship; it gives an orientation toward one's partner but not a specific plan of action. People learn their obligations within marriage by attending to the experience of others in long-term successful relationships, and by responding to the needs of their partners. To the extent that the marriage contract continues to serve a function after the relationship is established, it is primarily a symbolic one. It points to the commitment and mutual respect that constitute the essence of the bond between the partners.

Torah, for the covenantal ethicist, is just such a document. If, in reality, the Torah text provides more detailed directives than a typical marriage contract, these are understood as symbolic as well. They represent some of the ways in which the essential qualities of a covenantal bond can be expressed in deeds. It would be a mistake in this model, however, to read the Torah as a manual for creating a successful marriage between God and Israel; that can occur only if the partners do what is necessary day by day to create the ideal world that the marriage document envisions. So the covenantal ethicist rarely feels the need to engage in detailed explication of the Torah's rules, for they are taken as illustrative rather than definitive of one's moral responsibilities.

The narrative ethicist, in turn, views the Torah as a work of art, a painting of sorts. Its purpose is to open Jews' eyes to a certain way of perceiving reality. Just as viewing a work of art stimulates people to notice things about the world that they had not previously observed, the text expands one's moral vision. It invites Jews not only to see the world from a certain distinctive vantage point but also to carry that vision with them and to reproduce it in their responses to life. If they attend to it carefully, the text as work of art will transform them, directing them toward a new way of living in the world.

Torah, in the narrative model, instructs by guiding and stimulating Jews' moral imagination. Its value lies not in the rules it offers for how to behave but in the story it tells and asks Jews to internalize. In this sense, the text of the Torah is inherently incomplete, for it is the Jews themselves who complete the story as they use it to structure their moral lives. For the narrative theologian, the text of the Torah is not meant to legislate a pattern of Jewish behavior or even to establish the relationship between God and Israel, although the story contained in Scripture surely has much to say about that relationship. It primarily provides an overarching plot for Jews' moral lives, a meaningful structure that encompasses a conception of what the world is like and how God wants Jews to respond to it.

The point of the preceding analysis is that when Jewish ethicists read a text, they necessarily adopt a certain stance toward that text as a source of values. The way in which they appeal to the authority of the text and, consequently, the way in which they read its words and apply them to their lives depend on the type of relationship they have to the text. And, as I have noted, several quite distinct options are viable. Builders relate to blueprints very differently from the way spouses relate to their marriage contracts, which are both very different from the way people relate to works of art. It could be said, then, that although modern Jewish ethicists all appear to be engaged in a common enterprise and to claim the same Torah as the source of their values, they understand that task and the role of textual interpretation within it in radically different ways. In the final analysis, what distinguishes these models of Jewish ethics from one another are their respective ways of construing the tradition and, as you will discover, each way is in a sense self-verifying. In short, modern Jewish ethicists choose among competing conceptions of tradition, and the implications of that choice are very far reaching.

What it means to construe a tradition in one way rather than another has been elucidated by the legal theorist Ronald Dworkin. He discusses what it means for judges to feel bound by legal precedent yet to make free and creative choices about how to handle the cases before them. To illustrate his point, he considers what it would be like for several authors to collaborate in the writing of a single novel, each of the authors writing one chapter in the sequence. All of the novelists (after the first) enjoy a kind of constrained freedom, for their literary creativity to extend the story is necessarily limited by the parameters established by the story as developed by earlier authors in the chain. So too, Dworkin argues, judges are free to render their own decisions but in the context of an earlier legal tradition. He or she will need to justify any legal decision as coherent with the thrust of the legal tradition to this point as he or she interprets it.[22]

Modern Jewish ethicists, it seems, are exactly like the novelists or the judges in Dworkin's example. They are the latest link in a chain stretching back across centuries. They inherit a wealth of texts, decisions, stories, and practices that in no way form a seamless whole. Within this rich legacy, the modern Jewish ethicist will find many divergent philosophies and contradictory opinions as well as major themes and clearly articulated principles. No decision the contemporary ethicist makes can possibly be consistent with the whole of this tradition. Instead, the ethicist must (to paraphrase Dworkin) "determine what the point or theme of the tradition so far taken as a whole really is."[23] This means coming to a conclusion about what gives this multifaceted tradition its coherence and then acting to preserve that coherence as that interpreter sees it. It also means recognizing that other ethicists, like other novelists in the chain, could interpret the historical record differently; they could examine the facts and legitimately reach a different conclusion about what the tradition is and how to continue it.

The most basic question for modern Jewish ethicists, then, is this: How does a Jewish ethicist define the coherence of this religious tradition? What element or principle or method can provide a link between the efforts of past generations and the work that these ethicists do in this modern context? Torah is a rich and multifaceted resource for ethical reflection. The root meaning of Torah, after all, is "to provide direction or instruction," and surely Scripture does this in a variety of ways, frequently through specific legal injunctions but also through narratives and the depiction of a dynamic covenant relationship between God and Israel. Of course, this is true not only for the Biblical text but also for the entire corpus of rabbinic literature that flows from it. So each of these models (legal, covenantal, narrative) is firmly rooted in Jewish sources. Moreover, each can provide the thread of continuity that modern Jewish ethicists need to construct a serviceable concept of tradition. Finally, once the coherence of the tradition has been construed around any one of these elements, the relationship of the ethicist to the classical texts and so the proper strategy for interpreting them follow naturally.

Each of the three models of modern Jewish ethics explored here rests on a distinctive theory of Jewish tradition. The legalists have what could be called a "formalist" theory of coherence. In their view, the core of this religious-ethical tradition lies in its form or method, which is legal. In this model, talking about Jewish moral obligations outside the context of the law makes no sense. To do Jewish ethics is to stand within a legal tradition stretching back across the centuries. It is to see oneself as bound by legal precedents and to commit oneself to extending that system of legal injunctions to an ever changing world.

For covenantal ethicists, by contrast, the law is but one expression of something more fundamental that gives the tradition its coherence. The covenantal relationship binding God to Israel and Jews to one another is central. Within this relationship, a Jew discovers his or her moral obligations, partly, to be sure, by attending to legal precedents but also by drawing on other sources of moral wisdom. In this model, the foundation of the tradition is not a body of law but an existential commitment, the commitment of the Jewish people to live in a covenantal relationship with God and to explore ceaselessly the moral implications of such a relationship.

For narrative ethicists, the tradition's coherence is provided by the structure of its stories. It is the task of each successive generation to remain true to those stories and to add its own chapter to the unfolding plot. This concept of tradition is perhaps the most open ended of the three approaches. Jews have inherited a narrative legacy rich in possibilities; its plot gives structure and direction to the moral life but cannot fully determine how Jews should act in any given situation. Indeed, the narrative does not define the ethical choices Jews should make so much as it shapes their moral sensitivities, provides a vision of what the world is and can be, and alerts Jews to the possibilities for living faithfully. Jewish tradition can be perpetuated, in this view, only when Jews internalize the story it tells to such an extent that their lives come to embody its many themes and messages.

Finally, not all contemporary Jewish ethicists fall easily into one of the three categories outlined: legal, covenantal, and narrative. Indeed, many, if not most, employ what could be called "hybrid" methods, which draw on two or more of these perspectives. Some ethicists, while primarily legalists in their approach, draw upon theological concepts such as covenant in their interpretations of the law. By the same token, narrative ethicists might also pay close attention to some laws as examples of how themes in the Jewish story are translated into specific norms for behavior. The preceding discussion, therefore, should be understood as a summary of major trends within the field of contemporary Jewish ethics, not as a rigid typology.

Chapter Seven will examine Jewish positions on a range of moral questions. In this examination, keeping the differences among these approaches to Jewish ethics in mind will be important. Legal, covenantal, and narrative approaches to Jewish ethics are amply represented in the following debates about sexual ethics, abortion, and war. Indeed, these divergent perspectives surface in virtually every contemporary Jewish moral debate, for, as I have tried to show, contemporary Jewish thinkers differ from one another not only in their views of morality but also in their views of what makes something an authentic Jewish moral view in the first place. As the preceding analysis has also demonstrated, each approach can rightly claim to stand on firm ground, for each is rooted in some dimension of Torah, which, notwithstanding the contemporary debates about its meaning, continues to constitute the ultimate source of Jewish moral values.

KEY POINTS

- The Enlightenment gave rise to ideas of individualism, secularism, rationalism, and historicism, each of which challenged some of Judaism's basic beliefs.
- Subsequent political reforms, including the rise of the liberal, secular nation state, removed age-old social and political restrictions on Jews, and greatly expanded their opportunities and spheres of interactions with non-Jews.
- Modern Jewish liberalism responded to these challenges by casting universal ethics as the unchanging essence of Judaism and so promoted liturgical and ritual reform as well as revision or rejection of many traditional beliefs.
- In the late twentieth century, feminism, "postmodernism," and the expansion of the academic study of Judaism have all challenged liberal Judaism's approach to ethics.

- Among contemporary Jewish ethicists, three approaches predominate: legal, covenantal, and narrative. Each of these builds on one aspect of Torah, and so each provides the thread of continuity necessary for Jewish ethicists today to ground their values and decisions in the tradition.

QUESTIONS TO CONSIDER

1. Which aspects of modernity challenged Jews and Judaism most profoundly? Which changes do you think did the most to fuel the development of modern Judaism, the political and social changes in the status of Jews or the philosophical and religious changes in the intellectual climate of the time?

2. Try to project yourself into the debates that raged in the nineteenth century between traditionalists and reformers. What arguments would you offer in defense of each position?

3. Consider the various approaches to contemporary Jewish ethics presented here: legal, covenantal, and narrative. What do you see as the strengths and weaknesses of each?

4. In recent decades, many "postmodernists" have challenged the assumptions underlying liberal Judaism. Which of these assumptions do they find most problematic, and why? To what extent could liberalism continue to offer a viable response to the challenges of modernity despite the shortcomings noted by its critics?

5. Most Jewish thinkers in the early modern period were willing to make some accommodations to modernity provided that Judaism's "essence" was preserved. Given what you know about the development of Judaism, how would you define its essence?

Chapter Seven

Three Case Studies: Continuity and Diversity in Contemporary Jewish Ethics

Summary

This chapter explores three contemporary issues—sexual ethics, abortion, and war—from the perspectives of several Jewish ethicists. Each ethicist's assumptions and methods are analyzed to illustrate both the diversity of approaches that characterize contemporary Jewish ethics, and the ways in which each approach preserves elements of the classical tradition. Finally, the chapter notes the ways in which each debate exemplifies key methodological issues facing contemporary Jewish ethicists.

◆ ───────────────────────────────────

> *A new learning is about to be born. . . . It is a learning in reverse order. A learning that no longer starts from the Torah and leads into life, but the other way round: from life, from a world that knows nothing of the Law, or pretends to know nothing, back to the Torah. That is the sign of the time. It is the sign of the time because it is the mark of the men of the time. There is no one today who is not alienated, or who does not contain within himself some small fraction of alienation. All of us to whom Judaism . . . has again become the pivot of our lives . . . know that in being Jews we must not give up anything, not renounce anything, but lead everything back to Judaism. From the periphery back to the center; from the outside, in.*[1]

Contemporary Jewish ethicists have addressed an extraordinary array of moral issues from questions of social justice and capital punishment to questions about familial responsibility and ethics in the workplace, from the highly complex questions raised by advances in biotechnology (such as stem cell research and genetic engineering) to questions of politics, pluralism, and intergroup relations. Rather than attempting to survey a wide range of issues, this chapter provides a more in-depth analysis of the debates surrounding three issues. The issues of sexual conduct, abortion, and war have been selected both because readers are likely to be familiar with other moral perspectives on these issues and because they point to the various spheres of moral life from the very personal (sexual ethics) to the very social (war) to a personal issue with profound social implications (abortion). In addition, a number of prominent figures in the field of Jewish ethics have addressed these particular issues, so this summary and analysis also serves as something of an introduction to the work of these important thinkers.

The debates on these issues are illuminating in another sense as well. As the following analysis will demonstrate, these particular debates aptly illustrate a range of methodological issues that contemporary Jewish ethicists address regardless of the specific issue under discussion. The preceding chapter noted that the central issue for contemporary Jewish ethicists is how to provide a link between the ethics preserved within Jewish tradition and the effort to generate Jewish moral teaching for our time. This very general challenge can be broken down into several subissues, which include (1) how to mediate between traditional Jewish values and the values of contemporary society, (2) what assumptions guide the ethicist's reading of the traditional sources themselves, and (3) what role historical context plays in applying traditional sources to contemporary situations. The differences among contemporary Jewish authorities concerning sexual conduct, abortion, and war highlight diverse ways of tackling these specific challenges.

SEXUAL ETHICS

Humans are inherently sexual beings, both anatomically and psychologically. Our bodies and minds instinctively generate sexual desires and pursue ways of satisfying them. Sexual expression is an extremely powerful way to connect with others, to express deep emotions, to give ourselves and our sexual partners great pleasure, to create and maintain intimacy, and, of course, to procreate, thereby ensuring our genetic survival beyond our own inevitable deaths. Perhaps no other single aspect of our humanity is as deeply personal and as instrumental in shaping our relationships with others as is our sexuality. Given the centrality of sex within human experience, it is no wonder that it has been the subject of sustained ethical reflection in every culture and in all ages. How, when, and with whom should we express our sexuality? What sorts of social obligations do sexual contact in general and sexual intercourse in particular entail? Within the context of religious ethics, given that God created humans as sexual beings, how can we use our sexual energies to further, rather than hinder, the divine goals of human life?

Contemporary Jewish ethicists have addressed several dimensions of sexual ethics, including the appropriateness of sexual expression outside the context of marriage and of same-sex relationships. These ethicists have also attempted to articulate a theory of how human sexuality is, or can be made to be, sacred. In the process of doing so, each of the thinkers examined has, implicitly or explicitly, confronted the fact that traditional Jewish and contemporary views of human sexuality are often markedly different. This has meant that each ethicist has attempted to articulate a position that is both true to the teachings of the tradition in some way and responsive to the situation of contemporary Jews.

David Novak

An extremely prolific and erudite scholar, David Novak[2] has developed his ethical views using a unique combination of legal and philosophical analysis. His approach to traditional Jewish sources is consistent with the historical-critical approach embraced by the Conservative movement in which he was ordained while his philosophical orientation owes much to the tradition of natural law. Simply put, natural law is an ethical theory that defines what is morally good in terms of what is "natural"; given the nature of the world and of humankind, certain moral goals or principles inevitably follow. Because the natural world in the most basic respects is unchanging, so too are these moral guidelines. For Novak, natural law is the foundation for the sort of universal ethic discussed in Chapter Five, for it is binding on all people everywhere and at all times, and it can be discerned without recourse to any special divine revelation (such as Scripture). As you will see, this view animates Novak's approach to issues of human sexuality.[3]

Novak opens his essay on sexual ethics by offering a thesis and a set of questions.

> The thesis I propose: Judaism teaches that the human person is essentially (1) a sexual being; (2) a social being; and (3) the image of God. From this thesis I now ask two questions: (1) What is the relation between human sexuality and human sociality? and (2) How are human sexuality and human sociality related to God?[4]

His discussion of this thesis, like all of his work, draws heavily on biblical and classical rabbinic sources. He notes, for example, that the Mishnah asks at one point, "Was not the world created for procreation?" meaning that human sexuality is part of the "normative order of creation" and so the right to procreate is natural, prior to any biblical prescription. For Novak, the admonition in Genesis 1:28, "Be fruitful and multiply," "confirms the norm rather than establishing it *de novo.*" This commandment explains why Judaism has so consistently condemned celibacy, for "sexuality is rooted in the natural order created by God . . . [it] is not to be suppressed but channeled."[5] Relying on another set of rabbinic precedents, Novak argues that human sociality, no less than human sexuality, is natural, intrinsic to the human condition. In his words, "No innocent person is to be denied fulfillment of his or her sociality."[6]

In Judaism, Novak believes, social institutions are meant to channel our natural drives—both sexual and social—in appropriate and productive ways.

> . . . because sociality is the immediate source of society's *raison d'etre* and its guiding goal, society in its law and institutions channels sexuality in socially acceptable directions, thereby limiting its intentional range.[7]

This is accomplished for Novak primarily through the institutions of marriage and the family. For this reason, Judaism absolutely prohibits incest, which undermines appropriate familial relationships both across and within generations. Because sexuality primarily intends the union of male and female through intercourse, homosexual relationships are also prohibited.

> The rationale for the prohibition of homosexuality is closely connected to the prohibition of incest. Homosexuality is considered to be counterfamilial and, also, counterprocreative. Its intentionality is purely sensual.[8]

Novak cites the rabbinic midrash that the first human God created was half male and half female, that it was split into two beings, and that the longing of male for female and vice versa ever since is rooted in this desire to reconnect with one's missing half. Hence, homosexuality is "regressive" in that it does not seek its true "other." Homosexuality, in Novak's reading of the tradition, is unnatural and so forbidden because it is both counter to the intrinsic goal of human sexuality (procreation is impossible in same-sex relations) and inconsistent with the basic desire of male and female to complete one another.

Novak reviews the development of halakhah with respect to the status of women and suggests that there is a steady movement within the sources toward the equal treatment of women within sexual relationships. Though originally marriage and divorce could be initiated only by men, later rabbinic rulings affirmed that women could be neither married nor divorced without their consent. This development paralleled the move away from polygamy and concubinage for, like all forms of prostitution, these institutions turn women into objects of men's sexual desire rather than affirming their full personhood. Only in a marriage between two exclusively and mutually committed partners can natural human sexual desire achieve its authentic expression. In Novak's words, "It is only in a monogamous union that in effect *both* the man and the woman are exclusively sanctified to each other."[9]

In answer to the second of the two questions he poses—How are human sexuality and human sociality related to God?—Novak contends that within Judaism, sexual love is modeled on the relationship of love and mutual commitment between God and Israel. Noting that many traditional sources going back to the books of Hosea and Song of Songs draw an analogy between human and divine love, Novak argues that "sexual love in the sacred covenant of marriage is a participation in a higher relationship, that of God's everlasting love for his people."[10] Faithfulness is the foundation of both relationships, and this points to an understanding of human sexuality as based in spiritual, rather than physical, fulfillment. Sex, understood primarily as a physical need, is about pleasure and taking in the world. Sex, understood primarily as grounded in the imitation of God, is about self-transcendence, especially about transcending mortality through procreation and creating a bond that is everlasting. Ultimately, for Novak, "in Judaism human sexuality, socialized and sanctified in the covenant of marriage, becomes the way two mortal creatures together existentially affirm God's love, which alone never dies."[11]

In summary, Novak not only affirms the classical teaching that sexual relations must be restricted to heterosexual, married couples but also provides a thorough rationale for the whole treatment of sexuality in Judaism. He finds implicit within many classical sources a coherent theory of sexuality: Its origin is natural, an intrinsic feature of humankind; its expression is socially channeled through the maintenance of stable families within which the next generation can be created and raised; its purpose is the experience of God's love and faithfulness through committed relationship.

Arthur Waskow

A very different treatment of human sexuality emerges from the work of Arthur Waskow,[12] a leader in the renewal movement and the author of several books on contemporary Jewish spirituality and religious practice. Jews associated with the renewal movement, such as those in the 1960s who first established *havurot* ("fellowships") as an alternative to the large, suburban synagogues of that generation, believe that the spiritual insights of traditional Judaism must be blended with the wisdom of other traditions and infused with new creative energy. Only in this way can Judaism continue to speak to a new generation of mainly assimilated, secular Jews. So Waskow's work draws from feminist and ecological thought among other contemporary liberal ideologies in its interpretation of traditional Jewish sources and concepts.

Waskow traces the evolution of Jewish sexual ethics from the biblical period to the present day. Throughout this lengthy analysis, he notes the ways in which sociopolitical issues within and surrounding the Jewish community influenced the development of Jewish sexual values and practices. Waskow makes a special effort to review not only the classical positions about appropriate sexual relationships recorded in halakhic sources but also the less mainstream views of medieval erotic poets and mystics. In the contemporary world, Waskow argues, several important sociopolitical realities require Jews to reassess the applicability of classical norms, remain open to heretofore marginalized elements within the tradition, and search for new ways of sanctifying sexual relationships. He notes that in modern societies, people tend to marry much later than was the case in previous centuries, that modern technology has made birth control more effective, and that modern people interact far more frequently with those of other cultures than did their ancestors. As a result, people today are sexually active for much longer prior to marriage, are able to separate sexual intercourse from procreation more consistently, and are exposed to many more potential sexual partners (and so, to the threat of sexually transmitted diseases) than during the period when traditional Jewish sexual norms developed.

Most importantly, views of women have changed radically since rabbinic times. An entire tractate of the Talmud is devoted to issues surrounding sexual contact with women during their menstrual period based on the ancient taboo that blood (and other bodily emissions) were impure. Although women's legal status improved over the generations, substantial elements of misogyny remained as men were assumed to exercise authority over women. Within this system, sexual contact was channeled in ways designed to maximize the possibility of procreation. Although the pleasure of sexual union was acknowledged, and sometimes even celebrated, procreation remained the primary goal. The biblical Song of Songs with its depiction of sensual, passionate love between partners stands out in providing an alternative vision of sex as joyful in its own right, and the rabbis in effect subverted this by interpreting it allegorically as a story about the love of God and Israel.

The cornerstone of Waskow's sexual ethic is that, in an age of scarce resources and the threat of overpopulation, procreation should no longer be regarded as the primary goal of sexual intercourse. He states that in contrast to the male-dominated, legally structured model of marriage that prevailed in rabbinic times, Song of Songs provides a theory of sexuality appropriate for our time.

> In the Song of Songs, the Divine Parent is gone. Adam and Eve are grown up now, and the Parent has been absorbed into their own identities. . . . In the Song, their relationship with the earth is as fluid, playful, loving, and pleasurable as their relationship with each other.
>
> What if we were to take this as a teaching for our epoch? . . . As in the Song of Songs these grown-ups connect sexually for the sake of pleasure and love, so could the human race, or the Jewish people. Without denigrating the forms of sexuality that focus on children and family, we might find that forms of sexuality that are centered on pleasure are more legitimate at this moment in history than ever before.[13]

One key implication of this model is that it would undermine the traditional prohibition against homosexuality.

> . . . it is possible that the ethic of sexual pleasure and love celebrated by the Song of Songs . . . will come into its own alongside the ethic of family. It may seem ironic that the Song, one of the greatest celebrations of heterosexual sexuality in all of literature, could also affirm the homosexual community's bent toward sex as pleasurable and loving rather than as procreative.[14]

Waskow's search for an appropriate contemporary sexual ethic leads him to propose that we reconceptualize sexual relationships as shifting throughout the life cycle. Different models of appropriate sexual relationship, with varying levels of commitment, would suit adolescents, young adults, married couples, and single middle-aged adults. In part, this might motivate Jews to reconsider the wisdom of the long-abandoned tradition of the concubine (Hebrew, *pilegesh*), who had status in a man's household alongside his wife. Such a communally recognized sexual partnership, especially for those not yet ready for the long-term commitment of marriage (or for those recently widowed or divorced, or too elderly to make marriage practical), has roots within the tradition but also serves the particular sexual needs of a new generation of Jews. Similarly, Waskow considers embracing the notion of temporary couples (Hebrew, *zug*), who formalize in some socially recognized way a level of commitment, although not necessarily one that they expect to last a lifetime.

Waskow proposes that we think creatively about ways of honoring and sanctifying the various expressions of sexuality that occur at different life stages. He notes that some contemporary Jewish women have developed a menarche ceremony, sometimes held on the first New Moon following the onset of a young woman's menstrual period. He imagines that groups of young men or women could be guided, under synagogue auspices, on a kind of "vision quest" (perhaps modeled on the Exodus) in which older mentors would impart their wisdom about sexuality. Such an initiation ritual would parallel the bar or bat mitzvah, which is also a rite of passage, but focused on learning rather than on the sexual awakening that comes with puberty. He considers the possibility that a temporary or "experimental" relationship at any life stage could be formalized through a religious ceremony or in a declaration before the synagogue community that a particular couple has formed a *zug* and undertaken certain mutual responsibilities. Sexual encounters could be sanctified if the partners creatively appropriated the classical practice of reciting blessings at the moment of performing a holy act. In doing so, Waskow thinks, we could also bring greater moral awareness to our sexual behavior.

> . . . by clearly affirming that each sexual act is sacred, I hope to encourage a change in the quality of those acts; encourage honesty, caring, equality, and conscious choice rather than manipulation, coercion, and automatism in sexual relationships. Affirming that sex is holy may make it possible for sex to become more holy.[15]

Finally, Waskow invites Jews to consider the establishment of what he calls a *beit hesed*, "house of nurturing love" on the order of the traditional *beit din*, "house of judgment" or court. In a former age, when sexual relationships were understood as subject to legal regulation, questions about appropriate sexual behavior could be referred to a rabbinical court. In this generation, Jews need instead an institution that can provide religious guidance for people as they struggle with questions about appropriate sexual conduct. Such a *beit hesed* could offer individuals or couples "nurturing wisdom" and would "draw on Jewish tradition without rigidly obeying the strictures of the past."[16] Through such an institution, maintained within the synagogue or an alternative religious group, a new, yet traditionally based, sexual ethic could be developed that would speak to the needs of contemporary Jews and reaffirm that Jewish tradition has much guidance to offer them in this most personal area of their lives.

Waskow's approach to Jewish sexual ethics is marked by its sensitivity to the unique circumstances of contemporary Jews (and others) and by its willingness to creatively appropriate elements within Jewish tradition (e.g., the sensuality of Song of Songs or the notion of a sexual relationship, *pilegesh*, outside of marriage) in preference to the established halakhic standards of the past. He makes this choice quite deliberately and justifies it as follows:

> If we wish to make these choices based on Jewish spirituality, wisdom, and community, if we think there was some measure of wisdom in the Jewish past along with some outlooks that raise deep ethical and spiritual problems, then we need to have a way of drawing on Torah. One way, of course, is simply to bow to the authority of the past and of those who today repeat the content of its decisions.

Another path is to try to look into the deeper structure, the deeper intent, of the wisdom of the past.[17]

This approach leads Waskow to seek ways of affirming the sanctity of sexual relationships, including those traditionally proscribed, and well as to create new ways of providing Jewishly informed moral guidance to people in all stages of life as their sexual needs and relationships evolve.

Eugene Borowitz

Eugene Borowitz[18] is the most prominent liberal Jewish theologian and ethicist in the United States. In his capacity as a professor at Hebrew Union College, the seminary for Reform rabbis, and throughout his voluminous writings, he has championed the notion that covenant remains the central category through which contemporary Jews should interpret their experience and determine the norms for their lives. Such an approach attempts to balance the claims of the historical covenant community as embodied in its classical literature with those of contemporary liberal culture, especially the values of individual conscience, democracy, and personal freedom.

Borowitz is roundly critical of the sexual mores that emerged out of the "sexual revolution" of the 1960s with its emphasis on the almost unlimited endorsement of sexual experimentation and the assumption that "mutual consent" is sufficient to ensure the morality of any sexual encounter. For Borowitz

> the only human contact demanded under the consent criterion is first of wills and then of genitals. This makes too little of human beings and allows sexual relations to be another activity where we are seen in terms of our parts rather than summoned to full human interrelationship.[19]

Drawing on the theory of I–Thou relationships developed by Martin Buber, Borowitz argues that "we human beings are much more than our sexuality,"[20] and so, sexual relationships ought properly to be conducted in the context of a loving, mutual, committed relationship. He acknowledges that such relationships can exist outside the context of marriage, although he avers that "the most ethical form of human relationship I know is love-for-life."[21] Human sexuality ought to mirror and affirm our full humanity, and this can flourish only in a relationship built on commitment for the future rather than simply fulfillment in the present. Marriage is sanctified precisely because the exclusiveness and fidelity it entails are modeled on the faithful covenantal relationship between God and Israel, which is the source of all Jewish moral commitment.

With respect to marriage, Borowitz affirms the validity of much that the tradition teaches. Certainly, the tradition is right to affirm the sacredness of the marital bond and the centrality of sexual expression in that context. Marriage is meant to be very much a physical and sensual relationship, not only or even primarily a spiritual one. Moreover, the tradition rightly condemns incest and adultery, which unquestionably compromise the sacredness of a sexual relationship. Many traditional authorities understood that pleasure was a valid, if not primary, purpose for sex. By placing human sexuality in the context of covenantal living, Judaism both honors the sacred potential inherent in sexual relationship and insists that that potential be actualized in ways that honor our humanity as a whole.

Borowitz recognizes, however, that certain rabbinic attitudes are incompatible with our view of human sexuality and the circumstances of contemporary life. He notes that the rabbis, more interested in the social than the strictly personal dimensions of sexual life, offer little explicit guidance in how to maintain vitality in a relationship that spans a lifetime. More important, the tradition exhibits significant inhibitions about sexual fantasy as well as taboos about "spilling human seed" and menstrual blood and an undue emphasis on the procreative function of sex. Perhaps most significant, halakhic standards surrounding marriage are permeated with views of women as subordinate to men, which we now reject as incompatible with the inherent equality of men and women.

In typical fashion, Borowitz is less concerned to offer specific guidance about any of these issues than he is to explore the dialectic of traditional and contemporary perspectives. On the one hand, he concludes that the fundamental perspective of Jewish tradition's teaching on sexuality remains valid.

> In sum, the Jewish teaching on sexuality continues to express with compelling power the mandates of existence under the Covenant. It provides us with a ground of value, standards of practice, and ideals to which to aspire. It directs us to structure our existence so that our lives are not a random sequence of events or experiences. It puts us in a historical context so that the present moment takes its place not only within our personal history but that of our family, our people, and thus of humankind slowly moving toward God's kingdom. It invests our sexual lives with sanctity, raising our animality beyond the human to where something of the divine image may be seen in us.[22]

Nonetheless, Borowitz contends, traditional teachings need to be corrected in three areas. First, Judaism's preoccupation with abstract standards needs to be supplemented with concern for the individuality that we so value. Second, the traditional values that are grounded in a fear of sexuality and hence are potentially repressive must be reshaped into something that is more "therapeutically liberating." Finally, women's perspectives and experience must be incorporated into our sexual ethic alongside the traditionally male-oriented and male-dominated perspectives.[23]

In all, Borowitz's sexual ethic derives from a perspective that he calls "covenantal personalism":

> For me, Jewish teaching regularly, but not always, functions more significantly in my decision-making than does western culture, at least as far as values and grounding are concerned. These I interpret in a fundamentally personalistic way. . . .
>
> Applying this value stance to specific questions, I mediate between the demands of living in Covenant and the socio-historical, personal situation in which I find myself. My decisions and practice are, therefore, characterized by a dialectical flow. They are relatively steady and consistent insofar as my faith and personal integrity remain stable. They are also relatively free and changing insofar as I, at a given moment, detect a need to serve God as part of the people of Israel's historic Covenant in ways previously not utilized by me or the Jewish people.

Covenantal personalism makes me more "liberal" than the halachists and less universalistic and anarchic than the pure autonomists.[24]

With respect to sexual conduct, as we have seen, this leaves Borowitz affirming the central values of the tradition—that sexuality is natural, integral to human personhood, and a potential domain of sacredness—provided that its expression takes place in the context of loving, mutual, committed relationships, preferably within marriage. By the same token, he is openly critical of attitudes within the tradition that seem to him to inhibit the joy and playfulness of sexual expression, that minimize the personal (as distinct from social) dimensions of human sexuality, and that denigrate women.

Stepping back from this debate, you will notice that Novak, Waskow, and Borowitz represent three quite different ways of balancing the inherited wisdom of the tradition, on the one hand, and the insights and circumstances of contemporary Jews, on the other. For Novak, the truth of traditional sexual norms remains unchallenged; at no point in his discussion does he entertain the possibility that contemporary circumstances could invalidate a fundamental scriptural or rabbinic value. This appears to follow directly from his view that Judaism's theory of sexuality reflects certain basic and invariant features of human sexual and social life. For Waskow, just the opposite would appear to be the case. What Novak regards as "natural" and unchanging, Waskow relativizes as merely an expression of the social and historical circumstances prevailing at a certain time. His treatment of sexual ethics never seriously challenges the basic views of contemporary liberals, for example, about sexual orientation or sex outside the context of marriage. His goal, rather, is to find those aspects of the tradition that speak to the sexual realities that contemporary Jews live with and to find new ways of sanctifying contemporary practices. Borowitz stakes out an intermediate position. His dialectical approach leads him in some measure to critique contemporary sexual practices from the perspective of traditional values but also to challenge some traditional perspectives as incompatible with the needs and values of the modern Jew. Not surprisingly, he resists any formulaic approach to this balancing act, being fully aware that the moral demands that "covenantal personalism" places on him will be discovered only in the course of living in a dialectical tension between the two.

Underlying this debate, then, are various answers to a crucial question: To what extent do Jews view the values of the tradition as products of particular historical circumstances and to what extent, conversely, do they view them as transcending the time and place in which they were developed? There are multiple positions along this spectrum, and the views of Novak, Waskow, and Borowitz considered here represent only three possibilities. Plainly, however, if Jews incline toward one end of the spectrum, they will remain open to the possibility that, as circumstances change, the rules and values of an earlier era may be simply mistaken or, at very least, need significant revision. Jews will assign weight to these traditional ethical norms but not ultimate authority; in Mordecai Kaplan's famous phrase, tradition will get "a vote, but not a veto."[25] Any traditional moral position will have to be judged, at least in part, by the moral standards or the practical needs of the contemporary world. By contrast, if Jews incline to the opposite end of the spectrum, they will instead judge the contemporary world, at least in part, against the tradition's values. To whatever extent, and for whatever reason, they place the teachings of tradition in a realm of eternal and unchanging truth, to just that extent they will assign it authoritative status over against all relative and subjective truths.

It is tempting for many liberals to suppose that all values are relative and to eschew all moral absolutes. But, of course, liberals also affirm certain values as foundational and universal; in the words of the Declaration of Independence, "We hold these truths to be self-evident, that all men are created equal, endowed by their Creator with inalienable rights, that among these are life, liberty and the pursuit of happiness." Moral systems inevitably rest on some "first principles"; the question is how to determine what these are and how they function within a system that also responds to the changing social circumstances and prevailing values of those who are committed to it.

This contemporary Jewish debate about sexual ethics rests, in some measure, on a deeper theological debate: where to locate the absolute and eternal (that which is divinely ordained) in relation to the relative and changing (that which is merely the product of human reason and imagination). No contemporary Jewish ethicist, whatever his or her views on that matter, can avoid that fundamental question.

ABORTION

Since 1973, when the United States Supreme Court handed down its landmark decision in the case of *Roe v. Wade,* the debate within U.S. society over abortion has continued and even intensified. Advocates of a fetus's "right to life" and advocates of a "woman's right to choose" have faced off in local, state, and national political arenas, and the rhetoric on both sides of the debate has become increasingly extreme. Some have suggested that, more than any other moral debate, the controversy over abortion has defined the political climate of our time, at least in the United States. Of course, the morality of abortion has been debated for many centuries. Jewish sources dating to the early centuries of the Common Era addressed it, and an extensive literature has developed around both practical questions and theoretical concerns raised by abortion.

The question at the heart of the abortion debate cannot be reduced to the oft-repeated question, When does life begin? A more sophisticated analysis of the issue yields a more extensive and nuanced set of questions: What is the status of the embryo? Does it change during the course of its development? What sorts of protections, if any, are owed to prenatal life, and why? Under what circumstances can the fetus's "right to life" be overridden by other rights?

This overview of the problem of abortion focuses on three positions, moving from the most restrictive (Bleich), to a more moderate approach (Feldman), and finally to the most lenient view (Lubarsky). This recap of the views of these contemporary Jewish authorities highlights the ways in which they draw on and interpret the many classical sources that bear on the questions just listed.

J. David Bleich

J. David Bleich[26] is among the most respected and prolific Orthodox legal authorities in the United States. His many volumes of responsa together with his position as the *rosh yeshiva* (headmaster) of Yeshiva University establish him as an extremely influential *posek* (halakhic authority). His legal writings, especially in the area of biomedical ethics, are noteworthy for the careful way in which they guide readers through the intricacies of halakhic literature and for his attentiveness to the philosophical issues internal to halakhic discourse. Bleich's analysis of the abortion issue begins with this general statement:

> While Judaism has always sanctioned therapeutic abortion in at least limited circumstances, the pertinent halakhic discussions are permeated with a spirit of humility reflecting an attitude of awe and reverence before the profound mystery of existence and a deeply rooted reluctance to condone interference with the sanctity of individual human life.[27]

The subsequent review of halakhic sources—including many talmudic commentaries and responsa—is far too detailed to be summarized fully here. Instead, this discussion focuses on several key issues: the basis of the prohibition against abortion, the status of the embryo during the first forty days of gestation, the circumstances in which therapeutic abortions may be performed, and the question of aborting an abnormal fetus.

By common consent, the key early rabbinic text dealing with abortion is Mishnah, Ohalot 7:6:

> If a woman is experiencing difficulty in childbirth, the embryo within her must be dismembered and removed limb by limb [if necessary], because her life takes precedence over its life. Once its head [or its greater part] has emerged, one does not touch it, for one may not set aside one life for another.

The clear implication for most subsequent authorities is that abortion in general is prohibited but that an exception is made only when the mother's life is endangered. Still, there is no biblical statute explicitly prohibiting abortion, for rabbinic authorities explicitly exclude abortion from the purview of Exodus 21:12, "one who fatally strikes a *man* [but not a *fetus*] shall be put to death." Abortion is not generally permitted, the Mishnah implies, but neither is it a clear case of murder because the person who performs an abortion is not guilty of a capital offense as is someone who murders a human being outside the womb.

This ambiguity in the legal tradition surrounding abortion leads authorities to debate the rationale underlying the general prohibition. Many understand abortion as at least akin to murder, but others regard the prohibition as grounded in the rule against wasting or destroying semen (based on Genesis 38:9ff.) or as unlawful "wounding" (based on Deuteronomy 25:3). As Bleich notes, each of these rationales has difficulty explaining some aspects of the legal tradition on abortion, and each leads in somewhat different directions with respect to the circumstances in which an abortion is permitted.

If, as most authorities seem to believe, abortion is prohibited because it is close to murder, the question arises as to why the Mishnah cited above permits it at all—indeed, actually requires it—in cases where the mother's life is in danger. The Talmud takes up this issue and considers the argument that the fetus has the status of a "pursuer" (Hebrew, *rodef*) and, based on Exodus 22:1–2, if someone is pursuing you with intent to do you harm, you may justifiably defend yourself, even killing the pursuer, if this is necessary.[28] Of course, by this logic, we should be allowed to kill the fetus even after it begins to emerge from the womb, which the Mishnah expressly forbids. After all, it is still "pursuing" the mother even after its head emerges. The explanation offered in the Talmud that at this point the mother is actually being "pursued by Heaven [not the child]" is not very convincing, and, in any event, the Mishnah already provides rationale enough, that the mother's life takes precedence over the child's. Still, Maimonides relies on the principle of the pursuer in his explication of the law regarding abortion, and his view has been variously interpreted, and challenged, by many authorities in subsequent centuries.

The issue of the status of the fetus is further complicated by the famous Talmudic statement attributed to Rav Hisda that within the first forty days of gestation, the embryo is "mere water," and hence does not have the status of a person at all.[29] The implication would be that destruction of the fetus during this early period is entirely permissible, for any reason whatsoever.[30] This view, of course, could not be countenanced by those who regard the prohibition against abortion as a matter of "wasting seed," for on that theory there would be no distinction whatsoever between the first forty days and the remaining weeks of gestation. This notion that the fetus is "mere water" for the first forty days also poses problems for those who think of the prohibition against abortion in terms of "wounding" the mother, for if abortion entails prohibited wounding of the mother, this is just as true during the first forty days of gestation as afterward. So in this view abortion would have to be completely prohibited unless it is a matter of "wounding" the mother in order to save her life.

Bleich concludes from all this that, notwithstanding Hisda's view to the contrary, most abortion theories would fail to distinguish between the first forty days and the rest of the gestational period. Indeed, he notes that numerous authorities permit violation of the Sabbath to preserve fetal life in accord with the well-established principle that the Sabbath can be violated in order to preserve a life[31] and that this is so even in the earliest stages of pregnancy. The clear implication of this ruling is that fetal life, like human life outside the womb, is entitled to certain protections and is valued more highly than the observance of even the most important religious commandments. As Bleich puts it, "Anticipation of potential development and subsequent attainment of human status creates certain privileges and obligations with regard to the undeveloped fetus."[32]

Bleich, of course, endorses the long tradition, beginning with the Mishnah, which sanctions abortion when the mother's life is threatened. The matter becomes murkier when the pregnancy exacerbates a preexisting threat to her life but does not constitute a threat in itself. He notes that most authorities, relying on the logic of the "pursuer" argument, conclude that abortion is required, perhaps even permitted, only in cases where the fetus itself is the proximate cause of the threat to the mother's life. Moreover, if there is any doubt about the threat to the mother's life, we do not invoke the law of the pursuer and so do not permit abortions.

Still another complexity arises when the mother's health (including mental health) is threatened but not her life. With respect to such cases, the most lenient view of therapeutic abortion is that of Rabbi Jacob Emden (1697–1776):

> who permits performance of an abortion not only when the mother's health is compromised but also in cases of "grave necessity," such as when continuation of the pregnancy would subject the mother to great pain. Such abortions are sanctioned by R. Emden when performed before the onset of labor at which time the fetus has "torn itself loose" from the uterine wall [after which time the fetus may have status as an independent being].[33]

Bleich notes that Rabbi Eliezer Waldenberg, an outstanding contemporary authority on medical ethics, followed this precedent. Bleich implicitly rejects this more liberal view, however, concluding his discussion with a long list of traditional authorities who restrict therapeutic abortion to cases in which there is a definite threat to the mother's life.

A similar range of opinion exists, Bleich notes, with respect to abortions of abnormal fetuses. Again he notes that Rabbi Waldenberg is "the only authority who deems abnormality of the fetus to be justification for interruption of pregnancy and even he stipulates that the abortion must be performed in the very early stages of pregnancy.[34] Bleich again clearly sides with what he sees as the majority position of the halakhic authorities, that "there is no distinction in the eyes of the law between normal and abnormal persons either with regard to the statutes governing homicide or with regard to those governing feticide."[35]

Bleich concludes his analysis of this complex material with the following general statement of Jewish law's approach to abortion.

> Halakhah is motivated first and foremost by concern and solicitude for all living creatures. It is this extreme concern for man's inalienable right to life, both actual and potential, which permeates these many halakhic determinations.
>
> A Jew is governed by such reverence for life that he trembles lest he tamper unmindfully with the greatest of all divine gifts, the bestowal or withholding of which is the prerogative of God alone. Although he be master over all within the world, there remain areas where man must fear to tread, acknowledging the limits of his sovereignty and the limitations of his understanding. In the unborn child lies the mystery and enigma of existence.[36]

In summary, Bleich finds within the entire tradition of halakhic debate surrounding abortion a strong presumption in favor of protecting life in all its forms and a corresponding inclination on the part of most prior authorities to restrict abortion, as the Mishnah appears to do, to cases in which the fetus directly threatens the life of the mother. He acknowledges the existence of more lenient views, but he clearly favors the more conservative position and regards it as the majority view among traditional authorities.

David Feldman

A well-respected scholar as well as a practicing rabbi, David Feldman[37] is best known for his extremely well-researched and clearly written book, *Marital Relations, Birth Control and Abortion in Jewish Law*.[38] Feldman's work on this subject, which began with his doctoral dissertation at the Jewish Theological Seminary, encompasses hundreds of responsa on the subject. Most significant, he endeavors to lay bare the logic underlying the whole legal tradition with respect to abortion and offers important comparative judgments about Jewish and Christian views of the subject.

In discussing abortion, Feldman cites and discusses many of the sources already mentioned in Bleich's treatment of the subject. Feldman notes at the outset that abortion is not murder under Jewish law. The simplest evidence for this is the fact that the Mishnah cited earlier permits abortion for the purpose of saving the mother's life. Murder, however (together with public idolatry and gross sexual immorality), are classified in Jewish law as such weighty transgressions that they may not be performed even to save one's own life.[39] Abortion clearly is not in this category.

Moreover, Feldman notes the Talmudic dictum that "the fetus is the thigh [i.e., limb] of its mother," which means that within halakhah it has no "juridical personality."[40] The conversion of a pregnant woman, for example, automatically affects the unborn child within her, and one who purchases a pregnant animal automatically gains title to the embryo as well. This does not mean, however, that the fetus has no claim on us whatsoever or that a woman could treat it as *merely* a part of her own body. The threshold question, as Feldman defines it, is whether ending the life of a fetus constitutes a form of homicide.

The key biblical text in this regard is Exodus 21:22:

> When men fight, and one of them pushes a pregnant woman and a miscarriage results, but no other damage ensues, the one responsible shall be fined according as the woman's husband may exact from him. . . . But if other damage ensues, the penalty shall be life for life. . . ."

The straightforward implication of this text is that the death of the fetus is not treated as an accidental homicide but as a case of lost property for which the husband is entitled to monetary compensation. By contrast, if the mother is killed in the same encounter, the murderer is liable to the death penalty. So biblical law clearly distinguishes the taking of fetal life from the taking of human life outside of the womb. The reason here, as in the case of Mishnah Ohalot, is straightforward: The fetus is "not yet a person" until it emerges from the womb.[41]

After reviewing the debates surrounding the "pursuer" theory, Feldman summarizes two contrasting orientations within halakhah with respect to abortion:

> in fact, all rabbinic teaching on the subject of abortion can be said to align itself either with Maimonides, on the right, or with Rashi, on the left. The "rightist" approach begins with the assumption . . . that abortion is "akin to murder" and therefore allowable only in cases of corresponding gravity, such as saving the life of the mother. The approach then builds *down* from that strict position to

embrace a broader interpretation of lifesaving situations. These include a threat
to her health, for example, and perhaps a threat to her sanity in terms of suicidal
possibilities, but exclude any lesser reasons.

The more "liberal" approach, based on Rashi's affirmation that the fetus is
not a human person, . . . assumes that no real prohibition against abortion exists and
build *up* from that ground to safeguard against indiscriminate or unjustified
thwarting of potential life.[42]

As different as these two approaches might seem, Feldman notes that they share a
common assumption that the permissibility of abortion in all cases depends on
maternal, not fetal, considerations. In no sense does the fetus have a "right to be
born." In Feldman's words, "There is no right to be born any more than a right to be
conceived."[43] Rather, the presumption underlying the entire debate in Judaism is that
the mother has a right to life and to health. The only question is how broadly to interpret that right, that is, how seriously her life or health must be threatened before she
(or others) can take action to end the life within her. The more conservative approach
gives greater weight to the status of the unborn child and so permits abortion only
when the mother's life or health is gravely threatened. The more liberal approach
gives less status to the fetus and so gives the mother greater latitude in choosing to
perform an abortion.

This focus on maternal well-being leads Feldman to make the following intriguing observation. If a woman were to ask a rabbi for permission to abort because she
had reason to believe her child would be born deformed, the rabbi, following the
thrust of the tradition, would probably decline. The fact that a child may be born with
abnormalities, even if we can establish that with certainty, does not make its life less
valuable and certainly does not warrant taking its life. On the other hand, if the same
mother were to ask for permission to abort on the grounds that the fear of giving
birth to a deformed child was causing her extreme mental anguish, there would be
traditional grounds for granting her request. As Feldman puts it, "Now the fetal indication has become a maternal indication, and all the considerations for her welfare
are now brought to bear. The fetus is unknown, future, potential, part of the 'secrets
of God'; the mother is known, present, human and seeking compassion."[44] In this
regard he cites approvingly the ruling of Rabbi Mordecai Winkler, "Mental-health
risk has been definitely equated with physical-health risk. This woman, in danger of
losing her mental health unless the pregnancy is interrupted, would therefore accordingly qualify."[45]

In conclusion, Feldman notes that Judaism's approach to abortion is still a far
cry from the contemporary view that it is all a matter of a "woman's right to choose."
Abortion for population control, financial reasons, or for the sake of the woman's
career are all forbidden. Judaism, after all, regards procreation as a positive commandment and "casual abortion is accordingly abhorrent."[46] Recognizing that abortion is not the moral equivalent of murder (at least not in all cases) but also that
Judaism stresses reverence for life, Feldman concludes that "abortion can be understood in more than one way; the right to it under circumstances consistent with conscience should not be compromised or unduly stigmatized."[47]

Sandra Lubarsky

Sandra Lubarsky[48] is an associate professor of religious studies and director of the Master of Liberal Studies Program at Northern Arizona University. Her scholarly work focuses on interreligious dialogue, postmodern religious thought, process philosophy, feminism, and religion and nature. Lubarsky's analysis of the abortion issue begins with the acknowledgement that rabbinic authorities over the ages have been very reticent to sanction abortion except in cases of medical necessity. She finds, as well, a tension within the tradition between the legal status of the fetus and the generally conservative stance of most traditional authorities.

> In general, the rabbis do not find that the legal action guides given in *halakhic* literature sufficiently address the issue of abortion. The legal status of abortion is clear: the killing of an embryo is not murder. But what of the moral implications of abortion? . . . Abortion may not be a capital offense, but it is still morally reprehensible. Within Jewish circles, the discussion about abortion is a discussion about sufficient moral justification for an act that is not legally culpable.[49]

Following Feldman, Lubarsky notes that "in the greatest number of decisions made by members of both the 'lenient' and the 'stringent' schools, abortion has been permitted on medical grounds only."[50] She briefly reviews a few of the rabbinic texts that figure prominently in the abortion debate and articulates the central assumptions that she sees underlying the rabbinic rulings as follows:

> (a) Human fetal life has little independent value. It is certainly not "sacred."
> (b) The value that it has is far inferior to the value of a fully viable human being, so much so that only monetary recompense must be made for the destruction of fetal life. . . . (c) An existing human being has greater worth than a *potential* human being, that is, the mother is of greater value than the fetus.[51]

From Lubarsky's perspective, this set of assumptions alone should warrant abortion in a much wider range of situations than rabbinic authorities have recognized. They have been constrained in their views of abortion, however, by "extralegal" considerations and so have tended toward more conservative views on abortion than the legal sources alone would warrant. By uncovering these additional presuppositions and challenging their validity, Lubarsky makes the case for the permissibility of abortion for "ecological, sociological, economic, emotional, or intellectual reasons"—a far more lenient position than that of any traditional authority.[52]

Lubarsky's argument is best traced by listing each of these additional theological and moral presuppositions as she articulates them, followed by her critique. Because they are closely related, she deals with the first three as a unit.

> (1) "With the exception of God, human life is valued over every other kind of life."
> (2) "In almost all cases, an increase in human life amounts to an increase in value."
> (3) "All humans are of equal worth from God's perspective."

Lubarsky takes exception to these views. The anthropocentrism of Jewish tradition, according to which human life has an absolute value in contrast to all of God's other creations, fails to appreciate the interrelatedness of all life on the planet. Once we come to understand the essential interdependence of all life, we can no longer so easily dismiss concerns about overpopulation, for bringing new children into the world may threaten the environment and ultimately the long-term prospects for human survival. Moreover, a hierarchy of value is at work in Judaism that undercuts the presupposition that more human life, of any sort, necessarily entails an increase in value from God's perspective. Lubarsky writes:

> There is no equality of value between a fetus and a person because the experiences that define their existences are radically unequal—the fetus's experience lacks the richness, intentionality, and consciousness of a person's experience. We can affirm the intrinsic value of a fetus, an infant, and an adult, without also having to affirm an equality of value for them. And since we can do this, it is unreasonable to limit abortion to those instances in which a threat to the mother's health is present.[53]

Moreover, even the tradition recognizes that not all lives are of equal value because it requires that Jews sacrifice their lives in cases where continued life comes at the expense of grossly violating God's law and because it values maternal life over fetal life.

Lubarsky next articulates the presumption of the tradition that, fourth, "God is unchanging, or, at least, God's essence is unchanging." To this she counters that from biblical times on, Jews have understood God as manifest within the flow of history. Because God is in relationship with humankind, God is affected by that relationship and by the unfolding of events on earth. God, then, is responsive to historical circumstances, and the demands that God makes upon people vary depending on the current human situation. She writes:

> If the world is an unpopulated one, God may work to increase the richness of experience by urging the creation to reproduce at a higher level. If the world is an overpopulated one, God may work to increase the richness of experience by urging the creatures to reduce their rates of reproduction and to increase their enjoyment in other ways. . . . To say that abortion always "diminishes God's image" is to undermine God's ability to be responsive.[54]

The fifth belief that Lubarsky finds within the tradition is "the mental or psychological aspect of human life is (somehow) less basic than the physical aspect." In fact, however, the psychological aspect of human life is intrinsic to our humanity; indeed, it is in this way that God affects people most directly. Lubarsky proposes that the rabbis always tend to overlook or minimize the inner life of women, emphasizing their physicality. As a result of this bias, they minimize the emotional and psychological impact on women of carrying a child to term and so sanction abortion only when these factors pose a direct threat to the mother's physical health (or survival). If women are granted the full range of emotional and psychological experiences that the tradition readily acknowledges that men have, the range of considerations that are relevant to the ethics of terminating fetal life will necessarily be broadened.

Finally, Lubarsky challenges the assumption that "existing human life has precedence over potential human life." In one sense, of course, this principle supports the lenient view on abortion in that it weighs the actual life of the mother over the potential life of the fetus. Lubarsky insists, however, that ethicists need to take into account not only the potential life of the fetus (which is indeed less valuable than the actual life of the mother) but also the potential life of others: other children and family members, the population at large, and so on. To focus exclusively on the impact of abortion on mother and fetus is to overlook the implications for the future life of many persons who will be affected, directly or indirectly, by the decision whether or not to abort.

Lubarsky concludes her analysis of the abortion issue with the suggestion that, once these theological assumptions are corrected, Jews will be left with the plain thrust of the law itself, namely, that abortion is not murder and so can be justified for a range of reasons beyond just the mother's life or health. Indeed, within the tradition itself she finds warrant for these alternative theological perspectives:

> When these correctives are assumed, Judaism becomes a worldview that recognizes that all life—human, nonhuman, and divine—is interdependent and mutually responsive. Hence, a decision about abortion is a decision that must be made in light of both actual and potential human, nonhuman, and divine life.[55]

In summary, Lubarsky finds that the basic legal sources in Judaism, stripped of extraneous and erroneous theological views, give much wider latitude for performing abortion than has traditionally been recognized.

Reading this review of contemporary Jewish debate on abortion, you cannot help but notice the extent to which the same sources figure prominently in the work of Bleich, Feldman, and Lubarsky. All these writers are well aware of the range of positions and rulings to be found within classical Judaic sources, and they all believe that these sources are directly applicable to the current abortion debate, yet they draw quite different conclusions from the textual tradition. This is clear evidence that they bring a variety of perspectives to the interpretation of those sources.

As an Orthodox ethicist, Bleich works entirely within the assumptions of the halakhic system. The vast body of earlier rulings and opinions recorded in the halakhic literature must be sorted through and analyzed in order to derive a definitive answer to the question at hand. Within this tradition, many conflicting views may be expressed, but ultimately they must point in a single direction. As a *posek* (halakhic authority) Bleich's job, like that of a judge in our legal system, is to discern the main thrust of the tradition on the questions of abortion and to render a reasoned decision. If, as in the usual case, not all authorities agree on every point, Bleich will use all the legal and philosophical tools at his command to argue for the position that he regards as "correct." That process of deliberation encompasses judgments about the relative weight of different authorities, of "rulings" versus mere "opinions," and the ways in which individual views may rely on the interpretation (or misinterpretation) of prior views.

Feldman, in contrast, recognizes that two quite different approaches to abortion might be found within the tradition, and both might be equally valid. Like a contemporary scholar of U.S. law, he sifts through the sources not so much to find "Judaism's view on abortion" (presuming there is only one) but also to discern different legal philosophies and tendencies among earlier authorities. Within his analysis, minority views are no less viable than majority ones, for all have been preserved in the various layers of rabbinic literature. Hence, rather than trying to decide among various positions, Feldman carefully delineates the options and affirms the pluralism that he finds. His conclusions about abortion are less conservative precisely because he not only sees but also affirms the range of positions within the tradition.

Lubarsky, finally, approaches the very same texts with an eye to exposing and evaluating the unstated assumptions that animate the entire debate. Because she is not essentially a halakhist, she is concerned less with the fine distinctions to be drawn among different cases and rulings than with the broad principles and values that she sees at work within even the majority position. Also because she is not committed to discerning, much less abiding by, a single "traditional view," she is open to going where no traditional authority has gone before. For her, an authentic Jewish view on abortion is one that is consistent with the truest values and perspectives on human life whether these have been expressed in earlier rulings on abortion or not.

It is clear, therefore, that there are many ways of reading the traditional sources on a given moral issue and that this is true in more than one sense. Certainly many texts lend themselves to more than one interpretation: Maimonides' invocation of the law of the pursuer with respect to abortion is one salient example. Because that text plays a significant role in subsequent authorities' discussions (which are, themselves, subject to multiple interpretations), reaching different conclusions about the meaning of a whole line of traditional precedents is legitimate. Perhaps more significant, Bleich, Feldman, and Lubarsky clearly bring different assumptions to the whole enterprise of reading these textual sources, especially different ideas about the role that those sources play in the effort to discern a "Jewish view" of abortion. Does the tradition necessarily point in a single direction? What is the status of distinctly minority views within the tradition? Is it possible to reinterpret or even ignore sources if they are based on beliefs that seem to be mistaken or even at odds with other traditional beliefs? The way in which these basic methodological questions are answered will largely determine the conclusions an interpreter draws from this complex tradition of texts that spans many centuries and gives voice to many views.

Finally, it should be noted that the personal views of an author may color his or her reading of a text. Contemporary Jewish ethicists rarely, if ever, concede that they come to the sources with a preexisting position, on abortion, for example, and are drawn to read the sources in a way that tends to confirm what they already believed. Even if they do not admit this, however, given what we know about human nature, it would be naïve to suppose that they had no view at all on the ethics of abortion before they began their studies of the texts. The more important point, though, is that being predisposed to a particular position does not invalidate an ethicist's reading of the tradition. A person can see only with the eyes she has, and she can read and interpret the texts of a tradition only as a fully embodied person with experiences and values of her own. Whether consciously or unconsciously, these personal perspectives will probably inform a person's understanding of a moral tradition, of the words he reads, and of the way he responds both to the conflicting voices found there and to the values that found expression in the words of generations past.

At the same time, no contemporary Jewish ethicist would pretend that his or her view is "authentically Jewish" just because he or she subscribes to it. All understand that any position on a moral issue must be shown to be grounded in the tradition in some way. The classical sources may not speak for themselves, but contemporary Jewish ethicists speak only with the aid of those sources, which inspire, inform, and guide them in the process of developing a moral position.

WAR

Warfare has existed since the beginnings of recorded human history. Societies in all times and places have used violence for many purposes: to usurp the property of others, expand their territorial range, increase their economic prosperity, enhance their power and prestige, control alien populations, and defend themselves from the aggression (actual or intended) of others. During many periods in history, war has engaged the greater part of a society's energies, affected (directly or indirectly) the majority of its population, and preoccupied its greatest thinkers and strategists. As our technologies have advanced, especially in the areas of aeronautics, nuclear physics, and communications, the impact (both real and potential) of war has increased exponentially. Both because of its prevalence and the sometimes cataclysmic changes that it brings in its wake, warfare has unquestionably influenced the history of life on this planet as profoundly as any other single social activity.

As old and persistent as war itself is the effort to explore the ethics of warfare. Apart from pacifists, who oppose war at all times and in all forms, most thinkers in most religious traditions have considered at least some wars justified and have sought to define the moral parameters of war.[56] In what circumstances is waging war morally justified? What limits does morality place on the conduct of war, especially with respect to noncombatants? Are there categories of citizens who are exempt from the requirement of military service in time of war? Within the Roman Catholic tradition, the "just war" tradition has offered a set of principles designed to steer a middle course between pacifism and the indiscriminate sanctioning of war in all forms. Judaism has similarly sought to legitimize war within certain circumstances and for specific ends, although, as the following discussion indicates, the tradition's guidance on war is not always as clear as it appears at first glance.

In this section, I depart somewhat from the format of the preceding sections on sexual ethics and abortion. I review two presentations of the Jewish ethics of war and peace by Elliot Dorff[57] and Bradley Shavit Artson,[58] simultaneously. Elliot Dorff is one of the leading thinkers and ethicists in the Conservative movement. He is the author or editor of ten books and more than one hundred and fifty articles on Jewish law, theology, and ethics, and is a leading figure on the Law Committee of the Rabbinical Assembly (the organization of Conservative rabbis). Bradley Artson is the dean of the Ziegler School of Rabbinic Studies at the University of Judaism and the author of three books and many articles on contemporary Jewish life and values. The positions of these two thinkers are not strikingly different, but their analyses do raise somewhat different questions about the application of the classical sources to contemporary issues involving war.

Dorff and Artson both underscore the overriding value that Judaism places on peace and, accordingly, on the sanctity of human life. This is reflected in every genre of Jewish literature and in every stratum of the tradition. The ancient priestly blessing (Numbers 6:26) concludes with the words, "May the Lord bestow His favor upon you and grant you peace," and the concluding words of the *kaddish* prayer, which figures prominently in all worship services, are, "May the One who creates peace in the heavens grant peace to us and to all Israel." The biblical prophets envisioned the culmination of human history as a messianic time when nations will "beat their swords into plowshares and their spears into pruning hooks; nation shall not take up sword against nation; they shall never again know war" (Isaiah 2:4). Hillel, the first century C.E. sage, admonished his followers to "be among the disciples of Aaron, seeking peace and pursuing peace, loving God's creatures and drawing them close to Torah."[59] Indeed, the rabbis comment that of all the commandments in Scripture, creating peace is unique in that Jews must actively pursue opportunities to fulfill this obligation rather than observing the commandment only when conditions present themselves. Peace is taken to be an attribute of God, who, in the words of the liturgy, "makes peace and creates everything." Living according to the Torah will lead one to a life of peacefulness, for "her ways are pleasant ways, and all her paths, peaceful" (Proverbs 3:17). As the Bahya ben Asher wrote in the thirteenth century, "Peace is the foundation and principle of the entire Torah and the essential element in the creation of the world."[60] Indeed, one looks in vain for rabbinic statements glorifying war or praising the warrior.

Both Dorff and Artson acknowledge, however, that classical Judaism is not entirely pacifist despite this marked emphasis on the value of peace. Reviewing the classical sources, they find that the rabbis delineate three categories of war with varying degrees of legitimacy. Commenting on Deuteronomy 20:7, which specifies that a man is exempt from military service for the first year following his marriage, Mishnah Sotah 8:7 comments:

> To what does that apply? To discretionary wars, but in wars commanded by the Torah (*milhamot mitzvah*) all go forth, even a bridegroom from his chamber and a bride from her canopy. Rabbi Judah says: To what do these verses apply? To wars commanded by the Torah (*milhamot mitzvah*), but in obligatory wars (*milhamot hovah*) all go forth, even a bridegroom from his chamber and a bride from her canopy.[61]

The problem is that the critical terms in this mishnaic dispute—"discretionary," "commanded by the Torah," or "obligatory"—are not defined here. Rabbi Judah's opinion is especially perplexing because any war "commanded by the Torah" would seem to be "obligatory." Later rabbinic authorities suggest that the dispute concerns a category of wars that is neither specifically commanded by the Torah (e.g., the wars conducted by Joshua to conquer the Land of Israel), nor entirely discretionary (e.g., the wars of King David to expand the territory of the ancient Israelite empire). The disagreement is about "preemptive" strikes against other nations "to diminish the heathens so that they shall not march against them [Israel]." The general view is that such wars are discretionary, insofar as the Torah does not specifically command them, while Rabbi Judah holds that they are "commanded by the Torah" indirectly insofar as they are a matter of legitimate self-defense.

Leaving aside for now the status of preemptive wars, the broader distinction between obligatory and discretionary wars requires some clarification. In introducing these categories, the rabbis were apparently trying to make sense of those Scriptural passages in which God commands the Israelites to conduct wars (and in a rather unsparing, even brutal, way) against the Canaanites while acknowledging that other wars from later Israelite history were not specifically commanded by God. In the rabbis' classification, the "obligatory war" was limited to the one historical instance in which God commanded the Israelites to conquer the Land of Israel. By contrast, discretionary wars could be initiated, according to the rabbis, only by the king with the approval of the Sanhedrin (ancient council of Israelite elders) and with the confirming evidence of the breastplate (*urim v'tumim*) worn by the ancient high priest and used as a kind of oracle. The point, apparently, is that discretionary wars were justifiable only under very stringent conditions. The rabbis also distinguished these two categories of war in terms of the permissibility of violating the Sabbath; an obligatory war may be waged on the Sabbath, but a discretionary war may not be.

Artson raises important considerations that would render both sorts of war entirely impermissible in modern times. Because there is no longer a king, a Sanhedrin or a priestly breastplate to consult, there is simply no mechanism any longer for declaring a discretionary war. In Artson's words,

> None of the agencies necessary for the initiation of *milhemet reshut* [discretionary war] exists, and none of them can be restored through human action [since the restoration of the monarchy, the Sanhedrin and the priesthood await the advent of the Messiah]. Without these three, there can be no lawful *milhemet reshut*.[62]

As for commanded wars, Artson argues that the ancient wars of conquest cannot be a model of legitimate war in our generation on several grounds. First, he notes a tendency within rabbinic tradition to limit this category to the wars of the distant past. In his view, the rabbis emphasized the theological rather than the military meaning of these battles. They are to teach us about God's special relationship with Israel and to underscore God's battle with idolatry, which the biblical text cites as the reason the indigenous Canaanites had to be expelled from the land. In no way does the tradition look to these wars as a model of legitimate military strategy. Moreover, Artson suggests that these wars were *sui generis*, a one-time event, sanctioned by direct divine decree. He writes, "Because the war was initiated by special permission, it could occur only once. It was dependent on a revelation which would never be repeated within human history."[63] The ancient rabbis could not excise these passages from the Torah, but they could limit their applicability. Following their lead, Jews today should do the same. Artson writes,

> Any attempts to justify wholesale slaughters of civilians must be condemned as unethical and inhuman . . . any attempt to resurrect the crusading spirit would violate a clearly discernible trend which prominent Jewish sages have been encouraging since the Torah itself. While we cannot deny the past, we can insist on decrying its more brutal aspects.[64]

Dorff's much briefer treatment of this material does not categorically deny the contemporary relevance of the obligatory and discretionary war, but it does suggest several considerations—both historical and ethical—that mitigate against any Jewish endorsement of war. First, he notes that Jews have historically been the victims of war more often than its perpetrators. "As a result, waging war is not a significant part of the long-term Jewish historical memory and did not become an ideal filled with honor and glory, as it did in other cultures."[65] Second, Judaism has developed a healthy respect for governmental authority and so naturally tends not to support military intervention to change or overthrow governments. Third, as noted later, the Torah specifies important humanitarian limits on Israel's conduct in war, reflecting a deep-seated concern to minimize the inherently dehumanizing effects of warfare. Fourth, Judaism has always placed preeminent importance on the value of peace, both between individuals and among nations.[66] Finally, even when war was regarded as morally permissible, the rabbis insisted that it could be waged only if there was reasonable assurance of victory, for otherwise doing so was tantamount to suicide, which was forbidden.[67] For all these reasons, Jews historically have been reticent to engage in war even when they regarded it as morally permissible, and Judaism has been reluctant to sanction war except when it seemed there was no alternative.

The status of preemptive strikes has been a source of significant controversy within the tradition. Dorff notes that Maimonides' summary of halakhah is strikingly silent on the whole question and that subsequent sages have taken a wide range of positions. The most restrictive view would limit preemptive wars to circumstances in which the enemy has been engaged in taking Jewish lives, the most permissive view would sanction such wars "even when there is only a suspicion that they may attack us."[68] Moreover, some halakhic authorities considered preemptive wars as "commanded" while others deemed them "discretionary," a dispute which appears never to have been definitively resolved. At stake, as noted, are the legitimacy of engaging in such wars on the Sabbath and the applicability of the exemptions from military service for certain groups of people. Notwithstanding these differences, all traditional authorities appear to have agreed that preemptive attacks must be defensive in purpose, not aggressive or retributive.

This leaves the one category of war discussed by the sages that both Dorff and Artson believe has ongoing relevance to modern Jews, the defensive war. Maimonides, based on a talmudic discussion,[69] writes:

> If foreigners besieged Israelite towns, if they came for monetary reasons, it is not permitted to desecrate the Sabbath [to break the siege] nor do we make war against them [on the Sabbath] . . . if they came with the intention of taking lives, or if they established the lines for war, or if they simply besieged us [for no apparent reason], it is permitted to go forth against them with weapons and desecrate the Sabbath because of them. It is a commandment incumbent on all Israelites who can go out to come to the aid of their fellow Jews caught in a siege and to save them from the hand of foreigners on the Sabbath, and it is forbidden to wait until the Sabbath is over.[70]

Defending oneself against attack is plainly permissible; indeed, it is required. The principle in place here may be that society as a whole must defend itself when its life is in danger, just as Exodus 22:1 presupposes an individual's right to defend his household and family against hostile intruders. The alternative would entail a suicidal passivity in the face of blatant aggression. Such defensive wars, which Artson understands to be in the category of *milchemet mitzvah*, "wars commanded by the Torah," are based on this principle:

> that there are certain circumstances in which a people must fight; that life entails certain obligations, such as establishing families and communities, without which life itself is not fully life, without which peace is a euphemism for servitude. In such cases, being advocates of life demands a willingness to fight for life.[71]

As both Dorff and Artson read the tradition, defensive wars are not only permissible but morally required.

Apart from the question of distinguishing the types of conflicts and the respective legitimacy of each, Judaism provides a fairly extensive set of rules regarding the conduct of war, beginning with the provisions in Deuteronomy 20. Among the most striking features of this earliest code of warfare is that "when you approach a town to attack it, you shall offer it terms of peace" (Deuteronomy 20:10). If these terms are not accepted, the Israelites are to lay siege to the town but only subject to certain restrictions, principally that the fruit trees surrounding the city were not to be destroyed (Deuteronomy 20:19–20). This implies, for Artson, that even in the midst of a permitted war, Jews are not to pursue a "scorched-earth" policy. Later rabbinic commentary added the extraordinary requirement that a siege must not be total; one side of the city must be left unprotected to enable those civilians who wished to escape.[72] Thus, anyone who remained in the city was tacitly agreeing to join the combatants and so was a legitimate target of military action. This, as Artson notes, renders the siege all but useless as a military tactic, which may have been precisely the rabbis' intent. Here, again, humanitarian considerations figure prominently in the way that traditional authorities conceived the morality of war, even those limited forms of war that were legitimate in the first place.

This same concern to restrict the circumstances under which war could be waged is evident in the biblical rules that exempt from military service those who have built a house but not yet dedicated it, those who are engaged but not yet married, and even the bridegroom in the first year of his marriage (Deuteronomy 20:5–7; 24:5). Those in the midst of an especially joyous and promising time in their lives should not be subjected to the brutality of war, or made to risk losing their lives altogether. Even the faint-hearted are to be exempt from military service lest they weaken the resolve of their comrades (Deuteronomy 20:8). Although later tradition restricted these exemptions to the case of discretionary war (while requiring all to serve in the case of obligatory, i.e., defensive, war), it also expanded the category of exemptions to include those who were afraid, not of being killed in battle, but of taking the lives of others. In all, Artson concludes, these rules reinforce Judaism's emphasis on the value of life, its reticence to endorse war (except in the most limited circumstances), even its readiness to make war virtually impossible to wage effectively.

Consideration of the ethics of war in Judaism as it emerges from these two contemporary presentations, raises a number of methodological issues. First, a somewhat utopian approach to war is reflected in the classical sources. This may reflect the historical fact that, as Dorff puts it,

> It is only in three relatively short periods of Jewish history, though, that Jews also held political and military autonomy. . . . It is only in these periods that Jews directly confronted the realities of power and the agonizing decisions of determining when to use it.[73]

The rabbinic sources, in particular, derive from a time when Jews had no political autonomy, and so no direct experience with the exercise of military power. Moreover, the rabbis knew that the Romans had suppressed military action by a group of nationalist zealots in the second century C.E., leading to untold suffering among Jews in Palestine. Certainly, this experience colored their view of the ethics of war and probably contributed to their overall reticence to endorse military action, as well as the impractical restrictions that they placed on the conduct of warfare. Recognition of the historical context within which these views took shape still leaves this question: How should Jews apply these perspectives on war to the very different circumstances in which they live today, especially in the State of Israel?

Artson's response to this problem is clear:

> It can be argued that the Jewish refusal to see this war [of Conquest] as a justification for other wars was based on Jewish powerlessness. That may, in fact, be true, although it seems also to be irrelevant. In trying to estimate the moral worth of an argument, the contents of the argument, more than its source, determine its value. In this case, even if the source of the Jewish revulsion against war did spring from powerlessness, the ideas themselves might still be helpful in our efforts to delineate a way to conduct war justly. . . . Understanding the historical background of an intellectual or, in this case, legal position doesn't alter the fact of the position itself.[74]

This ahistorical view of Jewish ethics is not the only option. Strikingly, the Conservative movement, within which both Dorff and Artson are leading figures, has historically taken just the opposite view, that halakhah is subject to change precisely when historical circumstances have changed. The rationale is that Jewish law reflects the time and place in which it developed and was meant to respond to the needs of those communities to which it was addressed. Currently, a progressive, historically sensitive approach to halakhah arguably requires that Jews likewise remain open to the possibility of altering the inherited law so that it can remain responsive to the situation of contemporary Jews. Dorff hints at this problem when he notes that the entire tradition of Jewish reflection about war and peace is based on very limited historical experience with exercising political and military power. Had the rabbis been responsible for overseeing the conduct of Jewish armies, it is at least questionable whether they would, for instance, have insisted that sieges leave a path of escape for one's enemies. In any case, it is hardly self-evident that the moral views that made sense to Jews in ancient times are applicable, without modification, to the very different circumstances in which Jews now live.

Of course, times have changed dramatically in another way since the rabbis devised their three categories for exploring the ethics of war. Warfare in the twenty-first century is a different affair than it was in Roman times, or several centuries earlier, when the author of Deuteronomy lived. People now possess weapons vastly more powerful and destructive than anything that existed in earlier generations. Armies no longer lay siege to walled cities, and nuclear war can now be waged by the push of a button without bringing soldiers into direct contact with one another at all. Under such circumstances, waging war is potentially very different than it was before the advent of nuclear, biological, and chemical weapons. At a minimum, many intervening centuries of experience have shaped the way humans think about the circumstances that warrant war and the proper way to conduct it.

Moreover, the conduct of any nation must now be considered in the context of a whole framework of international relations, agreements (such as the Geneva Convention) and organizations (such as the United Nations) that radically change both the ways in which international aggression can be justified and the implications (both political and economic) of waging war. Questions regarding the ethics of war are quite different from those examined previously with respect to sexual relations and abortion. Arguably, the acts of sexual intercourse and of aborting a fetus have changed very little since ancient times. By contrast, the very act of waging war, as well as the international context in which nations take up arms against one another, has changed dramatically. How, if at all, should these changes be addressed by contemporary Jewish ethicists considering the ethics of war?

Dorff is quite clear that caution is required in this regard. He writes,

> Jews looking to Jewish sources for guidance in these matters should not expect clear, indubitable answers to all of their questions, for such answers are available only in much less complicated affairs. They can legitimately expect, however, a point of view emerging from the tradition that expresses its values and applies them in some concrete ways. That point of view may not determine a univocal answer to all situations, but it should enrich the moral thinking of Jews.[75]

Dorff does offer some tentative Jewish moral responses to the exercise of military power by Israel in several of its wars with the surrounding Arab states as well as to U.S. military actions from the Vietnam War to the present. He openly acknowledges that moving from theory to practice will always be open to debate among Jewish scholars drawing on the same body of traditional sources. Artson, for his part, offers strikingly little in the way of practical guidance, and nothing at all on the ethics of Israeli military action.[76]

Finally, although the Jewish view of war as Dorff and Artson present it seems remarkably consistent, there are clearly conflicting positions within the tradition. The biblical sources on the conquest of Canaan, even if mitigated by subsequent authorities, are dramatically more enthusiastic about war than later prophetic and rabbinic views. Artson is openly uneasy about the notion that at least one scriptural tradition unhesitatingly endorsed the mass slaughter of civilians and presented this as directly commanded by God, who is sometimes called "warrior" (Exodus 15:3). Artson understandably seizes on the efforts of the sages to relegate this view to a historical anomaly and to emphasize the more pacifist elements within Judaism. In fact, he is quite explicit about his methods in this regard. He draws a distinction between the "heritage" of Judaism—that is, the entire body of Jewish teachings—and a "tradition," which is a subset of the heritage, chosen subjectively by each Jewish ethicist or community as it draws from the heritage those elements that it finds most meaningful and applicable.[77]

> Not every thought ever conceived by every Jewish thinker needs to be presented and synthesized into some later whole. Instead, if we build on what, by community consensus, appears *to us* to be the *best* of Jewish insights and the *best* of Jewish morality, insisting at the same time on utilizing the full range of tools and approaches of modern thought, we can hope to do for Judaism today what our ancestors did in their day—present to the world visions developed by communities seeking to embody and enact God's will for a human society which is just, life-affirming, and at peace.[78]

Arguably, every Jewish ethicist who studies the complete heritage of Jewish reflection on any moral question must construct a "tradition" in Artson's sense, either explicitly or implicitly. The heritage of Jewish thought is simply too vast and encompasses too many divergent perspectives to be reduced to a single, internally consistent, view. All the pieces do not fit so neatly into a single jigsaw puzzle. As Artson realizes, constructing a Jewish view of war is possible only when the contemporary Jewish ethicist carefully selects, weighs, interprets and applies the many voices to be found within the Jewish heritage.

In all, then, this examination of the Jewish ethics of war highlights two important methodological issues—1) the extent to which contemporary ethicists should consider the historical circumstances that gave rise to various traditional views (as well as the historical circumstances that may define a current practice, such as war), and 2) the fact that every contemporary Jewish moral position is based on a "reading" of the sources, and that all such readings are necessarily selective. Moral judgments are not simply "there" in the sources, but are constructed by scholars whose interpretive skills and expert judgments must be brought to bear on the raw material that Judaism provides.

CONCLUSION

A review of this brief exploration of contemporary Jewish perspectives on selected moral issues, indicates just what is involved in generating a "Jewish view" of a moral problem. The preceding chapter noted that Jewish ethicists may be distinguished from one another by the way in which they view Torah, the type of instruction they find within it, and the way they relate to it. Having now delved into some of the ways that contemporary Jewish ethicists address concrete moral problems, you can now appreciate more fully the many dimensions of the relationship they strive to maintain with Torah.

The first and most notable fact about contemporary Jewish ethics is precisely that Torah remains the central and undisputed source of ethical insight. Notwithstanding their many differences, all of the Jewish ethicists examined here (I would argue, all Jewish ethicists worthy of the name) believe it is their task to mine the traditional religious and ethical writings of Judaism for the light that they can shed on the moral problems Jews face. Along the way, they may rely on modern historical scholarship, or draw from the work of secular thinkers, or include the insights of other religious traditions, but only Torah in the broadest sense remains sacred literature. Contemporary Jewish ethicists claim to speak for Torah, to bring its teachings to bear on the specific ethical challenges Jews face. For just this reason, they rightfully make a claim on the attention of contemporary Jews who share their commitment to seeing Jewish tradition as a repository of moral guidance.

That contemporary Jewish ethicists go about this task in such different ways should come as no surprise. Because modern Jews continue to struggle with the enormous theological and sociological changes that have transformed the Jewish community since the Enlightenment, they could hardly be expected to understand this tradition, or relate to it, in a single consistent way. What this chapter has indicated, instead, is that placing Torah at the center of the enterprise of "doing" contemporary Jewish ethics provides both an anchor and an essential link to the past while raising a number of pressing methodological problems.

First, as noted in the review of Jewish sexual ethics, the modern Jewish ethicist must mediate between the vision of a moral life contained in the classical tradition and that which is compelling to contemporary Jews. To what extent must Jews reconfigure their moral understanding of sexuality to conform with traditional rules and values? To what extent ought they find warrants within the tradition for sexual mores that feel consonant with their own moral perspectives? To what extent can they find a happy medium between these two? The answer to this important set of questions will depend, I suggest, on how Jews answer the deeper question about the authority of the tradition. Some ethicists will see in traditional moral guidelines the absolute standard against which all practices must be judged. Others will see in Torah a set of moral insights that must be interpreted in ways that speak to the situation of contemporary Jews.

Second, as the contemporary Jewish debate on abortion aptly illustrates, Jewish ethicists will approach these traditional sources with a whole range of different interpretive assumptions. Some assume that the tradition can ultimately speak with only one moral voice; hence, conflicting positions within the sources must be reconciled. Others take for granted that multiple, and equally legitimate, perspectives are preserved within the tradition. Still others attempt to see, and sometimes to challenge, the assumptions underlying the traditional views and then utilize that analysis in constructing a novel position. At issue here is the interpreter's stance, the way that he understands the very nature of the tradition, the assumptions that she brings to the work of interpreting traditional sources.

Finally, as the Jewish discussions of war indicate, much depends on the extent to which contemporary Jewish ethicists consider the historical conditions that existed when the traditional authorities lived. Can the moral perspectives found in the ancient sources be extracted from the political and historical conditions that prevailed when they were written? Can a traditional moral rule, even one with which contemporary Jews may be very sympathetic, legitimately be applied in the radically different historical circumstances of our day? The discussion also noted that the many voices preserved within the tradition do not all enter equally into the deliberations of the contemporary ethicist, who is always choosing to highlight some views and to minimize or ignore others. The contemporary Jewish ethicist draws on the tradition selectively.

In all, then, I hope that you, the reader, are now in a position not only to understand something of the range of contemporary Jewish views on sexuality, abortion, and war but also to grasp the complexities involved in generating such views. Most important, it should be apparent that, whatever else they may do, contemporary Jewish ethicists are committed to deriving moral guidance from the tradition they have inherited. Doing so necessarily involves invoking a host of other beliefs, judgments, and commitments about the character of the tradition itself and the proper means of interpreting it. Because doing Jewish ethics always entails interpreting sources and such interpretation always rests, at least in part, on the judgments of the interpreter, selectivity and subjectivity appear to be inherent in the enterprise at the most fundamental level. Any Jewish ethical position, then, must be justified with reference to the criteria of selection and interpretation that have guided the ethicist.

This entire set of issues is articulated succinctly and powerfully by Bradley Artson at the outset of his book on war and peace:

> Seeking God's will is a notoriously ambiguous exercise; it is difficult to understand how a Heritage may be used to address contemporary moral dilemmas. . . . Before we can establish what it is that Judaism says about issues of just war and the morality of nuclear weapons, we must first determine how a four thousand year old collection of traditions can speak at all. How may we use the past to understand the present more fully? Does Judaism speak with one voice or with many? Does it say now what it has always said? And how does the perspective of the viewer affect a presentation of the material which is viewed?[79]

Indeed, Judaism's ancient texts address modern moral issues only through the voice of the contemporary reader/ethicist. It follows that what the tradition says about any moral problem Jews might face will depend crucially on how ethicists understand the authority of the tradition and its relationship to contemporary values, how they deal with anomalous and contradictory views they find within the sources, and how much weight they assign to the historical conditions prevailing both at the time the sources were written and at present. This is not to suggest that Judaism is infinitely malleable, that it can be made to say anything one wishes it to or to endorse any moral position at all. Rather the point is that contemporary Jewish ethics is a *constructive* enterprise, that the sources out of which moral guidance is being drawn can always legitimately be construed in more than one way. This means that, in the final analysis, no sharp distinction can be drawn between what the traditional sources say "in themselves" and what contemporary interpreters have taken them to mean. Contemporary Jewish ethics is a living tradition precisely because living religious scholars bring those sources to life, and they can do this only by bringing to the sacred texts of this tradition their particular theological perspectives, their reading of history, their understanding of what this tradition essentially consists of, and their devotion to retaining and extending and sometimes modifying the moral wisdom of their ancestors. For precisely these reasons, contemporary Jewish ethics is simultaneously and inescapably both continuous with the past and remarkably diverse in its modes of expression.

KEY POINTS

- Contemporary Jewish ethicists faced with a specific moral issue draw on the resources of the Jewish tradition in diverse ways and so arrive at different conclusions.
- A number of different factors come into play when contemporary Jewish ethicists seek to interpret and apply the insights of their tradition:
    - The extent to which they regard the traditional sources as authoritative, a source of abiding truth, against which other values and contemporary needs must be evaluated;
    - The extent to which they regard the tradition as internally consistent and the way in which they deal with whatever inconsistencies and tensions among sources that they may find;
    - The personal biases that they bring to their reading of the tradition;
    - The extent to which they take into account the historical context in which traditional views were formulated;
    - The way in which they select from among the vast repertoire of traditional sources and perspectives those which figure most prominently in their analysis of the issue at hand.
- The subjectivity and indeterminacy inherent in this process of interpretation does not invalidate the enterprise of doing Jewish ethics; it does, however, underscore the fact that this is an inescapably constructive enterprise and that

those engaged in it should ideally be explicit about the methods and assumptions they bring to this work.

QUESTIONS TO CONSIDER

1. Most of the positions reviewed in this chapter, like most work in contemporary Jewish ethics generally, draw most heavily on halakhic sources. Nonetheless, can you discern within these presentations elements of the covenantal and narrative approaches?

2. How would you respond to a skeptic who argued that, given the diversity within the Jewish sources on any topic and the diverse ways in which contemporary authorities interpret them, all contemporary Jewish ethics is really subjective and arbitrary?

3. Of the various methodological issues discussed in this chapter, do any seem to bear more directly on those who adopt one or another of the approaches (legal, covenantal, or narrative) introduced in the previous chapter, or would all approaches face these methodological issues equally?

4. Consider other contemporary moral issues such as cloning, capital punishment, or the extent of corporate responsibility. How might the methodological issues considered here relate to these problems? Do certain types of moral issues challenge the contemporary Jewish ethicist more significantly than others? Why or why not?

Conclusion:
The Language
of Jewish Ethics

This book has explored the contours of the Jewish ethical tradition. I have identified certain theological beliefs at the core of classical Judaism and traced the ways in which these have given rise to both the substance of Jewish moral life and the theory that underlies this system of moral thought. I have also noted the numerous ways in which historical events central to Jewish experience—especially slavery, exile, and redemption—have shaped the content of Jewish moral reflection. I have shown Jewish ethics is expressed in its own distinctive idiom and is preserved through a centuries-old tradition of narratives, law codes, commentaries, and responsa. Finally, I have highlighted the various ways in which contemporary Jewish ethicists draw on this multifaceted tradition to address the moral problems Jews face in the modern world. Throughout, I have noted the unmistakable fact that neither classical nor contemporary Jewish ethicists speak in a single voice; indeed, this religious-ethical tradition encompasses multiple perspectives that, nonetheless, coalesce around certain common themes and concepts.

This book opened with the metaphor of embarking on an intellectual journey to a place that, in all likelihood, you had not visited before. In closing, I want to suggest that this journey into the world of Jewish ethics has been much like the process of learning a foreign language. For you have, in fact, been learning how to understand a special sort of discourse, the language of Jewish ethics. Reflecting now on the similarities between studying a foreign language and Jewish ethics will enable you to see more clearly just what is entailed in attempting to master this peculiar ethical discourse as well as what is to be gained from doing so.

When studying a foreign language, as many of you do in high school and/or college, you quickly discover that every language has certain features in common: a lexicon of words that refer to the whole array of objects, concepts, and actions needed to communicate about your experience of the world, as well as a set of grammatical rules that determine how to combine these linguistic elements into intelligible sentences. As you progress to more advanced study, you discover the great authors whose works have left their mark on the development of literature in that language, such as Dante in Italian, Goethe in German, and Shakespeare in English. And, at every turn, you discover how every language reflects a distinctive culture that develops over time, interacts with and borrows from other cultures, yet provides a unique window into the world of human experience. As you explore these aspects of a language and face the challenges in learning one, you will discover that all of these issues also arise in the study of Jewish ethics.

Every language has words in its lexicon that do not translate precisely into another. In part this is because within each language each word is related to others and so carries nuances and resonances with a cluster of related words. Even the closest parallel word in another language almost invariably fails to capture these subtle connotations. An example is the Hebrew word *teshuvah,* generally translated as "repentance." But *teshuvah* is related to the word for "turning," which suggests that repentance is essentially a turning or reorienting of oneself toward God, and to the word for "returning," as in returning to the proper path in life, and to the word for "responding" or "answering," which gives *teshuvah* the connotation of answering God's call to repent of one's moral failings. So the richness of a moral concept such as *teshuvah* is not easily captured in another language. Indeed, one challenge of learning a foreign language, like the language of Jewish ethics, is discovering the very interconnections among words that give every language its richness and subtlety.

Translating from one language to another poses other difficulties as well. Some concepts in one language have no direct parallel in another. The French *joie de vivre* means something in French culture that "the joy of living" simply doesn't convey in English. The phrase captures an attitude central to French culture, its values, and its way of experiencing the world, but the parallel phrase in English does not. By the same token, the Hebrew concept of *tikkun olam,* "repairing the world" refers to a whole complex of ideas: that God created the world but left the work of completing or repairing creation to humankind, that this work is done through acts of lovingkindness, and that every such act thus has a cosmic significance. All of this and more is conveyed in the phrase *tikkun olam,* a concept deeply rooted in Jewish ethical thought but that may be less central or even nonexistent in other systems of religious or moral reflection.

To master another language, then, is to discover both the myriad connections and connotations of each item in a certain lexicon and the significance that specific categories and concepts have within the culture that produced this language. You cannot understand Jewish ethical discourse without knowing that the Hebrew word for *charity* also means *righteousness* or that the Hebrew word for *compassion* is derived from the word for *womb.* The discovery of these connections brings with it an appreciation that every language has its own way of parsing and describing reality. How Jewish culture has understood moral experience, virtue, obligation, the quality of human relationships, the goal of living morally, and the consequences of failing to do so is all captured in the specific vocabulary that Jews have used over the centuries. Learning this distinctive moral language, then, is a matter of being introduced into a particular way of experiencing the moral dimensions of life. And, as with learning any foreign language, some of those experiences and corresponding concepts will be quite familiar to you from your native language and culture; others, inevitably, will seem alien. All, however, make sense within their own context.

As you know from English, reading and speaking a language requires understanding not only the meanings of individual words but also the proper way to combine them. The rules of grammar and syntax dictate that "the dog jumped easily over the fence" is a coherent sentence, while "easily the dog fence over the jumped" is gibberish. To learn a language, in other words, is to absorb the structures regularly used to organize the various nouns, verbs, adjectives, and other parts of speech. These structures direct your attention to the ways in which the various words within a string are interconnected into something like a sentence that conveys a complete and coherent thought. Every language has its grammatical rules that capture and dictate its inner logic; they generate coherence and meaning within that language.

The language of Jewish ethics likewise has its own "grammar," for, as you have seen, there are themes that weave their way throughout Jewish ethical life, giving coherence and meaning to the whole system. Here it is helpful to think of values, virtues, and obligations as the discrete elements (analogous to words) that comprise the vocabulary of Jewish ethics. Recall the ways in which Judaism portrays the value of justice, the virtue of humility, and the obligation to honor parents. None of these elements stands alone; each is connected in complex ways to the others, often through underlying theological concepts, into a web of moral meaning. So God's goodness is both a source of Jews' concept of justice and at the root of their sense of moral imperfection; thus, it both motivates them to create a world that mirrors God's justice and prompts them to cultivate an attitude of humility. When you further consider that God's goodness is expressed both through the gift of life and through a concern for those who are socially disadvantaged (especially through granting freedom to the enslaved), you see how a person's duty to honor parents is simply an extension of honoring the ultimate Source of life and how the duty to help widows, orphans, and the poor is modeled on God's own action in history. Thus, there are many thematic connections among the various elements in Jewish ethics. That is why, as you discovered earlier, even when Jewish ethics shares some vocabulary with other religious or secular systems of ethics (e.g., a basically conservative attitude toward abortion), it may construe that particular moral value or rule differently, for it occupies a different place within this particular web of moral concepts and theological beliefs.

On the level of moral theory, there also are deep structures that connect the various components of this ethical system. As discussed in Chapter Five, the way Jews have understood creation, revelation and the relationship between them has profound implications for the ways in which Jews understand universal ethics and its relationship to Jewish ethics. Similarly, the way they understand covenant affects how they understand the relationship between law and ethics within Judaism. Again, it is not as though Judaism's views toward law, moral obligation in general, and the moral obligations of non-Jews in particular are discrete elements. Rather, these views are reflections of underlying concepts and the relationships among them. The "logic" or grammar of Jewish ethical discourse, in this sense, is communicated through the theological concepts of covenant, creation, revelation, and redemption, for these categories and the relationships among them dictate what counts as a moral obligation (and how one obligation relates to another), just as the grammar of a natural language dictates what counts as a coherent sentence.

Of course, the point here is not that there is one "right" way to put together the various elements of Jewish moral life, either on the practical or the theoretical level. For, as you know, the rules of English grammar do not dictate that there is just one "right" way to construct a meaningful sentence. The point is rather that every meaningful sentence follows one of the many possible structures or patterns of coherence to which the language adheres. So, too, justice, humility, and honoring parents—as well as myriad other dimensions of ethical life—can be interconnected within Jewish ethics in many different ways, each of which creates a coherent and meaningful mode of Jewish ethical living. In Jewish ethics, as in every language, coherence and meaning are captured not by the individual elements, not in discrete words or acts, but in the many ways in which these can be linked to one another.

Every language, at least every written language that has existed over some stretch of time, has been shaped by certain great writers whose work can influence the development of that language for many centuries after them. Phrases such as "to be or not to be" or "we hold these truths to be self-evident" echo across the centuries, influencing generations of English authors and making their way even into casual speech. We continue to read Shakespeare and to refer to the Declaration of Independence because these words are beautiful and inspirational and because they capture important sentiments and perspectives so powerfully and eloquently that they have become "classics" within the culture. Indeed, English literary and political culture would be quite different and arguably much impoverished had these words never been written or, if once written, had been ignored instead of being celebrated and studied by generations of English speakers.

In a similar vein, particular works of Jewish ethics have exerted an influence on the whole history of the discourse. Examples include Maimonides' *Mishneh Torah*, which was influential for the elegance of its style and the clarity with which he organizes and explains Jewish law and his *Shemoneh Perakim* [Eight Chapters], which powerfully demonstrated the compatibility of Jewish and Aristotelian ethics. Bahya ibn Pakuda's *Duties of the Heart* spawned a whole movement of pietistic ethics, and many hasidic works influenced the perspective of Martin Buber who, in turn, influenced many contemporary Jewish thinkers. When you know a language and its literature well you are sensitive to these literary influences and can trace the roots of a writer's particular ideas or modes of expression to earlier figures or texts within that tradition.

This analogy points to yet another insight into Jewish ethics. Every language changes over time not only because new "classics" appear that influence new generations of writers and thinkers but also because its speakers interact with other cultures, and so words and concepts used by one group are "borrowed" by another and integrated into its language. Because groups of people rarely live in isolation from one another, this type of cultural and linguistic exchange is happening constantly. Over the course of centuries, many different cultural influences can shape the development of a language, including its vocabulary and its grammar. Rabbinic Hebrew included many words drawn from the Greek culture that spread throughout the Middle East in that period; more recently, English words have so infiltrated French that the French Ministry of Culture has launched a campaign to encourage the use of indigenous French words rather than the more colloquial English expressions. Of course, this type of influence is as old as language itself and becomes even more widespread as groups move across the globe and bring their languages with them.

Jewish ethics has similarly been shaped by numerous cultural influences. As you discovered, Maimonides' philosophy of Jewish ethics was heavily influenced by his study of Greek philosophy, especially of Aristotle. Cultural influence of this type is by no means restricted to the work of the great philosophers. Contemporary American Jewish ethicists have been deeply influenced by the quintessentially modern values of post-Enlightenment Western culture: autonomy, personal freedom, democracy, and liberalism. In this context, it is not surprising that Jewish theorists have struggled to determine the extent to which these values can be combined with those expressed in the classical Jewish literature written long before these Enlightenment ideas took hold. The influence of Western liberal values is evident in the ways these Jewish ethicists respond to issues involving sexuality, abortion, and political rights and responsibilities, but the blending of Jewish and secular values can be seen throughout contemporary Jewish ethical literature. Like all natural languages, the language of Jewish ethics is in flux for other cultural influences are constantly shaping the way this particular ethical discourse develops. If this has been true throughout history, it is particularly true today when the scope and intensity of cultural exchange has reached unprecedented proportions.

Of course, scientific discovery and technological innovation also introduce new concepts into our language. A generation or two ago there were no ATM's, bytes, or laser surgery, and a black hole would have meant something in the ground rather than in deep space. The language of Jewish ethics has likewise had to accomodate to the explosion of science and technology, for these have brought with them new ethical challenges. To take just one dramatic example, the decoding of the human genome promises to open the way to a new era in biology and medicine as the genetic basis of many illnesses is discovered and potentially becomes correctable through genetic engineering. In response, Jewish ethicists are beginning to grapple with how to understand the moral implications of this revolution in terms of classical concepts such as being created in the divine image and repairing the world. Over time, it is certain that Jewish ethicists will develop a new vocabulary and new ways to interpret Judaism's traditional vocabulary to meet these scientific and technological challenges.

Despite these dramatic changes, however, languages are fundamentally conservative, and necessarily so. To be a serviceable medium for communication, languages must remain relatively stable, for only then can people in one generation understand their own children and grandchildren. Just as English speakers can still read and understand Shakespeare's plays (despite the fact that some words have fallen into disuse), contemporary Jewish ethicists continue fundamentally to "speak the same language" as Rabbi Akiba, Maimonides, or Bahya ibn Pakuda. These ethicists not only read and understand these classics of Jewish ethics from centuries ago but also are influenced by them. Moreover, each time they use this language to address a contemporary moral problem, they help to preserve and extend it. In short, Jewish ethics, like most languages, is transmitted mostly intact from one generation to the next, not continually reinvented. So, just as native speakers of any language know that they stand within a linguistic tradition, having inherited a rich vocabulary in which to express themselves, contemporary Jewish ethicists are likewise heirs to a rich and multifaceted tradition of ethical reflection. They use this special language to create a moral life that is both true to their experience in the present and an authentic expression of the culture that produced this language in the first place. In the process, of course, they attempt to transmit this particular moral language/tradition to those who follow them.

Finally, it is worth noting that not all speakers of a language communicate in the same way. Languages frequently give rise to separate dialects that are spoken by distinct subpopulations within the larger group. Although local dialects can vary widely, they frequently remain similar enough that speakers of different dialects can continue to communicate with one another. Certainly, this is the case for speakers of English who come from different regions of the United States and for speakers of Spanish from Spain and Latin America. In parallel fashion, those who speak the language of Jewish ethics fall into distinct groups, not all of whom use precisely the same words in the same way or communicate in the same idiom. In your brief exploration of contemporary Jewish ethics you discovered that sometimes it appears that different authorities address an issue in such different ways that they seem to be speaking quite different languages. Yet they continue to speak to one another, and those who read and understand Jewish ethicists from all these subgroups continue to be a community. In that sense, surely, they can be regarded as living within the same linguistic/cultural sphere although differences of "dialect" can sometimes create obstacles to communication among them.

At the conclusion of this study, it makes sense to stop and ask yourself what you have gained from this foray into the world of Jewish ethics beyond the specific information covered in the preceding chapters. What, in the end, makes studying Jewish ethics or any unfamiliar ethical tradition worthwhile? To continue the language metaphor, if you can communicate effectively in your native language, why go to the trouble of learning a foreign one?

The answer, I believe, is two-fold. First, when you learn a foreign language, you often begin to notice and appreciate things about your native language that you would otherwise have taken for granted. The particular way in which a language describes reality, the grammatical rules that govern the way it constructs coherent thoughts, the ways in which it is simple or complex—all of this becomes clearer when you have a basis for comparison. Moreover, learning a foreign language expands your awareness of the richness of human experience. You begin to see that there are many more ways to see the world, describe it, and live within it than any one language can communicate. Indeed, the more languages you know, and the more deeply you know them, the more dimensions of human experience open up to you.

Studying another ethical tradition has precisely these benefits. As you learn the virtues that another culture honors or the ways in which it defines moral obligation, you become more self-aware and self-critical about the moral culture in which you were raised. You no longer take for granted the values and assumptions of that culture but can compare them with others and view them from another vantage point. Invariably, you discover subtleties and complexities in moral life that might have escaped your attention otherwise. For just as no single language can communicate all thoughts and feelings (and certainly not with equal ease), so too no single moral tradition has a corner on moral insight or wisdom. Entering into another moral tradition as you have here, expands your horizons and enriches your sense of what living a moral life can entail. As a result, you may reassess and change your own moral outlook, or you may simply come to understand your own moral values better and embrace them more fully.

Of course, it is possible to study a foreign language—or a different ethical tradition—at many levels, and "fluency" takes a long time to achieve. No one expects to be able to read Tolstoy or Dostoevsky in the original after a single term of Russian. But you know from experience that, as you become more fluent, you can comprehend more, begin to grasp the idioms and idiosyncrasies of a language or a writer, and ultimately communicate ever more sophisticated thoughts in that language.

This exploration of Jewish ethics has been limited; there is much that has not been presented or explained fully. What you have learned here can serve as the foundation for further study, for you now have a grasp of the basic vocabulary and grammar of this language. With this knowledge, you will be able to understand much of what makes Jewish ethics distinctive, and I hope you will be motivated to pursue an even deeper and more subtle understanding of this rich and complex ethical tradition.

A Note on Translations and Sources

Biblical references throughout the book appear within the text. I have followed the Jewish Publication Society (JPS) translation (Philadelphia: Jewish Publication Society, 1962, 1978, 1982), with certain exceptions. I have tried where possible to eliminate sexist language (e.g., rendering "God's" instead of "His," and "one may not" in place of "he may not"). Also, at times a rabbinic comment on a biblical verse is understandable only if the verse is rendered in a particular way, which sometimes deviates from the JPS translation. In such cases, I have provided the JPS translation in a note.

Except as noted, all references to traditional Jewish liturgy are cited from *Siddur Sim Shalom*, ed. Rabbi Jules Harlow (New York: The Rabbinical Assembly, 1985).

Translations of rabbinic sources are my own except as noted. The most frequently cited rabbinic texts are now available in English translation (e.g., Mishnah, Tosefta, Babylonian and Jerusalem Talmuds, as well as many collections of rabbinic midrash). In addition, to consulting these works, readers may wish to explore one of several English anthologies of rabbinic sources now available. The most extensive and best organized of these is Hayim Nahman Bialik and Yehoshua Hana Ravnitzky, eds., *The Book of Legends* [Sefer Ha-Aggadah, originally published in Hebrew, Odessa, 1908–1911], trans. William G. Braude (New York: Schocken, 1992). Earlier collections include Louis Ginzberg's monumental seven-volume *Legends of the Jews* (Philadelphia: Jewish Publication Society, 1968 [originally published 1909–1938]); and C. G. Montefiore and H. Loewe, eds., *A Rabbinic Anthology* (New York: Schocken, 1974 [originally published 1938]).

189

Notes

INTRODUCTION

[1] I have in mind here Geertz's famous analysis of religion as a synthesis of "ethos" (rituals, values, cultural practices) and "worldview" (beliefs about reality), as well as Hauerwas' identification of narrative as the source of Christian ethics. More will be said about these issues in Chapter One.

[2] While this book is explicitly intended to be useful to any reader interested in these issues, regardless of religious background, Jewish readers may find additional value in this presentation of Jewish ethics. For those already committed in some fashion to the Jewish tradition, I hope that this investigation of Jewish ethics will broaden their understanding and appreciation of their own tradition, help them to identify those elements of Judaism that may have shaped their own values and moral commitments, and inspire them to continue exploring the many facets of this rich tradition.

CHAPTER ONE: RELIGION, ETHICS, AND RELIGIOUS ETHICS

[1] Clifford Geertz, "Ethos, World View and the Analysis of Sacred Symbols," in *Interpretation of Cultures* (New York: Basic Books, 1973), 127.

[2] William Shakespeare, *Hamlet,* act 3, scene 1, line 58.

[3] Paul Tillich, *Dynamics of Faith* (New York: Harper & Row, 1957).

[4] This is in contrast to those, such as Sigmund Freud, who believed religion was simply the collective expression of a person's psychological dependence on an external source of moral authority and emotional comfort and Emile Durkheim, who believed religion was simply the authority and power of the community projected into a divine and eternal realm. Eliade and, before him, Rudolf Otto took exception to these efforts to explain religion in terms of some more basic human experience. See Rudolf

Otto, *The Idea of the Holy,* trans. John W. Harvey (New York: Oxford University Press, 1925) [originally published as *Das Heilige* (Breslau, 1917)].

[5] Mircea Eliade, *The Sacred and the Profane* (New York: Harcourt, Brace & World, 1959), 21.

[6] Eliade's vast corpus of scholarly work has been subjected to a wide range of criticisms: that his use of source material is irresponsible, that he forces data to fit within his preconceived categories and theories, that he improperly groups together contemporary nonliterate people and ancient cultures, that his purported "scientific" method is biased (especially by his religious beliefs and political values), and, perhaps most important, that his studies of religion in general and of myth in particular are ahistorical and so distort the meaning of the materials he analyzes. For fuller critical treatments of Eliade's work, see Ivan Strenski, "Mircea Eliade: Some Theoretical Problems," in *The Theory of Myth,* ed. Adrian Cunningham (London: Sheed and Ward, 1973), 40–78; Robert F. Brown, "Elaide on Archaic Religion: Some Old and New Criticisms," *Sciences Religieuses/Studies in Religion* 10:4 (1981): 429–49; Douglas Allen, "Recent Defenders of Elaide: A Critical Evaluation," *Religion* 24 (1994): 333–51. Notwithstanding these criticisms, Eliade remains a leading figure in the field of religious studies, which alone might justify my reliance on his work in this introduction to religion. But even allowing that many of the criticisms leveled against his work are justified, I am persuaded by his insistence on the immediacy of religious experience and his contention that religion is fundamentally about the ways in which experiences of the sacred orient people toward the world.

[7] William Shakespeare, *Macbeth,* act 5, scene 5, lines 27–28.

[8] Even this generalization is subject to some qualifications. Some have argued that certain religions, in particular certain Native American traditions, do not maintain a sharp distinction between the sacred and profane realms, and mystics in all traditions have at least blurred the distinction. For a lengthy and subtle treatment of these concepts and the relationship between them, see Carsten Colpe, "The Sacred and the Profane," in *The Encyclopedia of Religion,* ed. Mircea Eliade (New York: Macmillan, 1987), vol. 12, 511–26.

[9] William James, *The Varieties of Religious Experience,* (New York: Viking Penguin, 1982 [1902]), 31. James's concern was with individual rather than collective religious experience.

[10] Of course, the converse is also true in that institutional forms and social structures of a religious group can also influence their core beliefs and the interpretation of them. Max Weber, the influential early twentieth century sociologist and social theorist, explored these questions extensively; see especially *The Sociology of Religion,* trans. Ephraim Fischoff (Boston: Beacon Press, 1963 [1922]); and *From Max Weber: Essays in Sociology* trans. and eds. H. H. Gerth and C. Wright Mills (New York: Oxford University Press, 1946).

[11] Ludwig Wittgenstein, *Philosophical Investigations* (New York: Macmillan, 1953).

[12] I am not aware of any direct evidence that this ritual was practiced after the original event of the Exodus, but this appears to be implied in Exodus 12:21–27. The rite is prescribed as "an institution for all time," and when the Israelites are dwelling in the Land of Israel, their children are said to ask about the meaning of this strange ritual.

[13] Geertz's work has been criticized for relying on incompatible and incoherent theories of truth, for employing a notion of "symbol" and "model" that is excessively broad and vague, for relying on a reductionist theory of religion, for assuming that the social scientific method imposes constraints on the scholar that preclude assessing the truth of religious perspectives entirely, and for presupposing a dualism between symbolic models and the "world" as it is in itself. For a summary of all these criticisms, see Nancy K. Frankenberry and Hans H. Penner, "Clifford Geertz's Long-Lasting Moods, Motivations, and Metaphysical Conceptions," *Journal of Religion* 79:4 (1999): 617–40. Some similar criticisms may also be found in Aletta Biersack, "Local Knowledge, Local History: Geertz and Beyond," in *The New Cultural History*, ed. Lynn Hunt (Berkeley and Los Angeles: University of California Press, 1989), 72–96. Whatever the force of these criticisms (and many, arguably, would apply equally to any social scientific theory of religion), they do not fundamentally undermine the aspect of Geertz's work that I have found most useful: the description of the interplay and interdependence of worldview and ethos in religions. Geertz's work remains, despite his detractors, unquestionably the most influential and widely cited anthropological approach to religion to emerge in the late twentieth century.

[14] Clifford Geertz, "Religion as a Cultural System," in *The Interpretation of Cultures* (New York: Basic Books, 1973), 89.

[15] Ibid., 93–94.

[16] As I will indicate later, this way of delineating "religious" from "ethical" questions is somewhat artificial. All religions have, in fact, addressed questions of ethics, and arguably every ethical position, even if avowedly secular, rests on some suppositions about ultimate questions about the nature of reality and in this sense is "religious." Still, it is useful in a preliminary way to distinguish religion, which asks about the nature of reality as a whole and our relationship to it, from ethics, which asks about the good in human life and the right way to live in relationship to others.

[17] The question of who or what is entitled to moral consideration is a complex one. Those who have argued that animals have moral rights have relied on the idea that animals share with humans some feature (sentience, or the ability to suffer, for example), which is sufficient to establish a moral claim on us. This confirms the idea expressed here that moral obligations are always about relationships with other people (or creatures sufficiently like people to qualify for consideration). See Peter Singer, *Animal Liberation* (New York : Avon Books, 1977).

[18] This, of course, is the position taken by those who practice civil disobedience and conscientious objection to laws that they regard as immoral. See Henry David Thoreau, *Civil Disobedience* (New York: W. W. Norton, 1966).

[19] Tanna de bei Eliyahu, p. 135, trans. William G. Braude and Israel J. Kapstein (New York: Jewish Publication Society, 1981), 333.

[20] For a more detailed discussion of this issue, see "The Quality of Mercy: On the Duty to Forgive in the Judaic Tradition," in my *Past Imperatives: Studies in the History and Theory of Jewish Ethics* (Albany, New York: SUNY Press, 1998), 83–99.

[21] Babylonian Talmud, Sanhedrin 37a. The standard text of the Talmud reads: "a single soul *within Israel,*" but other manuscripts lack these words. The version translated here seems most in keeping with the universalist thrust of the creation story.

[22] This was the view of Saadia Gaon, *Book of Doctrines and Beliefs,* trans. Alexander Altmann in *Three Jewish Philosophers* (New York: Atheneum, 1969), 94 ff.

[23] See William K. Frankena, *Ethics* (Englewood Cliffs, N.J.: Prentice-Hall, 1973), 114–16.

[24] Mishnah, Peah 1:1.

[25] Here the standard translation is somewhat confusing. "Clean" (Hebrew, *tahor*) is a technical term in the priestly writings that refers to ritual cleanness or purity. It is not to be confused with the common meaning of "clean," or the absence of dirt.

[26] The listing of sins in the standard confessional prayer for the Day of Atonement is an alphabetic acrostic. This translation relies on that of Rabbi Morris Silverman, *High Holiday Prayer Book* (Hartford: Prayer Book Press, 1951).

[27] James M. Gustafson, "Can Ethics Be Christian? Some Conclusions," in *The Distinctiveness of Christian Ethics,* eds. Charles E. Curran and Richard A. McCormick, S.J. (New York: Paulist Press, 1980), 155.

[28] Stanley Hauerwas, "The Self as Story: A Reconsideration of the Relationship of Religion and Morality from the Agent's Perspective," *Vision and Virtue* (Notre Dame: Fides, 1974), 69.

CHAPTER TWO: JUDAISM AND JEWISH ETHICS

[1] Abraham Joshua Heschel, "The Meaning of Observance," from *Man's Quest for God* (New York: Charles Scribners' Sons, 1954), reprinted in *Understanding Jewish Theology,* ed. Jacob Neusner (New York: Ktav, 1973), 95.

[2] Song of Songs Rabbah, 1, 2–3.

[3] Avot 5:25.

[4] Tanhuma Bereshit 1 (66).

[5] The rabbis in the first few centuries of the Common Era were keenly aware of the suffering caused to the Jewish people under Roman rule. Later, in medieval Europe, Jews frequently suffered religious and political discrimination, as well as physical attack and repeated explusions, at the hands of both Church officials and feudal rulers.

[6] Lamentations Rabbah 3:21, 1.

[7] See Hosea, esp. chapters 2 and 4.

[8] Babylonian Talmud, Kiddushin 40b.

[9] See Franz Rosenzweig, *The Star of Redemption*, trans. William W. Hallo (Boston: Beacon Press, 1972).

[10] Author's translation.

[11] Here Harlow's translation reads "who loves His people Israel," but this obscures the all-important traditional doctrine of God's *choosing* Israel to be the recipient of Torah.

[12] Avot 1:2.

[13] See Babylonian Talmud, Eruvin 100b. A similar point is made, but using a different formulation, at Babylonian Talmud, Yoma 67b. For an extended discussion of natural law within Judaism, see "Nature and Torah, Creation and Revelation: On the Possibility of a Natural Law in Judaism," in my *Past Imperatives: Studies in the History and Theory of Jewish Ethics*, 117–38.

[14] Maimonides makes this point in *Eight Chapters*, ch. 8. See Isadore Twersky, ed., *A Maimonides Reader* (New York: Behrman House, 1972), 380.

[15] Mishnah, Avot 3:1.

[16] Babylonian Talmud, Eruvin 13b.

[17] From Martin Buber, *Tales of the Hasidim: Later Masters* (New York: Schocken, 1948), 249–50.

[18] The most significant body of material concerning the moral obligations of non-Jews falls under the rubric of "Noahide laws," those seven basic injunctions that the rabbis believed that God intended for all the descendants of Noah (i.e., for all people, not just the descendants of Abraham). For a complete discussion of these laws and their treatment in rabbinic literature, see David Novak, *The Image of the Non-Jew in Judaism* (New York: Edwin Mellon Press, 1983).

[19] By way of example, Mishnah Baba Kamma 4:3 states that when an Israelite's ox gores that of a non-Jew, the former is not obligated to pay (while, in the reverse situation, the non-Jew is obligated to pay). Interestingly, the Talmud records a discussion of the inequity of the law in this respect; see Babylonian Talmud, Baba Kamma 38a. The law also does not require Jews to return the lost property of non-Jews based on the wording of Deuteronomy 22:1–3; see Babylonian Talmud, Baba Kamma 113b. Also, at least one rabbi suggests (again based on the use of the word *neighbor* in Scripture) that the prohibition against shedding blood may exclude non-Jews (Mekhilta, Nezikin, ch. 4), though it is suggested that punishment for shedding a non-Jew's blood may be imposed by God if not by human courts. Notwithstanding these and other discriminatory provisions of the law, it should be noted that numerous passages in biblical and rabbinic literature emphasize the importance of treating non-Jews fairly. In part this reflected a concern to avoid "profaning God's name," for mistreatment at the hands of Jews would presumably bring dishonor to Israel, its law, and its God.

[20] Babylonian Talmud, Shabuot 39a.

[21] Babylonian Talmud, Baba Kamma 83b and Mekhilta, Nezikin, ch. 8.

[22] Sifra Leviticus, Kedoshim.

[23] The rabbis have totally changed the meaning of the phrase by quoting it out of context. The verse refers to *not* perverting justice by following (or inclining) after a multitude.

[24] Babylonian Talmud, Baba Metsia 59b.

[25] Of course, at various times in Jewish history, there were movements of imminent messianic expectation, as well as individual figures who were identified as the messiah (at least by some elements within the community). Simon bar Koziba (known as Bar Kokhba) who led a Jewish revolt against the Romans in the second century C.E. was regarded by some as the messiah; see the famous comment of Rabbi Akiba, Jerusalem Talmud, Taanit 4:5 [68d]. See also Gershom Scholem, *Sabbatai Sevi* (Princeton, N.J.: Princeton University Press, 1973) on the popular messianic figure in the 16th century.

[26] See Maimonides, Mishneh Torah, Laws of Slaves, for a summary of the rules that governed the treatment of indentured servants. From a contemporary perspective, any tolerance of slavery within this tradition appears to be immoral and at odds with its avowed commitment to freedom. In the context of the ancient Near East, however, the biblical and later rabbinic institution of slavery was extraordinarily progressive and tolerant.

[27] See the extended discussion of Lurianic kabbalah in Gershom Scholem, *Major Trends in Jewish Mysticism* (New York: Schocken, 1941), 244–86.

[28] See Babylonian Talmud, Sanhedrin 97b–98a, Song of Songs Rabbah 5, 2–2.

[29] Martin Buber, *Hasidism and Modern Man* (New York: Harper & Row, 1966), 175.

[30] See Babylonian Talmud, Sotah 49b, Sanhedrin 97a.

CHAPTER THREE: SOURCES OF JEWISH ETHICS

[1] Barry W. Holtz, ed., *Back to the Sources* (New York: Summit Books, 1984), 13.

[2] This was traditionally regarded as the date of the destruction of both the first and second Temples in Jerusalem, as well as the date on which various other national calamities occurred.

[3] Biblical scholars have named these separate authors whose work comprises the Pentateuch in part based on the names they typically use for God. The "E" author refers to God as "Elohim," the J author uses "Jehovah" (itself a later rendering of the four-letter Hebrew name YHWH), the P author is from the priestly caste and reflects that group's distinctive concerns. The book of Deuteronomy is attributed to a fourth author, "D."

[4] Jews traditionally have divided the Hebrew Bible into three main sections: Torah (the Pentateuch, or first five books), the Prophets (Joshua, Judges, Samuel, Kings, Isaiah, Jeremiah, Ezekiel, and the twelve "minor prophets"), and Writings (all the

remaining books, including Psalms, Proverbs, Job, Esther, Daniel, Ruth, and Chronicles). An acronym composed of the first letter of each of these three Hebrew words (T for Torah, N for Nevi'im, K for K'tuvim) yields the word *tanakh*, which refers to the Hebrew Bible as a whole.

[5] The vast majority of statements in the Mishnah are attributed to people who lived in this period. Some authorities who lived in the centuries before the Common Era are also cited, and even views attributed to later authorities may well be based on oral traditions going back centuries.

[6] See Jacob Neusner, *Judaism: The Evidence of the Mishnah* (Chicago: University of Chicago Press, 1981).

[7] The whole tractate is also known as *Pirke Avot* (literally, "Chapters of the Fathers" but sometimes rendered as "Ethics of the Fathers" because of the ethical nature of the content).

[8] It should be noted that of the sixty-three tractates in the Mishnah, only thirty-seven have a corresponding gemara in the Babylonian Talmud (compared with thirty-nine in the Jerusalem or Palestinian Talmud). Moreover, among Mishnaic tractates, some have a gemara in both Talmuds, some in neither, some in the Babylonian Talmud (but not the Jerusalem), and vice versa.

[9] The Jerusalem Talmud is sometimes also referenced to the first edition, printed in Venice, which has four columns on each folio page, or two on each side of each page. These are indicated with a page number followed by a letter a–d, to indicate the column (e.g., Shabbat 5d.). In these notes such citations appear in square brackets.

[10] The Talmud's question is based on a forced reading of the compound grammatical formulation (Hebrew: *v'nakeh lo yenakeh),* in which the first verb (here rendered "will clear the guilty") is actually meant to strengthen the force of the verb that follows ("will not clear the guilty"). Most contemporary translations render the phrase "will by no means clear the guilty."

[11] The Talmud again plays with the meaning of the Hebrew *('ohaveim n'davah).* The plain meaning is "I will love them freely, voluntarily," but the Talmud reads it as though it meant, "I will love the voluntary," that is, the voluntary offerings.

[12] This midrash is based on Jeremiah 3:1, in which the law of Deuteronomy is reiterated, and which ends with the words, "Now you have whored with many lovers; can you return to Me?"

[13] Jewish Publication Society (JPS): "appreciate your vigor in the days of your youth. . . ." But this represents the more standard translation and undoubtedly reflects Maimonides' understanding of the verse.

[14] Nowadays, many responsa can be found in computer databases or on the Websites of modern denominations of Judaism.

[15] I am grateful to Professor Eliezer Diamond of the Jewish Theological Seminary for bringing this text to my attention.

[16] JPS: "He donned victory like a coat of mail."

CHAPTER FOUR: CONTOURS
OF JEWISH MORAL LIFE

[1] Nahmanides' commentary on Deuteronomy 6:18.

[2] Avot 4:1.

[3] JPS: "Render true and perfect justice in your gates."

[4] Palestinian Talmud, Ta'anit 4:2, [68a].

[5] The consideration of the broad principles of justice developed in Jewish tradition is limited here and so leaves aside many rules concerning the administration of justice. Examples of the latter would include the insistence that a conviction in capital cases requires the testimony of two witnesses (Deuteronomy 17:6) and the rabbinic dictim that rabbis shouldn't create laws that the community will not abide (and thereby encourage disrespect for the law) (Babylonian Talmud, Baba Batra 60b).

[6] See Pesikta d'rav Kahana, 23:8.

[7] See, for example, Gustavo Gutierrez, *Essential Writings*, ed. James B. Nickoloff (MaryKnoll, N.Y.: Orbis Books, 1996).

[8] Of course, historically many Jews have been attracted to socialism, partly for political reasons but also because it has some affinity with a radical strain within Jewish tradition. See Nora Levin, *While Messiah Tarried* (New York: Schocken, 1977).

[9] By contrast, the earlier Mesapotamian law, as preserved in the famous Code of Hammurapi, provided for penalties in some instances that were more severe than the original crime and for differential penalties depending on the social status of the offender or the offended party.

[10] Mishnah Sanhedrin 4:1–6:6.

[11] Immanuel Kant, *Groundwork of the Metaphysic of Morals*, trans. H. J. Paton (New York: Harper & Row, 1964).

[12] Jerusalem Talmud, Nedarim 9:4, [41c]; Genesis Rabbah 24:7.

[13] Babylonian Talmud, Sanhedrin 7a. The passage from Psalms is ambiguous. The JPS translation reads, "God stands in the divine assembly; among the divine beings he pronounces judgment."

[14] Deuteronomy Rabbah 5:6.

[15] Babylonian Talmud, Sotah 14a.

[16] Babylonian Talmud, Avodah Zarah 20b.

[17] I am grateful to Byron Sherwin for drawing this distinction, although he makes the mistaken claim that Judaism endorses only the second of these two types; see Byron L. Sherwin and Seymour J. Cohen, *How to Be a Jew: Ethical Teachings of Judaism* (Northvale, N.J.: Jason Aronson, 1992), 86.

[18] Pride is an ambiguous term, sometimes signifying an attitude of arrogance or self-importance and sometimes referring to a sense of satisfaction with ourselves or others (as when we speak of being proud of our children's accomplishments). The former attitude is universally condemned in Jewish sources, and the latter is the subject

of some disagreement. Some would regard attributing significance to our own or oth-ers' accomplishments as problematic while others consider some degree of pride as natural and even necessary for human striving. On this issue, see Isaac Herzog, "Man's Smallness and Greatness," in *Judaism: Law and Ethics* (New York: Soncino Press, 1974), 29–33; and Sol Roth, "Toward a Definition of Humility," in *Contemporary Jewish Ethics and Morality: A Reader,* eds. Elliot N. Dorff and Louis E. Newman (New York: Oxford University Press, 1995), 259–268. Throughout this dis-cussion, I consider pride in any form to be antithetical to humility and hence to be avoided as much as possible.

[19] Babylonian Talmud, Sanhedrin 38a.

[20] Mishnah, Avot 4:4.

[21] Bahya ibn Pakuda, *Duties of the Heart,* Gate Six (Humility), Chapter Five.

[22] Moses Hayyim Luzzatto, *Mesilat Yesharim—The Path of the Upright,* trans. Mordecai M. Kaplan (Philadelphia: Jewish Publication Society, 1936), 414.

[23] Babylonian Talmud, Sotah 4b. The JPS translation of the passage from Deuteronomy reads, "beware lest your heart grow haughty" based on a textual emendation.

[24] JPS: "I cannot endure the haughty and proud man," but this translation would not capture the rabbis' play on the Hebrew word translated here as "him."

[25] Babylonian Talmud, Sotah 5b. JPS translation: "I cannot endure the haughty and proud man." But this translation makes the wordplay of the midrash clearer.

[26] Babylonian Talmud, Berakhot 43b.

[27] Martin Buber, *Tales of the Hasidim: Early Masters* (New York: Schocken, 1947), 149.

[28] Derekh Eretz Zuta 7.

[29] Derekh Eretz Zuta 5.

[30] Maimonides, Mishneh Torah, Laws of the Foundations of the Torah, 2:2.

[31] Babylonian Talmud, Eruvin 13b.

[32] The JPS translation actually has "in the dust," but this is not literal and does not capture the rabbis' clever exegesis of the passage.

[33] Babylonian Talmud, Sotah 5a.

[34] Avot d'Rabbi Nathan, 26.

[35] Babylonian Talmud, Sotah 5a.

[36] Babylonian Talmud, Sotah 5a. The rabbis assumed that Mt. Sinai was lower and less majestic than other mountains where God might have chosen to reveal the law to Israel.

[37] Traditional prayerbook, my translation.

[38] It must be remembered, as we noted in Chapter Two, that this emphasis on humil-ity is mitigated by an appreciation for the standing that human beings have in God's eyes. Both as humans created in God's image and as Jews in covenant with God, Jews believe they have the right to stand before God and even, at times, to make demands

on God. Indeed, the paragraph in the liturgy that immediately follows the one just cited reads, "But we are Your people, partners to Your covenant, descendants of Your beloved Abraham to whom you made a pledge on Mount Moriah. . . ." Notwithstanding this interplay between the Jews' relative powerlessness in relation to God and the Jews' status as God's beloved children, the ethical tradition seems to commend the virtue of humility far more than that of pride. Perhaps this is because traditional authorities understood that excessive pride is a far more common and more dangerous moral failing than excessive humility. I am indebted to Elliot Dorff for calling my attention to this issue.

[39] More radical view: True humility is obliterating ego entirely, hence not being preoccupied with one's failings.

[40] Ronald Green, "Jewish Ethics and the Virtue of Humility," *Journal of Religious Ethics* 1:1 (1973): 58.

[41] Babylonian Talmud, Kiddushin 31b.

[42] Ibid. This translation is gender inclusive, as indeed the commandment applies to both father and mother. The rabbis also find significance in the contrasting word order of the two verses. "The Creator knew that a son honors his mother more than his father, because she sways him by persuasive words—therefore, the Torah gave precedence to the honor of one's father. . . . The Creator knew that a son fears his father more than his mother, because he teaches him Torah—therefore, the Torah gave precedence to the reverence due one's mother. . . . Where a deficiency exists—God filled it." (Mekhilta, Bahodesh 8)

With respect to contradicting a parent, it should be noted that some authorities differentiated between secular matters and discussions of Torah. In the latter case, children are permitted to contradict their parents, presumably because here the search for truth is paramount and the rabbis presume that this requires unfettered discussion and open debate. See Israel ben Joseph Alnakawa, *Menorat Ha-maor,* cited in Gerald Blidstein, *Honor Thy Father and Mother: Filial Responsibility in Jewish Law and Ethics* (New York: Ktav, 1975), 41.

[43] Other rabbinic sources add to the list of responsibilities: "washing his [the father's] face, hands and feet" (Tosefta Kiddushin 1:11) and "sprinkling the floor before him, washing and anointing him, and putting his shoes on." (Pesikta Rabbati, 122a).

[44] Quoted in Blidstein, *Honor Thy Father and Mother,* 53.

[45] Strikingly, the classic rabbinic sources do not mandate *loving* parents, only honoring and revering them. This may be because parents are covered by the commandment "love one's neighbor," or because the rabbis realistically understood that affection could not really be commanded. Indeed, they may have been so emphatic in their insistence on the honor and reverence due parents precisely because, in the absence of filial love, such behavior will not come naturally.

[46] Jerusalem Talmud, Kiddushin, 1:7, [61b].

[47] Babylonian Talmud, Kiddushin 32a.

[48] Babylonian Talmud, Kiddushin 31a.

[49] Jerusalem Talmud, Peah 1:1.

[50] Maimonides, Mishneh Torah, Mamrim 6:7.

[51] Tanhuma, Ekev, 2.

[52] Babylonian Talmud, Kiddushin 31b and Rashi, *ad. loc.*

[53] Sifra, Kedoshim 1:10.

[54] Babylonian Talmud, Kiddushin 32a.

[55] See the discussion of these responsa in Blidstein, *Honor Thy Father and Mother,* 84–85.

[56] It is interesting to note that all these sources deal with the case of a son's responsibilities to his parents when they are in conflict with their daughter-in-law.

[57] Cited in Blidstein, *Honor Thy Father and Mother,* 105.

[58] Sefer Hasidim, 564, cited in Blidstein, *Honor Thy Father and Mother,* 106.

[59] Other qualifications of the commandment to honor parents involve cases in which the parents are guilty of abandoning or abusing the child.

[60] See sources cited in Sherwin, and Cohen, *How to Be a Jew: Ethical Teachings of Judaism* (Northvale, N.J.: Jason Aronson, 1992), 164.

[61] Babylonian Talmud, Kiddushin, 30b–31a. Other versions of this text, in whole or in part, appear in Sifra 86d; Mekhilta (ed. Horowitz), p. 232; Jerusalem Talmud, Peah 1:1 [15c]; Jerusalem Talmud, Kilayim 8:4, [31c]; and Babylonian Talmud, Niddah 31a.

[62] See Jerusalem Talmud, Kilayim 8:4, and Babylonian Talmud, Niddah 31a.

[63] The biblical imagery used in connection with God is overwhelmingly masculine. Similarly, the rabbis' discussion of honoring parents focuses on the treatment of fathers more than of mothers.

[64] Nahmanides' commentary to Exodus 20:12, 13.

[65] I have in mind here those places where aspects of religious ritual are invested with ethical significance, as when the rabbis teach that removing the leaven from one's home on Passover is also about discarding all that is "puffed up" and arrogant in oneself; see Shalom Meir Wallach, *Haggadah of the Chassidic Masters* (Jerusalem: Mesorah Publications, 1990), 19. A fuller introduction to Jewish ethics would treat all such instances of the moralization of Jewish religious behavior, in addition to the strictly ethical aspects of life and their religious foundations, which is the subject of this study.

CHAPTER FIVE: FOUNDATIONS OF JEWISH MORAL OBLIGATION

[1] Douglas Knight, "Cosmogony and Order in the Hebrew Tradition," *Cosmogony and Ethical Order,* eds. Robin Lovin and Frank Reynolds (Chicago: University of Chicago Press, 1985), 143–44.

[2] The obvious exceptions to this generalization are the works of medieval philosophical writers, like Maimonides, who attempted to develop a systematic statement of the Jewish ethics. See, for example, his *Shemoneh Perakim* [Eight Chapters], which offers a distinctly Aristotelian theory of Jewish ethics.

[3] There are texts within the tradition that suggest otherwise. The parade example is the story in Genesis 18 of Abraham arguing with God over the propriety of destroying the cities of Sodom and Gomorrah, even if a number of righteous people live there. Indeed, some have suggested that this sort of moral argument with God is characteristic of a certain strand within Judaism, one that especially suits the sensibilities of modern Jews, who tend to be uncomfortable with the notion of an authoritarian God. Yet the whole tradition of Jewish reflection on matters of proper religious and moral behavior rests on the assumptions that God's Torah is the perfect and complete record of divine revelation, the ultimate source of truth and religious instruction, and so needs merely to be interpreted properly to provide answers to all Jews' moral questions. Of course, rabbis across the centuries sometimes interpreted biblical laws in ways that diverged radically from their plain meaning but did so confident that they were simply making plain God's will for their own time.

[4] See Allan E. Farnsworth, *Contracts* (Boston: Little, Brown & Co., 1982), 374 ff. for a discussion of the Statute of Frauds, which requires that certain types of contracts are enforceable only if written.

[5] See also Deuteronomy 7:9–11.

[6] See also Exodus 15:26 and Deuteronomy 12:28.

[7] Similarly, Wurzburger argues that at Sinai Israel experienced primarily a revelation of God's presence and only secondarily specific rules as the content of revelation. There are thus covenantal imperatives "which confront us with God's demands upon us in the here and now in all their uniqueness and particularity." Walter Wurzburger, "Covenantal Imperatives," in *Samuel K. Mirsky Memorial Volume: Studies in Jewish Law, Philosophy and Literature*, ed. Gersion Appel, Morris Epstein, and Hayim Leaf (New York: Yeshiva University Press, 1970), 11.

[8] This view, which is prevalent among Christian biblical scholars, tends to contrast the covenant, which is dynamic, with the law, which is static. See, for example, Dennis McCarthy, *Treaty and Covenant* (Rome: Pontifical Biblical Institute, 1963), 175–76.

[9] See, for example, Eliezer Bashan, "Lifnim mishurat hadin besifrut hahalakhah" (Hebrew) *Deot* 39 (Spring 1970): 236–43; Saul Berman, "Lifnim mishurat hadin" *Journal of Jewish Studies* 26 (1975): 86–104 and 28 (1977): 181–93; Shear-Yeshuv Cohen, "Lifnim mishurat hadin" (Hebrew) in *Adam-Noah Baron Memorial Volume* (Jerusalem, 1970), 165–88; and Tzvee Yehuda Meltzer, "Megadray lifnim mishurat hadin" (Hebrew) *Hadarom* 12 (1960): 33–36.

[10] See Babylonian Talmud, Baba Metsia 30b.

[11] See Babylonian Talmud, Hullin 130b.

[12] See Mishnah Shebiit 10:9.

[13] See also Leviticus 24:20 and Deuteronomy 19:21, where the same injunction appears.

[14] See Babylonian Talmud, Baba Kamma 83b.

[15] For other examples, see Seymour Siegel, "Ethics and the Halakhah," *Conservative Judaism* 25 (1971): 35–36, who writes, "From these and many other examples it is clear that the sages modified the law when they saw that following another norm would result in unfavorable results. Ethical considerations and public policy were sufficient to change the decision."

[16] For other examples and for a complete discussion of this issue, see my *Past Imperatives: Studies in the History and Theory of Jewish Ethics* (Albany: State University of New York Press, 1998), esp. Chapter Two, "Ethics as Law, Law as Religion: Reflections on the Problem of Law and Ethics in Judaism."

[17] Aharon Lichtenstein, "Does Jewish Tradition Recognize an Ethic Independent of Halakhah?" in *Modern Jewish Ethics,* ed. Marvin Fox (Columbus: Ohio State University Press, 1975), 62–88.

[18] Elliot N. Dorff, "The Covenant: The Transcendent Thrust in Jewish Law," *The Jewish Law Annual* 7 (1988): 79. (Reprinted in Dorff and Newman, eds., *Contemporary Jewish Law and Ethics* (New York: Oxford University Press, 1995), 59–78.

[19] The *musar* movement was founded by Rabbi Israel Salanter in Vilna, Lithuania, in the 1840s and spread throughout eastern Europe. Its goal was the moral revitalization of Jewry through fearless moral introspection and ongoing penitence. See Lester Samuel Eckman, *The History of the Musar Movement, 1840–1945* (New York: Shengold Publishers, 1975).

[20] Hasidism was founded in the late eighteenth century by Israel Baal Shem Tov, a charismatic religious leader and itinerant storyteller, who emphasized the joy of serving God, ecstatic worship, and the *tzaddik,* or righteous individual, as a mediator between the community and God.

[21] Eugene B. Borowitz, *Exploring Jewish Ethics* (Detroit: Wayne State University Press, 1990), 188.

[22] In the later account of Abraham's argument with God over the fate of Sodom and Gomorrah, the patriarch challenges God with the rhetorical question, "Shall not the judge of all the earth do justly?" (Genesis 18:25) Abraham's question would make no sense if he did not have access to moral standards independent of God's direct commands.

[23] Babylonian Talmud, Yoma 67b.

[24] Jerusalem Talmud, Nedarim 9:4 [41c]. This same view is reflected in another striking rabbinic statement: "R. Joshua ben Levi said: When one walks on the highway, a company of angels goes ahead announcing: 'Make way for the image of the Holy One, blessed be He' " (Midrash Psalms 17:8; Deuteronomy Rabbah 4:4).

[25] Babylonian Talmud, Erubin 100b.

[26] Saadia Gaon, *Book of Doctrines and Beliefs*, 98.

[27] Avot 3:14.

[28] In his exhaustive and masterful study of this material, David Novak has demonstrated that the concept of a universal law, applicable to all descendants of Noah, arose in the early rabbinic period and continued to be a source of theological and legal interest throughout the centuries. See Novak, *The Image of the Non-Jew in Judaism* (Lewiston, N.Y.: Edwin Mellen Press, 1983).

[29] In some editions of Tosefta, this is 9:4.

[30] See Novak, *The Image of the Non-Jew*, 4–5, for a comparison of two later rabbinic passages that find allusions to other biblical verses, and thereby to these specific commandments, in each of the words in Genesis 2:16.

[31] See Tosefta Avodah Zarah 8:6–8; Babylonian Talmud, Sanhedrin 56b. In Babylonian Talmud, Hullin 92a–b, Rav Ulla opines that God gave the Noahides 30 commandments, but they only scrupulously observe three of them. Many rabbinic sources berate non-Jews either for their refusal to accept the Torah (insofar as it demanded that they abandon their immoral practices) or for their inability to observe even the few commandments that they were given.

[32] Novak, *The Image of the Non-Jew*, 412–13.

[33] Judah Halevi acknowledges that Genesis 2:16 is not the source of Noahide law but merely a mnemonic device for remembering it. See *Kuzari*, 3.73.

[34] Tosefta Sotah 8:6.

[35] Maimonides' view has generated significant controversy; see Steven Schwarzschild, "Do Noahides Have to Believe in Revelation?" in *The Pursuit of the Ideal*, ed. Menachem Kellner (Albany: State University of New York Press, 1990), 29–59.

[36] Mishneh Torah, Laws of Kings 18:11. Maimonides' precise meaning here is open to question, since some manuscripts vary from the standard printed texts of Mishneh Torah, in which the last sentence reads "nor is he one of" rather than "but he is one of." The transposition of a single letter in this case completely reverses the meaning of the sentence. At stake is how to understand those non-Jews who observe Noahide law "based on reason"—are they deserving of the designation "righteous of the nations" or, since their observance lacks a religious basis, are they simply "wise men"? In either case, the point here is that Noahide law *could* be justified on a purely rational basis, according to Maimonides.

[37] Bernard S. Jackson correctly comments on this passage, "What is clear here is that a Gentile who observes these commandments because he judges them to be rational, rather than because he wishes to obey the command of God, loses such religious merit (and reward) as is normally attendant upon observance of divine commands" ("Natural Law Questions and the Jewish Tradition" *Vera Lex* 6, no. 2 (1986): 1–2, 6, 10. Of course, any non-Jew who accepts the Torah (including its doctrine of Noahide law) as a record of divine revelation would be theologically practically an adherent of

classical Judaism, which is what Maimonides means by referring to such a person as a "resident alien."

[38] See Babylonian Talmud, Sanhedrin 59 and Hullin 33a.

[39] Genesis Rabbah 1:4

[40] According to some midrashic texts, it is the oral law that distinguishes Israel from the nations. God has given Scripture to all, but the remainder of God's revelation in the form of oral tradition is communicated to Israel alone. See Tanhuma B, Ki Tissa 17; Tanhuma, Ki Tissa, 60; Exodus Rabbah 47:1.

[41] David Novak, *Jewish Social Ethics* (New York: Oxford University Press, 1992), 15.

[42] The very same issue faced Christian thinkers in the early centuries of the Church. The new revelation through Christ required Christian thinkers to confront the extent to which the earlier revelation through Torah had continuing validity. On the one hand, to the extent that the earlier revelation had continuing validity for Christians, it seemed to minimize the significance of the new revelation. On the other hand, Torah was a genuine revelation of God (albeit perhaps a limited one) and so the new revelation had to be understood in a way that encompassed rather than obliterated the old one.

[43] For a clear discussion of the tension between universalist and particularist dimensions of Israel's covenant, see Elliot N. Dorff, "The Covenant: How Jews Understand Themselves and Others," *Anglican Theological Review* 64 (1982): 481–501; reprinted in revised form in Elliot Dorff, *To Do the Right and the Good* (Philadelphia: Jewish Publication Society, 2002), pp. 61–95.

CHAPTER SIX: JEWISH ETHICS IN MODERN TIMES

[1] Eugene Borowitz, *Renewing the Covenant: A Theology for the Post-Modern Jew* (Philadelphia: Jewish Publication Society, 1991), 1.

[2] Samson Raphael Hirsch, *Judaism Eternal: Selected Essays from the Writings of Rabbi Samson Raphael Hirsch*, ed. and trans. I. Grunfeld (London: Soncino Press, 1956), excerpted and reprinted in Paul Mendes-Flohr, ed., *The Jew in the Modern World: A Documentary History*, 2 ed. (New York: Oxford University Press, 1995), 200.

[3] Contrast the dictum of the Hatam Sofer (1762–1839), "Everything new is forbidden by the Torah" with Samson Raphael Hirsch's motto, "Torah together with worldly knowledge."

[4] See Samuel C. Heilman and Steven M. Cohen, *Parochials and Cosmopolitans: Modern Orthodox Jews in America* (Chicago: University of Chicago, 1989).

[5] Arthur Hertzberg, *Being Jewish in America* (New York: Schocken, 1979), 19.

[6] The Pittsburgh Platform (1885), cited in Paul Mendes-Flohr, ed., *The Jew in the Modern World*, 469.

[7] Kaufman Kohler, *Jewish Theology: Systematically and Historically Considered* (New York: Macmillan, 1918), 8

[8] Leo Baeck, *Das Wesen des Judentums*, 2d ed. (Frankfort, 1922), 54, as cited in Simon Bernfeld, ed., *The Foundations of Jewish Ethics* (New York: Ktav, 1929), 33. Baeck's book was translated into English by Victor Grubewieser and Leonard Pearl, *The Essence of Judaism* (New York: Schocken, 1948).

[9] For a cogent critique of this view, see Ahad Ha'am's essay "The Transvaluation of Values," in Asher Ginsburg [Ahad Ha'am], *Selected Essays of Ahad Ha'am*, trans. Leon Simon (Philadelphia: Jewish Publication Society, 1962), 231.

[10] See the online journal of the Society of Textual Reasoning (http://etext.lib.virginia .edu/journals/tr.html). To date, the most comprehensive exploration of this postmodern approach to Jewish ethics is Robert Gibbs, *Why Ethics?* (Princeton, N.J.: Princeton University Press, 2000).

[11] J. David Bleich, "Introduction: The A Priori Component of Bioethics," in *Jewish Bioethics*, eds. Fred Rosner and J. David Bleich (New York: Hebrew Publishing Co., 1979), xix.

[12] Elliot N. Dorff, *Matters of Life and Death: A Jewish Approach to Modern Medical Ethics* (Philadelphia: Jewish Publication Society, 1998), 413.

[13] Eugene B. Borowitz, *Exploring Jewish Ethics*, (Detroit: Wayne State University Press, 1990), 24–25.

[14] Ibid., 134–36.

[15] Ibid., 165–92.

[16] Stanley Hauerwas, *Vision and Virtue* (Notre Dame, Ind.: Fides, 1974), 45–46.

[17] For a critique of the narrative approach, see Paul Lauritzen, "Is 'Narrative' Really a Panacea: The Use of 'Narrative' in the Work of Metz and Hauerwas," *Journal of Religion* 67 (1987): 322–39.

[18] Michael Goldberg, *Jews and Christians: Getting Our Stories Straight* (Nashville, Tenn.: Abingdon, 1985), 127.

[19] Laurie Zoloth, *Health Care and the Ethics of Encounter: A Jewish Discussion of Social Justice* (Chapel Hill: University of North Carolina Press, 1999).

[20] Stanley Hauerwas, *Vision and Virtue*, 22.

[21] I intend these metaphors to be suggestive of basic differences between the three models explained here, although none of these metaphors precisely captures the methods of the Jewish ethicists whose work is described. In particular, I want to acknowledge that legalists have a good deal more latitude in interpreting the Torah's injunctions than a builder does in relation to a blueprint. Still, in comparison to the other models, the legalist is committed to being guided by the details of the Torah's laws, much as the builder must be guided by the detailed instructions of the blueprint. I am grateful to Elliot Dorff for pointing out to me the limitations of this metaphor.

[22] Ronald Dworkin, *A Matter of Principle* (Cambridge, Mass.: Harvard University Press, 1985), 159 ff.

[23] Ibid., 159.

CHAPTER SEVEN: THREE CASE STUDIES: CONTINUITY AND DIVERSITY IN CONTEMPORARY JEWISH ETHICS

[1] Franz Rosenzweig, *On Jewish Learning* (New York: Schocken, 1965), 98.

[2] All references in this section are to David Novak, "Some Aspects of Sex, Society and God in Judaism," in his *Jewish Social Ethics* (New York: Oxford University Press, 1992), 84–103.

[3] Novak has developed his theory of Jewish natural law most fully in his *Natural Law in Judaism* (New York: Cambridge University Press, 1998). For a critical appraisal of Novak's work on natural law, see my "The Law of Nature and the Nature of the Law: David Novak and the Role of Natural Law in Judaism," in *Ethical Monotheism, Past and Present: Essays in Honor of Wendell S. Dietrich* eds. Theodore M. Vial and Mark A. Hadley (Providence, R.I.: Brown Judaic Studies, 2001), 259–77.

[4] Novak, *Jewish Social Ethics* 84.

[5] Ibid., 85.

[6] Ibid., 86.

[7] Ibid.

[8] Ibid., 89.

[9] Ibid., 94.

[10] Ibid., 96.

[11] Ibid., 98.

[12] All references in this section are to Arthur Waskow, *Down-to-Earth Judaism: Food, Money, Sex and the Rest of Life* (New York: William Morrow and Co., 1995), 243–349.

[13] Waskow, *Down-to-Earth Judaism* 315–16.

[14] Ibid., 322.

[15] Ibid., 340.

[16] Ibid., 331.

[17] Ibid., 318.

[18] All references in this section are to Eugene B. Borowitz, *Exploring Jewish Ethics: Papers on Covenant Responsibility* (Detroit, Mich.: Wayne State University Press, 1990), especially Chapter 19, "When Is It Moral to Have Intercourse?" and Chapter 20, "Reading the Jewish Tradition on Marital Sexuality."

[19] Borowitz, *Exploring Jewish Ethics*, 247.

[20] Ibid., 248.

[21] Ibid., 253.

[22] Ibid., 268.

[23] Ibid.

[24] Ibid., 261.

25 Mordecai Kaplan, *Not So Random Thoughts* (New York: Reconstructionist Press, 1966), 263.

26 All references in this section are to J. David Bleich, "Abortion in Halakhic Literature," *Tradition* as reprinted in Fred Rosner and J. David Bleich, eds., *Jewish Bioethics* (New York: Hebrew Publishing Co., 1979), 134–77.

27 Ibid., 134.

28 The right of self-defense is well established in Jewish law. The basic principle is "if a person comes to kill you, rise up to kill him [first]" (Babylonian Talmud, Sanhedrin 72a). When applied to third parties, this yields what is known as the "law of the pursuer," that we have the right to protect the innocent lives of others being pursued by an enemy. This principle has been variously applied to the case of the fetus who threatens the life of the mother. Some authorities have argued, contra Maimonides, that the fetus cannot be considered a "pursuer," since it is incapable of having malicious intent.

29 Babylonian Talmud, Yebamot 69b.

30 Actually, this view is expressed in the context of another issue entirely, whether the daughter of a priest who has married an Israelite man and immediately afterwards is widowed may eat *terumah,* the priestly offering. By law she is entitled to do so only if she has no children, but it is unknown in this case whether she could have become pregnant before her husband died. Hisda's claim, then, is that for the first forty days after her marriage, even if she becomes pregnant, she is regarded as childless, for the fetus at this stage is "mere water," and so she is entitled to eat the *terumah.*

31 Babylonian Talmud, Shabbat 151b.

32 Bleich, "Abortion in Halakhic Literature," 144.

33 Ibid., 152.

34 Ibid., 161.

35 Ibid.

36 Ibid., 163.

37 All references in this section are to David M. Feldman, "This Matter of Abortion," from *Health and Medicine in the Jewish Tradition* (New York: Crossroad, 1986), as reprinted in Elliot N. Dorff and Louis E. Newman, eds., *Contemporary Jewish Ethics and Morality* (New York: Oxford University Press, 1995), 382–91.

38 He is also the author of *Health and Medicine in the Jewish Tradition* (New York: Crossroad, 1986).

39 Feldman, "This Matter of Abortion," 383. The paradigm case here is that of a tyrant who demands that a Jew violate one of the biblical commandments or else be killed. Rabbinic law is clear that to save one's life one must violate all commandments, except the three noted here. In such cases, sacrificing one's life is preferable to violating the law. See Babylonian Talmud, Sanhedrin 74a.

40 Feldman, "This Matter of Abortion," 384.

41 The classic formulation of this view is that of Rashi in his commentary to Babylonian Talmud, Sanhedrin 72b.

[42] Feldman, "This Matter of Abortion," 388.

[43] Ibid., 389–90.

[44] Ibid., 389.

[45] Ibid.

[46] Ibid., 390.

[47] Ibid.

[48] All references in the following section are to Sandra Lubarsky, "Judaism and the Justification of Abortion for Nonmedical Reasons," *Journal of Reform Judaism* 31 (1984): 1–13, as reprinted in Elliot N. Dorff and Louis E. Newman, eds., *Contemporary Jewish Ethics and Morality* (New York: Oxford University Press, 1995), 392–402.

[49] Lubarsky, "Judaism and the Justification of Abortion for Nonmedical Reasons," 392.

[50] Ibid.

[51] Ibid., 394–5.

[52] Ibid., 392.

[53] Ibid., 398.

[54] Ibid., 399.

[55] Ibid., 400.

[56] Some contemporary Jews identify with the pacifist tradition and see Judaism as favoring nonviolence over aggression in almost all circumstances. For a study of this position, see Evelyn Wilcock, *Pacifism and the Jews: Studies of Twentieth Century Jewish Pacifists* (Gloucestershire: Hawthorn Press, 1992). Other resources reflecting this view may be found on the Websites of the Jewish Peace Fellowship (www.jewishpeacefellowship.org) and Shalom Center (www.shalomctr.org). I have chosen here to analyze positions that are more centrist and that illustrate the problems of applying ancient sources endorsing war to contemporary circumstances.

[57] All references here are to Elliot N. Dorff, *To Do the Right and the Good: A Jewish Approach to Modern Social Ethics* (Philadelphia: Jewish Publication Society, 2002), Chapter Seven, A Time for War and a Time for Peace: The Ethics of War and International Intervention.

[58] All references here are to Bradley Shavit Artson, *Love Peace and Pursue Peace: A Jewish Response to War and Nuclear Annihilation* (New York: United Synagogue of America, 1988).

[59] Mishnah Avot 1:12.

[60] Kad ha-Kemakh, *Shalom,* (New York: Shilo, 1980), 398, as cited in Artson, *Love Peace and Pursue Peace* 57.

[61] As cited in Dorff, *To Do the Right and the Good,* 166.

[62] Artson, *Love Peace and Pursue Peace* 190.

[63] Ibid., 116.

[64] Ibid., 139.

[65] Dorff, *To Do the Right and the Good,* 178.

[66] Ibid., 179.

[67] Ibid., 174.

[68] Ibid., 172–73. Dorff notes a range of intermediate positions that have been articulated by various authorities over the centuries, including the view that such wars are
permitted in response to intermittent attacks even in the absence of full-scale war,
that they are permitted only in response to a military build-up, that they are permitted to prevent such a build-up, and that they are permitted only in response to a clear
threat of aggression.

[69] Babylonian Talmud, Eruvin 45a.

[70] Mishneh Torah, Laws of the Sabbath, 2:23.

[71] Artson, *Love Peace and Pursue Peace* 196.

[72] Sifre Deuteronomy, 203.

[73] Dorff, *To Do the Right and the Good,* 162.

[74] Artson, *Love Peace and Pursue Peace* 106.

[75] Dorff, *To Do the Right and the Good,* 163–64.

[76] Notably, Artson does offer an extended analysis of nuclear war which, not surprisingly, he categorically condemns based on the values he finds within Judaism.

[77] Artson, *Love Peace and Pursue Peace* 5.

[78] Ibid., 11.

[79] Ibid., 4.

Glossary

aggada, aggadah—(Hebrew, "narrative, lore") a general term referring to the non-legal components of rabbinic literature, including interpretations of biblical narratives, stories about rabbis, and aphorisms.

B.C.E., C.E.—Before the Common Era, Common Era; the commonly accepted scholarly method of referring to dates otherwise identified as B.C. and A.D. Current usage avoids the Christological assumptions of the older terminology.

gemara—(Aramaic, "study, learning") the commentary on the Mishnah composed by the rabbis known as amoraim, who lived from the second to fifth centuries C.E.

haggada, haggadah—(Hebrew, "narrative, telling") the name of the text used on the eve of Passover in which the narrative of the exodus from Egypt is retold, replete with rabbinic commentary, and the order of rituals at the Passover meal (seder) is detailed.

halakha, halakhah—(Hebrew, "a way, path"), adj., *halakhic*; Jewish law, encompassing both biblical and rabbinic injunctions; the path that one ought to follow in life; halakha can refer either to a specific law or to the entire body of Jewish law.

Hasidism—(from Hebrew, "pious"), adj., **hasidic**; a popular religious movement that arose among eastern European Jews in the eighteenth century. With roots in kabbalah, Hasidism is noted for its emphasis on joyful, ecstatic worship and for the stories told by and about its popular teachers. Hasidism developed into numerous sects, each headed by a charismatic leader, or rebbe.

kabbala, kabbalah—(Hebrew, "tradition") and **kabbalistic**; the Jewish mystical tradition that encompasses many different schools of thought from ancient times to the present; kabbalists claim access to esoteric teachings about God, creation, and the redemption of the world; kabbalistic works emphasize the use of prayer, meditation, and the study of mystical texts as means of achieving a higher spiritual plane.

messiah—(Hebrew, "anointed"), adj., **messianic**; the name given to the figure who was to appear at the end of days ushering in an idyllic period in history. The messiah was to be a descendant of King David, the greatest of Israel's monarchs, whose dynasty was to last forever.

midrash—(Hebrew, "investigation, explication") the investigation of the meaning of a text, typically biblical text; midrash is a form of biblical commentary, often quite imaginative and only very loosely connected to the plain meaning of the text; rabbinic midrash employs a number of characteristic interpretive techniques and ranges across both legal and narrative materials within the Bible.

Mishnah—(Hebrew, "teaching") a Hebrew law code written in Palestine in circa 200 C.E., traditionally ascribed to Rabbi Judah the Prince; mishnah is divided into six "orders" (seeds, festivals, women, damages, holy things, and purities), which, in turn, are subdivided into a total of sixty-three tractates, covering ritual, civil, criminal, domestic and agricultural law.

musar—(Hebrew, "admonition, ethics") the closest Hebrew equivalent for ethics as a distinct aspect of human behavior; also, the name of a pietistic movement that began in Lithuania in the nineteenth century, noted for the strict, moralistic literature it produced.

Pentateuch—(from Greek, "five books"), Hebrew: chumash; the first five books of the Hebrew Bible: Genesis, Exodus, Leviticus, Numbers, and Deuteronomy; traditionally regarded by Jews as revealed by God to Moses and the Israelites, the Pentateuch relates the history of the Israelites and spells out the divine laws which they are to follow as God's holy people.

rabbi—(Hebrew, "teacher"); adj., **rabbinic;** the name given to ancient Jewish teachers of Scripture and of the proper method for its interpretation; in ancient and medieval times, rabbis also functioned as judges in Jewish courts of law (and still do, within orthodox communities); most contemporary rabbis function as clergy to the Jewish community, although their primary duties remain educational, rather than clerical.

responsa—(sing., **responsum**), Hebrew: teshuvot; a genre of halakhic literature beginning in post-Talmudic times, encompassing the letters written by rabbinic authorities in response to specific legal questions that had been addressed to them.

Sh'ma—(Hebrew, "hear") the name of a central Jewish prayer text taken from the first word of Deuteronomy 6:4 ("Hear, O Israel, the Lord is our God, the Lord alone."); the Sh'ma includes three biblical texts: Deuteronomy 6:4–9; 11:13–21 and Numbers 15:37–41; observant Jews recite the Sh'ma twice daily, in the morning and evening prayer services.

siddur—(Hebrew, "order") the traditional Jewish prayerbook, which establishes the set order of prayers for daily and festival worship.

Talmud—(Hebrew, "learning") the compendium of Jewish teaching, consisting of the mishnah together with the gemara; the Palestinian Talmud, composed circa 400 C.E. includes the commentary on the mishnah of the rabbis living in Palestine; the Babylonian Talmud, far larger and better known, was completed circa 500 C.E. and includes the gemara of the Babylonian rabbis; since its composition, the Talmud has itself been the subject of numerous commentaries; traditionally, study of the Talmud was itself an act of piety and the hallmark of learned Jews.

Tanakh—(acronym for Hebrew words, "Torah," "prophets" and "writings") the name for the Hebrew Bible or Old Testament

Temple—the central religious institution of ancient Israel, originally built by Solomon in Jerusalem in 954 B.C.E. Priests officiated at the Temple, offering sacrifices on the altar, and Israelites were commanded to make a pilgrimage to the Temple three times each year.

teshuva, teshuvah—(Hebrew, "turning, responding") repentance, the process of reflecting on one's own failings and resolving to turn again toward God and to recommit oneself to a life of piety.

tikkun olam—(Hebrew, "repair of the world") the concept that God gave humankind the capacity and the responsibility to complete the work of creation, that the world in its present state is imperfect and requires "repair"; in some views, each divine commandment the Jews perform contributes to the tikkun olam.

Torah—(Hebrew, "instruction, direction") God's instruction to the Jewish people, contained primarily in the Pentateuch; in its narrowest meaning Torah connotes the first five books of the Hebrew Bible; in its broader meaning, however, Torah encompasses all rabbinic interpretation of Scripture that is all that one needs to know to follow God's law properly.

Tosefta—(Aramaic, "addendum") an addendum to the Mishnah containing other contemporaneous rabbinic views that either supplement or contradict those codified in the Mishnah; like the Mishnah, it is divided into sixty-three tractates.

Suggestions for
Further Reading

The scholarly literature on religion, Judaism, and ethics is vast and complex. The following very limited list of titles is intended for the general reader who wishes to continue exploring the issues raised in this volume. I have intentionally included some general introductory textbooks in addition to books widely regarded as classics in the field.

CHAPTER ONE: RELIGION, ETHICS, AND RELIGIOUS ETHICS

On Religion

Berger, Peter. *The Sacred Canopy*. Garden City, N.Y.: Doubleday, 1969.

Eliade, Mircea. *The Sacred and the Profane*. New York: Harcourt Brace Jovanovich, 1959.

Ellwood, Robert S. Jr. *Introducing Religion: From Inside and Outside*. Englewood Cliffs, N.J.: Prentice-Hall, 1978.

Smith, Wilfred Cantwell. *The Meaning and End of Religion*. New York: New American Library, 1963.

Streng, Frederick J. *Understanding Religious Life*. Encino, Calif.: Dickinson Publishing, 1978.

On Ethics

Frankena, William K. *Ethics*, 2d ed. Englewood Cliffs, N.J.: Prentice-Hall, 1973.

MacIntyre, Alasdair. *After Virtue*, 2d ed., Notre Dame, Ind.: University of Notre Dame Press, 1984

Norman, Richard J. *The Moral Philosophers: An Introduction to Ethics.* Oxford: Oxford University Press, 1983.

Stout, Jeffrey. *Ethics After Babel.* Boston: Beacon Press, 1988.

On Religious Ethics

Chidester, David. *Patterns of Action: Religion and Ethics in a Contemporary Perspective.* Belmont, Calif.: Wadsworth, 1987.

Little, David, and Sumner B. Twiss, Jr. *Comparative Religious Ethics.* San Francisco: Harper & Row, 1978.

Outka, Gene, and John P. Reeder, Jr., eds. *Religion and Morality.* Garden City, N.Y.: Anchor/Doubleday, 1973.

Reeder, John P., Jr. *Source, Sanction, and Salvation: Religion and Morality in Judaic and Christian Traditions.* Englewood Cliffs, N.J.: Prentice-Hall, 1988.

CHAPTER TWO: JUDAISM AND JEWISH ETHICS

On Jews and Judaism

Ben-Sasson, H. H., ed. *A History of the Jewish People.* Cambridge, Mass.: Harvard University Press, 1976.

Cohn-Sherbok, Dan. *The Jewish Heritage.* Oxford: Basil Blackwell, 1988.

Fishbane, Michael. *Judaism.* San Francisco: Harper & Row, 1987.

Glatzer, Nahum N. *The Judaic Tradition.* New York: Behrman House, 1969.

Hertzberg, Arthur, ed. *Judaism.* New York: Simon & Schuster/Touchstone, 1991.

Neusner, Jacob. *The Way of Torah: An Introduction to Judaism,* 7th ed., Belmont, Calif.: Wadsworth, 2004.

Seltzer, Robert M. *Jewish People, Jewish Thought: The Jewish Experience in History.* New York: Macmillan, 1980.

———. *Judaism: A People and its History.* New York: Macmillan, 1989.

On Jewish Ethics

Borowitz, Eugene B. *Exploring Jewish Ethics.* Detroit, Mich.: Wayne State University Press, 1990.

Borowitz, Eugene B., and Frances Weinman Schwartz. *The Jewish Moral Virtues.* Philadelphia, Pa.: Jewish Publication Society, 1999.

Dorff, Elliot N., and Louis E. Newman, eds. *Contemporary Jewish Ethics and Morality.* Oxford: Oxford University Press, 1995.

Fox, Marvin, ed. *Modern Jewish Ethics: Theory and Practice.* Columbus, Ohio: Ohio State University Press, 1975.

Gordis, Robert. *Judaic Ethics for a Lawless World.* New York: The Jewish Theological Seminary of America, 1986.

Kellner, Menachem Marc, ed. *Contemporary Jewish Ethics*. New York: Sanhedrin Press, 1978.

Newman, Louis. *Past Imperatives: Studies in the History and Theory of Jewish Ethics*. Albany, N.Y.: State University of New York Press, 1998.

Novak, David. *Jewish Social Ethics*. Oxford: Oxford University Press, 1992.

Sherwin, Byron L., and Seymour J. Cohen. *How to Be a Jew: Ethical Teachings of Judaism*. Northvale, N.J.: Jason Aronson, 1992.

CHAPTER THREE: SOURCES OF JEWISH ETHICS

General Introductions to Jewish Literature

Finkelstein, Louis, ed. *The Jews: Their History, Culture and Religion*. New York: Harper, 1949.

Holtz, Barry W., ed. *Back to the Sources: Reading the Classic Jewish Texts*. New York: Summit Books, 1984.

Waxman, Meyer. *A History of Jewish Literature*. 5 vols. New York: T. Yoseloff, 1960.

On the Bible

Buber, Martin. *On the Bible: Eighteen Studies*. New York: Schocken Books, 1968.

Childs, Brevard S. *Introduction to the Old Testament as Scripture*. Philadelphia, Pa.: Fortress Press, 1979.

Irwin, William A. "The Hebrews." In *The Intellectual Adventure of Ancient Man*, ed. Henri Frankfort and H. H Frankfort. Chicago: University of Chicago Press, 1946.

Kaufman, Yehezkel. *The Religion of Israel*. New York: Schocken Books, 1972.

Levenson, Jon D. *Sinai & Zion: An Entry into the Jewish Bible*. San Francisco: Harper & Row, 1985.

Sandmel, Samuel. *The Hebrew Scriptures: An Introduction to Their Literature and Religious Ideas*. New York: Oxford University Press, 1978.

On Rabbinic Literature

Jaffee, Martin. *Early Judaism*. Upper Saddle River, N.J.: Prentice-Hall, 1997.

Kaddushin, Max. *The Rabbinic Mind*, 2d ed. New York: Jewish Theological Seminary of America, 1965.

Neusner, Jacob. *The Formation of the Babylonian Talmud*. Leiden: E.J. Brill, 1970.

———. *Method and Meaning in Ancient Judaism*. 3 vols. Missoula, Mont.: Scholars Press, 1979–1981.

———. *Judaism in Society: The Evidence of the Yerushalmi*. Chicago: University of Chicago Press, 1983.

———. *Judaism: The Evidence of the Mishnah*. Chicago: University of Chicago Press, 1981.

———. *Judaism: The Classical Statement: The Evidence of the Bavli*. Chicago: University of Chicago Press, 1986.

———. *The Midrash: An Introduction*. Northvale, N.J.: Jason Aronson, 1990.

———. *Introduction to Rabbinic Literature*. New York: Doubleday, 1994.

Strack, Hermann L. *Introduction to the Talmud and Midrash*. New York: Atheneum, 1969.

On Jewish Philosophy, Mysticism, and Law

Cohen, Boaz. *Law and Tradition in Judaism*. New York: Ktav, 1959.

Dan, Joseph. *Jewish Mysticism and Jewish Ethics*. Seattle: University of Washington Press, 1986.

Dorff, Elliot, and Arthur Rosett. *A Living Tree: The Roots and Growth of Jewish Law*. Albany: State University of New York Press, 1988.

Guttmann, Julius. *Philosophies of Judaism*. New York: Schocken Books, 1973.

Hecht, N. S., B. S. Jackson, S. M. Passamaneck, D. Piattelli, and A. M. Rabello, eds. *An Introduction to the History and Sources of Jewish Law*. Oxford: Clarendon Press, 1996.

Husik, Isaac. *A History of Mediaeval Jewish Philosophy*. New York: Atheneum, 1969.

Jacobs, Louis. *Theology in the Responsa*. London: Routledge & Kegan Paul, 1975.

———. *A Tree of Life: Diversity, Flexibility and Creativity in Jewish Law*. Oxford: Oxford University Press, 1984.

Roth, Joel. *The Halakhic Process: A Systemic Analysis*. New York: The Jewish Theological Seminary of America, 1986.

Scholem, Gershom. *Major Trends in Jewish Mysticism*. New York: Schocken Books, 1954.

Twersky, Isadore, ed. and trans. *Introduction to the Code of Maimonides (Mishneh Torah)*. New Haven, Conn.: Yale University Press, 1980.

CHAPTER FOUR: CONTOURS OF JEWISH MORAL LIFE

On Justice

Bick Etta, ed. *Judaic Sources of Human Rights*. Tel Aviv: Israel-Diaspora Institute, 1987.

Dorff, Elliot N. *To Do the Right and the Good: A Jewish Approach to Modern Social Ethics*. Philadelphia, Pa.: Jewish Publication Society, 2002.

Goodman, Lenn Evan. *On Justice: An Essay in Jewish Philosophy*. Yale University Press, 1991.

———. *Judaism, Human Rights, and Human Values*. New York: Oxford University Press, 1998.

Konvitz, Milton, ed. *Judaism and Human Rights*. New York: W.W. Norton, 1972.

On Humility

Belkin, Samuel. *In His Image: The Jewish Philosophy of Man as Expressed in Rabbinic Tradition.* Westport, Conn.: Greenwood, 1979.

Feldman, David. *The Right and the Good.* Northvale, N.J.: Jason Aronson, 1999.

Fendel, Zechariah. *The Ethical Personality.* New York: Hashkafah Publications, 1986.

Green, Ronald M. "Jewish Ethics and the Virtue of Humility." *Journal of Religious Ethics* 1:1 (1973): 53–63.

Roth, Sol. "Toward a Definition of Humility." *Tradition* 14 (1973–1974): 5–22.

On Honoring Parents

Dorff, Elliot N. "Parents and Children," In *Love Your Neighbor and Yourself: A Jewish Approach to Modern Personal Ethics.* Philadelphia, Pa.: Jewish Publication Society, 2003, Chapter 4.

Sherwin, Byron. *Jewish Ethics for the Twenty-First Century: Living in the Image of God.* Syracuse, N.Y.: Syracuse University Press, 2000.

CHAPTER FIVE: FOUNDATIONS OF MORAL OBLIGATION IN JUDAISM

Appel, Gersion. *A Philosophy of Mizvot.* New York: Ktav Publishing Co., 1975.

Fox, Marvin. "Philosophical Foundations of Jewish Ethics." The Second Annual Rabbi Louis Feinberg Memorial Lecture, Judaic Studies Program, University of Cincinnati, 1979.

Freedman, Benjamin. *Duty and Healing: Foundations of a Jewish Bioethic.* New York: Routledge, 1999.

Novak, David. *Covenantal Rights: A Study of Jewish Political Theory.* Princeton, N.J.: Princeton University Press, 2000.

Shubert, Spero. *Morality, Halakha and the Jewish Tradition.* New York: Ktav Publishing House and Yeshiva University Press, 1983.

CHAPTER SIX: JEWISH ETHICS IN MODERN TIMES

On the Emancipation and Its Aftermath

Katz, Jacob. *Out of the Ghetto: The Social Background of Jewish Emancipation, 1770–1870.* Cambridge, Mass.: Harvard University Press, 1973.

Mendes-Flohr, Paul, and Jehuda Reinharz, eds. *The Jew in the Modern World: A Documentary History* 2d ed. New York : Oxford University Press, 1995.

On the Holocaust and Its Aftermath

Blumenthal, David. *The Banality of Good and Evil: Moral Lessons from the Shoah and Jewish Tradition*. Washington, D.C.: Georgetown University Press, 1999.

Morgan, Michael. "Jewish Ethics After the Holocaust." *Journal of Religious Ethics* 12:2 (Fall 1984): 256–77.

On Feminism and Jewish Ethics

Adler, Rachel. *Engendering Judaism: An Inclusive Theology and Ethics*. Philadelphia, Pa.: Jewish Publication Society, 1998.

Zoloth, Laurie. *Health Care and the Ethics of Encounter: A Jewish Discussion of Social Justice*. Chapel Hill: University of North Carolina Press, 1999.

On Postmodern Jewish Ethics

Breslauer, S. Daniel. *Toward a Jewish (m)orality : Speaking of a Postmodern Jewish Ethics*. Westport, Conn.: Greenwood Press, 1998.

Gibbs, Robert. *Why Ethics? Signs of Responsibilities*. Princeton, N.J.: Princeton University Press, 2000.

CHAPTER SEVEN: THREE CASE STUDIES: CONTINUITY AND DIVERSITY IN CONTEMPORARY JEWISH ETHICS

On Sexual Ethics

Ackelsberg, Martha A. "Jewish Family Ethics in a Post-*halakhic* Age." In *Contemporary Jewish Ethics and Morality*, ed. Elliot N. Dorff and Louis E. Newman, 300–14. New York: Oxford University Press, 1995.

Adler, Rachel. "Justice and Peace Shall Kiss: An Ethics of Sexuality and Relationship" and "*B'rit Ahuvim:* A Marriage Between Subjects." In *Engendering Judaism: An Inclusive Theology and Ethics*. Philadelphia, Pa.: Jewish Publication Society, 1998.

Dorff, Elliot N. *Love Your Neighbor and Yourself: A Jewish Approach to Modern Personal Ethics*. Philadelphia, Pa.: Jewish Publication Society, 2003.

On Abortion

Jakobovits, Immanuel. *Jewish Medical Ethics*, 4th ed. New York: Bloch, 1975.

Rosner, Fred. *Modern Medicine and Jewish Ethics*. New York: Ktav Publishing Co., 1986.

Rosner, Fred, and J. David Bleich. *Jewish Bioethics*. Hoboken, N.J.: Ktav Publishing Co., 2000.

On War

Landes, Daniel, ed., *Confronting Omnicide: Jewish Reflections on Weapons of Mass Destruction*. Northvale, N.J.: Jason Aronson, 1991.

Novak, David. "Nuclear War and the Prohibition of Wanton Destruction." In *Jewish Social Ethics*. New York: Oxford University Press, 1992.

Shapiro, David S. "The Jewish Attitude Toward War and Peace." In *Studies in Jewish Thought*, vol 1. New York: Yeshiva University Press, 1975.

Though now somewhat out of date, the following entries contain valuable references to books on all aspects of Jewish ethics.

Breslauer, S. Daniel. *Contemporary Jewish Ethics: A Bibliographical Survey*. Westport, Conn. : Greenwood Press, 1985.

———. *Modern Jewish Morality: A Bibliographical Survey*. New York: Greenwood Press, 1986.

———. *Judaism and Human Rights in Contemporary Thought: A Bibliographical Survey*. New York: Greenwood Press, 1993.

Index